Union Representation Elections:
Law and Reality

Union Representation Elections: Law and Reality

JULIUS G. GETMAN
STEPHEN B. GOLDBERG
JEANNE B. HERMAN

Russell Sage Foundation   New York

PUBLICATIONS OF RUSSELL SAGE FOUNDATION

Russell Sage Foundation was established in 1907 by Mrs. Russell Sage for the improvement of social and living conditions in the United States. In carrying out its purpose the Foundation conducts research under the direction of members of the staff or in close collaboration with other institutions, and supports programs designed to develop and demonstrate productive working relations between social scientists and other professional groups. As an integral part of its operation, the Foundation from time to time publishes books or pamphlets resulting from these activities. Publication under the imprint of the Foundation does not necessarily imply agreement by the Foundation, its Trustees, or its staff with the interpretations or conclusions of the authors.

Russell Sage Foundation
230 Park Avenue, New York, N.Y. 10017

Library of Congress Catalog Number: 76–13271
Standard Book Number: 87154–302–8

Second Printing

Contents

Tables

Figures

Foreword

For many years, lonely voices have repeatedly been heard proclaiming the need for more empirical research in the field of law. In most areas of legal study, the results have been less than impressive. Law professors are seldom trained in the use of sophisticated techniques of data collection and analysis. Social scientists have not been much inclined to take an interest in the development of the law. More important still, most significant legal questions turn in the end on the weighing of interests and values that cannot be quantified or measured with any exactitude. As a result, although empirical research can help to illuminate parts of many legal problems, it seldom has a sufficiently dramatic impact on the shape of legal doctrine to excite the imagination of the scholar.

Against this backdrop, the work of Professors Getman, Goldberg, and Herman is particularly interesting because the authors have chosen to launch a major assault upon an area of the law in which a large and complex body of rules has been built upon assumptions of human behavior that are subject to empirical examination. The area involves the voting behavior of employees, and the rules are those established by the National Labor Relations Board to regulate elections to determine union representation.

The book is doubly interesting because it examines the basis for an elaborate body of rules at a time when thoughtful people are increasingly skeptical about the growth of government regulation in the economy. Those who share this interest will not be disappointed by the work of Getman, Goldberg, and Herman. Earlier writers had seriously questioned the government's policy of establishing detailed election rules to protect employee free choice from a long list of questionable campaign practices on the part of unions and employers. What Getman, Goldberg, and Herman have done is to investigate the voting behavior of employees in a large number of elections to determine whether the Labor Board rules are really needed to guarantee a free and uncoerced choice. Unlike many empirical studies, their work arrives at clearcut conclusions that make a massive attack on the assumptions that support an entire body of regulatory law.

I leave to others, more expert than myself, the task of evaluating the research methodology and the ultimate validity of the conclusions reached. If the results stand up under scrutiny, however, it is tempting to speculate on the effects of the study on the behavior of the National Labor Relations Board.

Ironically, one must recognize at the outset that the Board is singularly ill-equipped to evaluate the study. Neither the members of the Board nor its staff are social scientists, and the research unit established in the early years of the NLRB was long ago dismantled by Congress as a result of repeated charges that it was infested by persons of Communist persuasion. The shortsightedness of Congress is sharply revealed by this book, for the study carried out by Getman, Goldberg, and Herman is precisely the type of work that the Board ideally should have conducted decades ago to make certain that its rules were truly based on the best available data. As it is, the present study must be received by a Board that is poorly prepared to evaluate its findings and ill-disposed at this late date to accept a body of conclusions that calls in question a whole multitude of rules that have been in force for many years.

Yet let us suppose that the findings cannot be readily refuted. What then? Of course, if it were *completely* clear that the conclusions were correct, the Board would virtually feel compelled to rescind many of its rules. Indeed, the very need for the rules would greatly diminish since knowledgeable unions and employers would have little reason to make campaign threats and misrepresentations or to fire union leaders once it was clear that such actions could not affect the outcome of the election.

But findings of this sort can seldom be proved to be a certainty. There will always be lingering doubts that *some* elections may be influenced by questionable tactics, at least where the results are close or other special circumstances are present. Under these conditions, it is very likely that employers and unions will still be tempted to engage in questionable tactics in the hope that they may possibly succeed. The government's predicament, however, is more difficult. If it accepts the study and rescinds the rules, the risk will remain, however slight, that some elections will be decided unjustly by threats, misrepresentations, and other tactics that seem inherently improper. On the other hand, if the Board rejects the study, there is little danger of such injustice but a high probability of much unnecessary red tape and needless expense, running into the millions of dollars, for taxpayers, unions, and employers.

In the end, therefore, the judgment the Board must make will be political, in the best and broadest sense of the term. What matters more: a continuing burden of highly questionable expenditures and bureaucratic regulation or the bare possibility of reaching results in a number of elections that do not reflect the true wishes of the employees?

To me, the choice is not a difficult one since I am persuaded that even the existing rules give rise to delays, distortions, and game playing that create risks of injustice at least as great as those which might occur if the current rules were relaxed. (How many unions have withered while the employer has pursued his right to appeal each arguable violation of the Board's rules? How many employers have been unjustifiably subjected to the expense of defending themselves against complaints brought by unions to serve some unrelated tactical objective?) But the Board is much less likely to view the matter in this light. Certainly, in the past, neither the courts nor the regulatory agencies have been much inclined to place significant weight on administrative burdens in deciding the shape of legal doctrine. The interesting question is whether this tendency will be seriously reexamined in an era when so many voices, including that of the President, have spoken out on the dangers of overly ambitious efforts to regulate the economy.

Having recently experienced at first hand the problems of adjusting to government intervention, I can only applaud the efforts of Professors Getman, Goldberg, and Herman. Whatever the eventual impact of their study, work of this kind will surely be important to a society that seeks to weigh the benefits and costs of regulation with greater sensitivity and discrimination.

Derek C. Bok

Harvard University

Acknowledgments

It would have been impossible to conduct a study of this magnitude without the assistance of many people and institutions. What follows is a brief acknowledgment of that assistance.

We owe substantial thanks to Melvin J. Kohn, director of the Laboratory for Socio-Environmental Studies, National Institute of Mental Health. During the early stages of this study, when many doubted its feasibility, Mel provided encouragement and advice. When we had completed a first draft of the manuscript, he made suggestions which, we think, led to a deeper and more thoughtful interpretation of our findings. Others who read early drafts and made useful suggestions were Professor Carol Dweck, University of Illinois, and attorney Janet Kohn.

Our primary intellectual debt is owed to Derek Bok, president of Harvard University, whose work on Board regulation of union representation elections suggested the need for a study such as ours.[1] When we first considered doing the study, we received encouragement and support from William Harvey, then dean of the Law School at Indiana University and Dean John Cribbet, College of Law, University of Illinois.

Charles Cannell, director of Field Studies, Institute for Social Research, University of Michigan, was most helpful in designing the data collection procedures. We also profited greatly from early discussions with Professor Seymour Sudman, Survey Research Laboratory, University of Illinois. Professors Bernard Meltzer, Merton Bernstein, and Clyde Summers reviewed our initial interview schedules and made useful suggestions. Professor Meltzer also provided helpful criticism of an early draft of Chapter 1. Similarly helpful criticisms of that chapter were made by attorneys Lee Cross and Robert Williams.[2]

---

[1]See Bok, *The Regulation of Campaign Tactics in Representation Elections Under the National Labor Relations Act,* 78 HARV. L. REV. 38 (1964).

[2]We also made extensive use of Mr. Williams' book on the law governing Board elections. See R. WILLIAMS, P. JANUS & K. HUHN, NLRB REGULATION OF ELECTION CONDUCT (1974).

In order to obtain the names and addresses of employees in the elections we wished to study, it was necessary to sue the Board under the Freedom of Information Act.[3] We were ably represented in that litigation by attorney Lee Modjeska. Advice and affidavits were provided by Charles Cannell, Seymour Sudman, and Professor Albert Klassen, Indiana University. When we were later sued to enjoin us from studying an election, attorney Solomon Hirsh successfully defended us.

Dozens of people were involved in the collection of data. Jeffrey Goldberg, then of the Survey Research Laboratory (SRL), University of Illinois, worked hard and efficiently as our field coordinator. Matt Hauck, also of SRL, provided overall supervision. The interviewers themselves, students at the University of Illinois, Indiana University, Northwestern University, and the University of Chicago, were crucial to the success of the study. They brought to their work enthusiasm and willingness to spend long hours on the trail of elusive respondents. Some of the interviewers also helped in other ways. Barbara Farrell was a valuable coding assistant, and Janet Pauls and Bruce White contributed legal research.

Data collection was assisted by the National Labor Relations Board's regional offices in Chicago, Peoria, Indianapolis, Cincinnati, and St. Louis. The regional directors and election clerks in each of those offices provided us with daily reports on hundreds of elections in order that we might select those we wished to study. John Truesdale, executive secretary, NLRB, responded promptly and cheerfully to our frequent requests for information on the Board's operations.

Melvin J. Welles, administrative law judge, National Labor Relations Board, to whom Professors Getman and Goldberg were intellectually indebted long before this study began, read all the campaign material and, acting as he would in his official role, provided an unofficial decision as to its legality. Judge Welles's willingness to help us was vital to our analysis of the impact of unlawful campaigning.

Careful and efficient typing of the manuscript at various stages of completion was provided by Linda Peterson, Brenda Nolan, and Jane King, University of Illinois; Vickie Wilgus and Marci Shulman, University of Michigan; Francine Spearman, Northwestern University; and Jan Wagner, University of Indiana. Curtis Groves and John Klesh assisted in data analysis while students at the University of Illinois.

The bulk of the funding for this study was provided by the National Science Foundation (grant GS–3030) and Russell Sage Foundation.

---

[3]See Getman v. NLRB, 450 F.2d 670 (D.C. Cir., 1971).

Seed money was furnished by the University of Illinois and Indiana University. The American Bar Foundation provided Professor Goldberg with time off from university duties to work on this project in 1973–74 and Northwestern University did the same in 1974–75. Both also provided generous supporting services. The Institute for Social Research, University of Michigan, provided similar services for Professors Herman and Goldberg in 1975–76.

Professor Getman was provided with time off and supporting services by Indiana University in 1970–71. He was also provided with supporting services by the University of Chicago during the winter and spring quarters of 1972 and by Stanford University in 1975–76. He acknowledges his thanks to Bobby Filzer Getman for much help and advice on every aspect of the study and to Dan, Mike, and Poppy Getman for being themselves.

Our most substantial debt is owed to the men and women who provided the data on which this book is based—union officials, organizers, employers, attorneys, and most important, the working men and women who voted in the elections we studied. Without their willingness to talk to us candidly and at length, this book would not have been possible. We came away from the study with a heightened awareness of the fundamental decency and intelligence of the American worker.

The order in which the authors are listed on the title page is alphabetical. It is not intended to indicate the magnitude of their respective contributions.

Julius G. Getman
Stephen B. Goldberg
Jeanne B. Herman

July 1976

Union Representation Elections:
Law and Reality

CHAPTER 1

NLRB Regulation of Campaign Tactics: The Behavioral Assumptions on Which the Board Regulates

The process by which a single union is selected to represent all employees in a particular unit is crucial to the American system of collective bargaining. If a majority votes for union representation, all employees are bound by that choice and the employer is obligated to recognize and bargain with the chosen union. The selection process is controlled by the National Labor Relations Act,[1] which applies to almost all nongovernmental employees[2] and takes place primarily through elections conducted by the National Labor Relations Board.[3] In the decade from 1966–1975, the National Labor Relations Board conducted approximately 85,000 elections, in which over five million workers voted.[4] In 1975 alone, nearly 8,500 elections took place, with more than 500,000 people voting on the question of union representation.[5]

The first step toward union representation is typically an organizing drive in which the union solicits employee signatures on cards authorizing it to represent the signer in bargaining with his or her employer about wages, hours, and other working conditions. The cards are generally submitted to the Board along with the union's petition for an election to satisfy the Board's rule that such petitions must be supported by at least 30 percent of the employees.[6]

---

[1] 29 U.S.C.§§ 141–87 (1970).

[2] 29 U.S.C.§§ 152(2)–(3) (1970).

[3] 29 U.S.C.§§ 159(a), (c)(I) (1970). The largest groups not covered by the National Labor Relations Act are agricultural employees, domestic employees, and employees in industries subject to the Railway Labor Act, 45 U.S.C.§§ 151–88 (1970).

[4] 40 NLRB ANN. REP. 226 (1975); 39 NLRB ANN. REP. 217 (1974); 38 NLRB ANN. REP. 226 (1973); 37 NLRB ANN. REP. 242 (1972); 36 NLRB ANN. REP. (1971); 35 NLRB ANN. REP. 172 (1970); 34 NLRB ANN. REP. 215 (1969); 33 NLRB ANN. REP. 218 (1968); 32 NLRB ANN. REP. 234 (1967); 31 NLRB ANN. REP. 202 (1966).

[5] 40 NLRB ANN. REP. 225 (1975).

[6] See NLRB Statements of Procedure, sec. 101.18.

1

When a union election petition is filed, the Board first decides if there is any reason why an election should not be held, such as an unexpired collective bargaining agreement[7] or pending unfair labor practice charges.[8] The next question is which employees should be included in the election unit. This is most often resolved between the employer and union who then enter into a consent election agreement.[9] If they cannot agree, the Board will determine the appropriate unit and issue a decision and direction of election. In most cases, the parties also agree on the election date, but if they cannot, the Board will set a date.[10]

The period between the signing of the consent election agreement or the decision and direction of election and the election date is generally between fifteen and thirty days. During this time, the parties typically engage in a campaign—much like a political campaign—in which the union tries to persuade employees to vote for union representation and the employer tries to persuade them to vote against it. The Board has developed an elaborate system of rules[11] to govern campaign tactics:

> The Board has said that in election proceedings it seeks "to provide a laboratory in which an experiment may be conducted, under conditions as nearly ideal as possible, to determine the uninhibited desires of the employees." Where for any reason the standard falls too low the Board will set aside the election and direct a new one. Unsatisfactory conditions for holding elections may be created by promises of benefits, threats of economic reprisals, deliberate misrepresentations of material facts by an employer or a union, deceptive campaign tactics by a union, or by a general atmosphere of fear and confusion caused by a participant or by members of the general public.[12]

The Board enforces its rules relating to campaign conduct in two

---

[7] 40 NLRB ANN. REP. 53 (1975).

[8] 38 NLRB ANN. REP. 54 (1973).

[9] In fiscal 1975, 79 percent of all representation elections were arranged by agreement of the parties. 40 NLRB ANN. REP. 16 (1975).

[10] Most of the Board's powers in election cases are exercised by its regional directors, subject to limited review by the Board. See NLRB Rules and Regulations, sec. 102.67.

[11] These rules have been established by Board case law. The Board possesses authority to promulgate rules under the procedures of the Administrative Procedure Act, but has not done so. See Bernstein, *The NLRB's Adjudication-Rule Making Dilemma under the Administrative Procedure Act,* 79 YALE L.J. 571 (1970).

[12] Sewell Mfg. Co., 138 NLRB 66, 69–70 (1962). See also Modine Mfg. Co., 203 NLRB 527, 530 (1973). ("We . . . have thus opted for safeguards more rigorous than those applied in the arena of democratic procedures which lie at the very heart of our form of government.")

ways. The losing party may file objections to conduct allegedly affecting the outcome of the election; if the Board finds such objections valid, it will set aside the election and order a new one.[13] Alternatively, the loser may file unfair labor practice charges, alleging that the winning party has interfered with the right of employees to "bargain collectively through representatives of their own choosing."[14] Interference with this right constitutes an unfair labor practice, which the Board is empowered to remedy by ordering the offending party, employer or union, to cease and desist from the forbidden practice.[15] The Board also possesses the power, if it deems the interference with employee choice sufficiently serious, to order an offending employer to recognize the union as the representative of his employees and bargain with it even though the union lost the election.[16]

An unfair labor practice will almost always constitute grounds for setting aside an election.[17] Moreover, "conduct that creates an atmosphere which renders improbable a free choice will sometimes warrant invalidating an election, even though that conduct may not constitute an unfair labor practice."[18] Campaign tactics found by the Board to be both unfair labor practices and grounds for setting aside an election are typically those that trade on the employer's economic power over employees—threats and acts of reprisal and promises and grants of benefit. Campaign tactics that are only grounds for setting aside an election are those thought to impede a reasoned choice, such as misrepresentations of fact or law or appeals to racial prejudice.[19] The

---

[13] The Board's authority to promulgate election rules and to enforce them by setting aside an election in which they have been violated was nowhere spelled out in the original National Labor Relations Act, which stated only, "Whenever a question ... arises concerning the representation of employees, the Board may ... certify ... the representatives that have been designated or selected." Act of July 5, 1935, ch. 372 § 9(c), 49 Stat. 449 (1935). The Board's power to set aside an election it deems to have been unfairly conducted has, however, long been assumed. See Miami Newspaper Printing Pressmen's Local 46 v. McCulloch, 322 F.2d 993, 997–998 (D.C. Cir. 1963), and cases there cited.

[14] 29 U.S.C.§ 157 (1970). The power to file such charges is technically open to either party, but it will rarely, if ever, be utilized by the winner.

[15] 29 U.S.C.§§ 158(a)(1), 160(c) (1970).

[16] NLRB v. Gissel Packing Co., 395 U.S. 575 (1969). A bargaining order may also be issued when no election has been held. Thus, if the union believes it has little or no chance of winning an election due to the employer's unfair practices, it may prefer to withdraw its election petition and rely solely on unfair labor practice charges to achieve bargaining rights. *Id.* at 580–81.

[17] Dal-Tex Optical Co., 137 NLRB 1782, 1787 (1962).

[18] General Shoe Corp., 77 NLRB 124, 126 (1948).

[19] See R. WILLIAMS, P. JANUS & K. HUHN, NLRB REGULATION OF ELECTION CONDUCT 19–25, 93–99 (1974).

Board thus possesses the power, either through objections or unfair labor practice proceedings, to regulate broad spectrum of pre-election conduct.

Board regulation traditionally has been defended by reference to the Board's expert ability to determine which campaign tactics are likely to interfere with employee freedom of choice. The Board has claimed such expertise,[20] and the courts have generally acquiesced in this claim.[21] In recent years, however, courts and commentators have begun to challenge the assumption of Board expertise, pointing out that the source of the Board's presumed special knowledge has never been identified. Judge Skelly Wright described the Board as "an institution which in over thirty years has itself never engaged in the kind of much needed systematic empirical effort to determine the dynamics of an election campaign or the type of conduct which actually has a coercive impact."[22] Indeed, the Board has not permitted the introduction of evidence as to whether particular conduct had a harmful impact on employees involved in a given election.

> In evaluating the interference resulting from specific conduct, the Board does not attempt to assess its actual effect on employees, but rather concerns itself with whether it is reasonable to conclude that the

---

[20] See, e.g., General Stencils, Inc., 195 NLRB 1109, 1111 (1972), in which the Board set out "to draw upon [its] knowledge and expertise in evaluating the effects of any misconduct. . . ." In Modine Mfg. Co., *supra* note 12, at 531, the Board claimed the ability to "take into account the current degree of sophistication of the voters at a particular time or in a particular area of the country." See also General Electric Co., 156 NLRB 1247, 1251 (1966); Peerless Plywood Co., 107 NLRB 427 (1953).

[21] The Supreme Court has stated that the Board can take into account "imponderable subtleties" in weighing the effect of employer speech on employee exercise of the right of self-organization, NLRB v. Virginia Electric & Power Co., 314 U.S. 469, 479 (1941), and that the Board is capable of engaging in an "expert estimate as to the effects on the election process of unfair labor practices of varying intensity," NLRB v. Gissel Packing Co., 395 U.S. 575, 612 n.32 (1969). Cf. NLRB v. United Steelworkers (Nutone, Inc.), 357 U.S. 357, 362–364 (1958); NLRB v. Babcock & Wilcox Co., 351 U.S. 105, 111–112 (1956); Republic Aviation Corp. v. NLRB, 324 U.S. 793, 798–800 (1945).

[22] Getman v. NLRB, 450 F.2d 670, 675 (D.C. Cir. 1971). See Getman & Goldberg, *The Myth of Labor Board Expertise*, 39 U. CHI. L. REV. 681 (1972). Cf. Bok, *The Regulation of Campaign Tactics in Representation Elections Under the National Labor Relations Act*, 78 HARV. L. REV. 38, 46–53, 88–90 (1964); Lewis, *Gissel Packing: Was the Supreme Court Right?*, 56 A.B.A.J. 877 (1970); Note, *Behavioral and Non-Behavioral Approaches to NLRB Representation Cases*, 45 IND. L. J. 276 (1970). See also Samoff, *NLRB Elections: Uncertainty and Certainty*, 117 U. PA. L. REV. 228 (1968). An early call for empirical research into the impact of campaign tactics is found in Summers, *Politics, Policy Making and the NLRB*, 6 SYRACUSE L. REV. 93, 106–108 (1954).

conduct tended to prevent the free formation and expression of the employees' choice.[23]

The Board's rules concerning the circumstances under which it will find a tendency to coerce employee choice are thus not grounded on factual data, but on guesses or assumptions. However, nothing in the collective activities or experience of the Board insures the accuracy of these assumptions. To be sure, many of the Board's members and staff have spent years interpreting and applying Board rules in terms of the policies, language, and legislative history of the NLRA. But the process of elaborating and harmonizing rules of decision provides no information about the validity of the assumptions underlying those rules.

Some Board members and staff have served as lawyers for employers or unions involved in organizing campaigns, while others have been attorneys in NLRB regional offices, engaged in investigating objections and unfair labor practice charges. Many of these people have observed that a particular employer campaign tactic was followed on one or more occasions by a union loss. Therefore, they may have assumed that the union loss was due to this tactic. There are two possible flaws in this assumption. Initially, the observations on which it is based may not be representative. The same tactic may be followed just as frequently by a union victory. Alternatively, the union loss may have been caused by factors other than the tactic that impressed the observer.

The Board has no means of determining the actual effect of the tactics used in union representation elections. Prior archival and field studies, though limited in scope, have indicated the potential value of empirical research in resolving this question.[24] Our study was designed

---

[23] 33 NLRB ANN. REP. 60 (1968). See Shovel Supply Co., 118 NLRB 315, 316 (1957). Cf. Modine Mfg. Co., *supra* note 12, at 531. See also Murry Envelope Corp., 130 NLRB 1574, 1576 (1961); Lane Drug Stores, Inc., 88 NLRB 584, 586 (1950).

[24] See Brotslaw, *Attitude of Retail Workers Toward Union Organization,* 81 LAB. L.J. 149 (1967); Field & Field, "*. . . And Women Must Weep" v. "Anatomy of a Lie": An Empirical Assessment of Two Labor Relations Propaganda Films,* 1 PEPPERDINE L. REV. 21 (1973); Comment, *An Examination of Two Aspects of the NLRB Representation Election: Employee Attitudes and Board Inferences,* 3 AKRON L. REV 218 (1970); San Fernando Valley State College Political Science Department, A Survey of Voters in National Labor Relations Board Elections (unpublished report prepared for the Los Angeles and Orange Counties Organizing Committee, AFL-CIO, 1968); Pollitt, *NLRB Re-Run Elections: A Study,* 41 N.C. L. REV. 209 (1963); Blackman, *Relative Severity of Employer Unfair Labor Practices,* 28 LAB. L. J. 67 (1971). See also Roy, *The Role of the Researcher in the Study of Social Conflict: A Theory of Protective Distortion of Response,* 24 HUMAN ORGANIZATION 262 (1965).

to provide the broadly based empirical data necessary to evaluate the effectiveness of campaign tactics used in union representation elections and the propriety of the Board's regulation of those tactics.

THE CONCEPT OF A FREE AND REASONED CHOICE: AN IMPLICIT MODEL OF VOTING BEHAVIOR

The Board has frequently stated that its objective in regulating the pre-election campaign is to protect employee freedom of choice.[25] By "freedom of choice" the Board means the opportunity to exercise a "reasoned, untrammeled choice" for or against union representation.[26] Board opinions presuppose that in a properly conducted election employees will reserve their final decision until the campaign ends and then make a "sober and thoughtful choice" based on the arguments for and against union representation.[27] In this respect, the Board assumes, or at least seeks to encourage, a model of employee voting behavior similar to that at one time contemplated in political elections.[28]

While the campaign preceding a political election is generally free of restrictions on campaign tactics, the Board, explicitly rejecting this aspect of the political analogy, closely regulates such tactics.[29] The decision to regulate closely was a natural outgrowth of the historical circumstances and economic philosophy that led to the passage of the National Labor Relations Act. The decades preceding passage of the Act were marked by stormy efforts to organize employees in major industries. Employers often sought to defeat unionization by capitalizing on their economic power over employees. The techniques employed included mass discharges, yellow dog contracts, and company unions. In response to the use of such tactics, the framers of the Act established unfair labor practice procedures.[30] They hoped thereby to overcome "the relative weakness of the isolated wage earner."[31] In this

---

[25] See, e.g., General Shoe Co., 77 NLRB 124, 126 (1948).

[26] Sewell Mfg. Co., 138 NLRB 66, 69 (1962). See R. WILLIAMS, P. JANUS & K. HUHN, *supra* note 19, at 19–23.

[27] Peerless Plywood Co., 109 NLRB 427, 429 (1953).

[28] Sears, *Political Behavior* in G. LINDZEY & E. ARONSON (eds.) HANDBOOK OF SOCIAL PSYCHOLOGY, vol. 5, 324 (2d ed. 1969).

[29] Sewell Mfg. Co., 138 NLRB 66, 69–70 (1962).

[30] The framers of the Wagner Act were also concerned with less obvious attempts to use the employer's economic power: "It is impossible to catalog all the practices that might constitute interference, which may rest upon subtle but conscious economic pressure exerted by virtue of the employment relationship." S. Rep. No. 573, 74th Cong., 1st Sess. 8–11 (1935).

[31] *Id.* at 3.

context it was probably inevitable that the Board would reject the model of political elections and seek to prevent employers from relying upon the threat or use of economic power to influence employee voting decisions.[32]

The Board also assumes that if employee voters are to be free to exercise a reasoned choice, they need protection from some types of emotional appeals not based on the employer's economic power. The Board has used the metaphor of "laboratory conditions" to describe the atmosphere necessary for a fair election.[33] The comparison with a laboratory suggests that an atmosphere of pristine calm and purity is both attainable and necessary to determine the uninhibited desires of the employees.[34]

The Board must also assume that emotional appeals will cause employees to vote differently from their reasoned choice. If emotional appeals were not believed to affect vote, the Board, which views its primary mission as that of protecting free choice, would be unlikely to regulate those appeals.

THE BOARD'S ASSUMPTIONS

The Board rarely articulates its assumptions. Frequently, when it sustains objections to an election, it asserts only that the "totality" of the conduct alleged to be unlawful was such as to interfere with free choice.[35] In such cases it is difficult to determine precisely which conduct was objectionable, let alone why. Moreover, the Board is not consistent. The same assumption is given different weight in different cases, and, at times, one assumption is discarded in favor of its opposite.[36] Nonetheless, certain assumptions can be identified as more or less central to the Board's regulation of pre-election campaign tactics.

[32] Because a union seeking representation rights will not usually possess economic power vis-à-vis the employees involved, elections are rarely set aside on the basis of such power being used improperly. But see NLRB v. Savair Mfg. Co., 414 U.S. 270 (1973), discussed *infra* in text accompanying note 131. The economic pressure to accept unionization that is exerted by organizational picketing is regulated by § 8(b)(7) of the National Labor Relations Act, 29 U.S.C.§ 158(b)(7) (1970).

[33] The phrase "laboratory conditions" was used first in General Shoe Co., 77 NLRB 124, 127 (1948), and has been used regularly since that time. See, e.g., Sewell Mfg. Co., 138 NLRB 66, 69 (1967).

[34] In furthering its goal of laboratory conditions, the Board has outlawed such tactics as appeals to racial prejudice, Redbaiting, and, on occasion, the showing of films portraying the harmful effects of a strike. See notes 86–88, 118 *infra* and accompanying text.

[35] Cf. Arch Beverage Corp., 140 NLRB 1385, 1387 (1963); Bernstein, *supra* note 11, at 576.

[36] See notes 108–118 *infra* and accompanying text.

The Assumption That Employees Are Attentive to the Campaign

Many of the Board's rules presuppose that employees are paying close attention to the campaign. This assumption is perhaps most noticeable in Board cases setting aside elections due to misrepresentations of fact or law. In *Haynes Stellite Co.*,[37] the Board set the election aside on the basis of the employer's statement that

> . . . in some cases we are the sole source of supply at present for some of our customers. We have been told that we would not continue to be the sole source of supply if we become unionized, due to the ever present possibility of a work stoppage due to strikes or walkouts.[38]

One customer had so informed the company, but the Board found that by using "some" instead of "one" the employer had materially misrepresented the facts.[39] In setting the election aside the Board assumed that employees would distinguish between the use of "one" and "some" and that their vote might be affected by the difference. On other occasions the Board has set aside elections because of a union's misstatement of wage rates at another firm[40] and because of an employer's misrepresentation of the amount of union dues that would be required of employees.[41]

The Board will also set aside an election when the employer misstates, however slightly, the legal or practical implications of a union victory. For example, an employer may state that a union victory will preclude his dealing directly with employees regarding their wages, hours, or working conditions. If, however, his statement implies that employees will be unable to present grievances directly to him, the

---

[37] 136 NLRB 95, enforcement denied sub nom. Union Carbide Corp. v. NLRB, 310 F.2d 844 (6th Cir. 1962).

[38] 136 NLRB at 96–97.

[39] *Id.* at 97.

[40] Kawneer Co., 119 NLRB 1460 (1958) (union claimed that wages were $1.81 per hour when they actually ranged from $1.73 to $1.90 per hour).

[41] In Trane Co., 137 NLRB 1506 (1962), the employer deducted an amount from the employees' paychecks which he said was "the estimated amount" of monthly union dues and paid it in a separate envelope. Since the employer deducted $5 and the union dues were $4, the Board found this to be a substantial misrepresentation which constituted partial grounds for setting the election aside. Implicit in this holding is the assumption that some employees would note the amount of money deducted, recall that amount when making their voting decision, and be influenced by that recollection to vote differently than they otherwise would have. The Board sustained the union's objection on the additional grounds that the employer had misrepresented the nature of Tennessee's right-to-work law and that the distribution of literature on the eve of the election had not given the union time to reply.

election will be set aside, since the right to have grievances adjusted without the intervention of the bargaining representative is protected by the first proviso to §9(a) of the Act.[42] Similarly, an employer is free to point out that a strike is possible, indeed likely, if the union wins, but he may not state that there will be a strike or convey the impression that a strike is inevitable.[43] Here too, the assumption is that employees are attending to the campaign so closely that they will perceive the difference.[44]

The Assumption That Employees Will Interpret Ambiguous Statements by the Employer as Threats or Promises

Employers are free to inform employees of their opposition to unionism and frequently do so.[45] However, when the employer makes ambiguous statements about the effect of unionism, the Board frequently assumes that employees will infer threats of reprisal or promises of benefit. For example, in *Singer Co.*,[46] the employer stated that one of his chief reasons for opening a plant in the particular community was to take advantage of lower labor costs. He further stated that costs had risen at other plants after unionization and as a result work had been transferred and nearly 1,000 people lost their jobs. Although the employer's remarks could have been interpreted as a lawful prediction of the economic consequences of unionization, the Board found they contained an implied threat of reprisal if the employees voted for union representation. In *Thomas Products Co.*,[47] the employer's constant reference to strikes was found not to suggest that

---

[42] 29 U.S.C.§ 159 (a) (1970). See Saticoy Meat Packing Co., 182 NLRB 713, 714–715 (1970); Winn-Dixie Stores, Inc., 166 NLRB 227, 234 (1967); Graber Mfg. Co., 158 NLRB 244, 246–247 (1966).

[43] Unitec Industries, 180 NLRB 51, 52–53 (1969); Thomas Products Co., 167 NLRB 732, 733 (1967).

[44] As a corollary of the assumption of attentiveness, the Board assumes that employees will discuss employer actions among themselves. In Great Atlantic & Pacific Tea Co., 140 NLRB 133 (1962), the employer operated sixteen stores with approximately 120 employees. The area supervisor asked five employees about the merits of unionization. The Board set aside the election, stating: "Individual interviews took place in 25 percent of the total number of stores in the unit. This is hardly an isolated number of interviews, and it is not unreasonable in the circumstances to infer, as we do, that the ramifications of the interviewing technique extended beyond the employees immediately involved." *Id.* at 135.

[45] This freedom is guaranteed by the First Amendment and, in unfair labor practice cases, by § 8(c) of the National Labor Relations Act, 29 U.S.C.§ 158(c) (1970). Cf. Dal-Tex Optical Co., 137 NLRB 1782 (1962).

[46] 199 NLRB 1195 (1972).

[47] 167 NLRB 732, 733 (1967).

union intransigence might cause a strike, but that the employer would take an unyielding bargaining stance, forcing employees to strike to obtain benefits. This statement, too, was thus seen as a threat of reprisal. In *Rein Co.*,[48] the employer said that he was neither required to negotiate present benefits into a union contract nor prohibited from telling employees that such benefits could be discontinued. Although these statements were legally accurate, they were found to threaten the loss of existing benefits in retaliation for unionization.[49]

Questions as well as statements can be found to contain implied threats of reprisal or promises of benefit. If the employer tries to find out which employees support the union, the Board assumes that absent specific safeguards his questioning will be understood as a threat of reprisal against union supporters.[50] If the employer asks employees why they want a union, or what their grievances are, the Board assumes the employees will infer a promise to correct the grievances leading to the desire for unionization.[51]

Efforts by the employer to determine the identity of union supporters through surveillance of union activities have been held unlawful, even when the employees involved are unaware of such surveillance.[52] The theory on which secret surveillance is forbidden is

---

[48] 111 NLRB 537, 538–539 (1955).

[49] See also Bok, *supra* note 22, at 77–82. The assumption that employer speech will be scrutinized by the employees for indications of coercion has been applied by the Board even where the employer makes no statement about his reaction to unionization. In Tunica Mfg. Co., 182 NLRB 729, 741 (1970) (Trial Examiner's decision, adopted by the Board) the Board held that a company cartoon that showed hands above water grasping for a life preserver with the caption "Don't run the risk" was likely to be considered a threat of retaliation.

[50] See, e.g., Isaacson-Carrico Mfg. Co., 200 NLRB 788 (1972); Spartus Corp., 195 NLRB 134 (1972); General Automation Mfg. Inc., 167 NLRB 502 (1967); Abex Corp. 162 NLRB 328–329 (1966); Standard Products Co., 159 NLRB 159 (1966) (Trial Examiner's decision, adopted by the Board). The safeguards necessary, in the Board's view, to render interrogation noncoercive are: (1) the employer must communicate his purpose for the interrogation of the employees; (2) the purpose must be legitimate; (3) the employees must be assured there will be no reprisals; (4) there must be an overall background free of anti-union hostility. Blue Flash Express, Inc., 109 NLRB 591, 593–594 (1954). If the interrogation is characterized as "polling," or systematic interrogation as to union preference, there are additional requirements that the poll be by secret ballot and that its purpose be to determine the truth of a union's claim of majority. Struksnes Construction Co., 165 NLRB 1062, 1063 (1967).

[51] See Flight Safety, Inc., 197 NLRB 223, 227–228 (1972); Reliance Electric Co., 191 NLRB 44, 46 (1971); Raytheon Co., 188 NLRB 311, 312 (1971) (concurring opinion); Tom Wood Pontiac, Inc., 179 NLRB 581 (1969); Texaco. Inc., 178 NLRB 434 (1969).

[52] Bethlehem Steel Corp., 14 NLRB 538, 628 (1939), enf'd, 120 F.2d 641 (D.C. Cir. 1941); Grower-Shipper Vegetable Ass'n. of Central Calif., 15 NLRB 322,

not that it will directly affect employee free choice, as it obviously cannot, but that it is the first step leading to discriminatory actions against union supporters.[53] Known surveillance is impermissible, because it demonstrates the employer's anxiety regarding unionization, thus causing the employees to fear economic retaliation.[54]

The Assumption That Employees Are Unsophisticated about Labor Relations

Many of the Board's decisions setting aside elections on the basis of employer speech appear to rest on the assumption that employees know little about labor-management relations or the effect of unionization on such relations. It is assumed that all or nearly all their information on this subject will be a product of the campaign. In *Boaz Spinning Co., Inc.*,[55] the employer set out in some detail the history of other plants (one of which it had operated) that closed after prolonged strikes called by a union seeking representation rights. He discussed possible results of a strike, including loss of jobs, loss of income, violence, bloodshed, and disruption of family and community life. The Board set aside the election on the ground that the employer had unfairly given the employees the impression that their only choice was between no union and a strike. It stated

> In arguing against unionism, an employer is free to discuss rationally the potency of strikes as a weapon and the effectiveness of the Union seeking to represent his employees. It is, however, a different matter when the employer leads the employees to believe that they *must* strike in order to get concessions. A major presupposition of the concept of collective bargaining is that minds can be changed by discussion, and that skilled, rational, cogent argument can produce change without the necessity for striking. . . . Policy considerations dictate that employees should not be led to believe, before voting, that their choice is simply between no union or striking. That narrow choice is essentially what this Employer gave them.[56]

---

356 (1939), enf'd. in part, 122 F.2d 368 (9th Cir. 1941); Cannon Electric Co., 151 NLRB 1465, 1468–1469 (1965); Elder-Beerman Stores Corp., 173 NLRB 566 (1968).

[53] Cannon Electric Co., *supra* note 52, at 1468–1469. While the Board has found secret surveillance to be an unfair labor practice, we are aware of no case in which it has set an election aside on the basis of secret surveillance.

[54] Hendrix Mfg. Co. v. NLRB, 321 F.2d 100, 104, n. 7 (1963), enf'ng 139 NLRB 397 (1962).

[55] 177 NLRB 788 (1969).

[56] *Id.* at 789.

Implicit in this decision is the assumption that the employees had not previously considered the possibility of a strike and were unaware of the possible negative consequences of striking. Also implied in the Board's discussion is the assumption that employees will see their choice as presented by the employer—no union or strike—and will be unaware that many employers who adamantly oppose unionization ultimately accept a union contract rather than risk a damaging strike.[57]

In *Bausch & Lomb, Inc.,*[58] the employer stated that the union seeking to represent the employees ". . . agreed last November that the four Bausch & Lomb employees represented by them will not receive a Christmas bonus. The Union also agreed they will not get the new pension plan."[59] The Board set aside the election because the company "created the false impression that the Minneapolis Local gave up the valuable right of the Minneapolis employees to receive the Christmas bonus without receiving anything in return."[60] In fact, the union had negotiated for new benefits. The opinion assumes that employees will not know enough about collective bargaining to recognize that the surrender of existing benefits is generally in return for other benefits that the union considers more important.[61]

---

[57] See Ideal Baking Co. of Tenn., 143 NLRB 546, 551–52 (1963). Cf. Utica-Herbrand Tool Div. of Kelsey-Hayes Co., 145 NLRB 1717 (1964).

[58] 185 NLRB 262 (1970).

[59] *Id.* at 264.

[60] *Id.* at 262.

[61] The assumption that employees lack sophistication also underlies the doctrine that an employer may not bargain with one union when a rival union claim raises a question concerning representation. Midwest Piping & Supply Co., 63 NLRB 1060, 1070 (1974). Bargaining with one union, the Board has said, bestows an "unwarranted prestige" on the recognized union and thereby prevents a free choice by the employees. Scherrer & Davisson Logging Co., 119 NLRB 1587, 1588–1589 (1958). It is by no means clear why, in the Board's view, the prestige that might accompany employer recognition interferes with the freedom of employees to choose the union they prefer. Something more than the mere expression of employer preference must be involved, inasmuch as the Board does not condemn an expression of preference unaccompanied by negotiations.

The Board's theory must be that substantial prestige will accrue to the recognized union due to the position of authority that it will occupy in the plant. Union leaders will be dealing with management officials with respect to grievances and the negotiation of an agreement. From these dealings the union will acquire an aura of responsibility that will give it a significant advantage over rivals in a forthcoming election. This theory presupposes that employees will be so impressed by the union's acting in a responsible role that they will be unable to consider the likelihood that another union could do likewise. Hence, they are deprived of freedom of choice. See Getman, *The Midwest Piping Doctrine: An Example of the Need for Reappraisal of Labor Board Dogma,* 31 U. CHI. L. REV. 292, 309 (1964).

The assumption of unsophistication, even if accurate, could not justify the Board in setting aside elections because of employer campaign tactics without assuming further that the union cannot neutralize the impact of such tactics. If the employer threatens to close the plant contingent on a union victory, the union organizer presumably will respond that the employer cannot do so as a matter of law, will not do so as long as the plant is profitable, and that the union has no intention of making it unprofitable. If the employer promises to raise wages contingent on a union loss, the organizer undoubtedly will respond that mere words are not equal to a union contract. The Board must assume either that employees will not attend to the union's counter-assertions or that the impact of the employer's use or threatened use of his economic power *vis-à-vis* employees is so great that counter-assertions will be ineffective. Hence, self-policing of the campaign by the parties is ruled out and governmental regulation required.[62]

The Assumption That Free Choice Is Fragile

The Board assumes that an employee's pre-campaign intent to vote for or against union representation is tenuous and easily altered by the campaign. This assumption is so inherent in Board regulation that it is rarely articulated, save when the Board discusses those tactics it considers particularly effective in unfairly influencing vote. Foremost among these impermissible tactics are threats and acts of reprisal and promises and grants of benefit. The Board has concluded that such tactics interfere with free choice, because they sensitize employees to the employer's economic power and his ability to use it in a retaliatory fashion. This conclusion rests on two major assumptions: (1) unless reminded of the employer's economic power and his ability to use that power to further his opposition to unionization, employees will not fully appreciate its existence or the possibility of its use; (2) once reminded of that power, by threats, promises, or their effectuation, employees will vote against the union. The second assumption implies that employees planning to vote for the union will vote against it either to prevent the employer from using his economic power against them or to encourage him to use that power in ways favorable to them.

---

[62] The rejection of self-regulation is not absolute. The Board stated in Hollywood Ceramics Co., 140 NLRB 221, 224 (1962), that it would not set aside an election despite misrepresentations made by the winner unless, *inter alia,* these misrepresentations are made "at a time which precludes the other party or parties from making an effective reply...." Apparently, the Board assumes that the impact of misrepresentations on voting choice can be neutralized by counter-representations, but the impact of other types of campaign propaganda cannot.

Threats and Acts of Reprisal

Of all reminders of employer power, threatened or actual loss of employment is considered among the most coercive. In *Cornelius American, Inc.*[63] the Board held that the discriminatory discharge of a single worker was cause to invalidate the election.[64] Threats, even when implicit, are also thought to have a substantial impact if the speaker is in a position to effectuate them. In *Thomas Products Co.*,[65] the president of the parent company of the employer stated that operations had not been successful and that other plants that had not succeeded had been closed, including one that had endured one union turmoil after another. He also told the employees, "I am a businessman and I have to make business decisions."[66] The Board found his comments likely to coerce employees into voting against the union in order to prevent retaliation. The Board's assumptions in setting aside the election were clearly stated.

> Power can persuade, and substantial power can persuade substantially. When an employer who controls a multiplant operation stands before employees and verbally juggles the factories, blithely reminding them of his ability to close this, that, or the other one, it is a display of enormous economic power, calculated to put the fear of unemployment in the minds of employees. Such a demonstration is unnecessary to a reasoned discussion of the pros and cons of unionism and can only tend to make employees believe that, should they incur the employer's displeasure, he could easily find a formidable way to express his dissatisfaction.[67]

In *General Stencils, Inc.*,[68] the Board went a step further and issued a bargaining order based upon a threat of discharge.[69]

Promises and Grants of Benefit

Promises or grants of benefits intended to discourage union support are considered exceedingly potent, whether or not made contingent on the union's defeat. The Board stated in *Hudson Hosiery:*[70]

---

[63] 194 NLRB 909 (1972).
[64] *Id.* at 920.
[65] 167 NLRB 732 (1967).
[66] *Id.* at 733.
[67] Cf. Graber Mfg. Co., 158 NLRB 244, 248–249 (1966).
[68] 195 NLRB 1109 (1972).
[69] "A direct threat of loss of employment . . . is one of the most flagrant means by which an employer can hope to dissuade employees from selecting a bargaining representative." *Id.* at 1109.
[70] 72 NLRB 1434 (1947).

... the presentation of economic benefits to employees in order to have them forego collective bargaining is a form of pressure and compulsion no less telling in its effect on employees because benign. ... We can perceive no logical distinction between threats to withdraw economic benefits, for the purpose of thwarting self-organization of employees, and promises of better things to come, for the same objective. ... What is unlawful under the Act is the employer's granting or announcing such benefits (although previously determined bona fide) for the purpose of causing the employees to accept or reject a representative for collective bargaining. ... [71]

On occasion, the grant of benefits is held to exert so powerful an influence on employee free choice that setting the contaminated election aside and holding another is considered futile. In issuing a bargaining order in one such case, the Board stated

There are few unfair labor practices so effective in cooling employees' enthusiasm for a union than the prompt remedy of the grievances which prompted the employees' union interest in the first place.[72]

The theory on which promises or grants of benefits are assumed to interfere with rational decision making has never been fully articulated by the Board. In *NLRB* v. *Exchange Parts Co.*,[73] the Supreme Court found the grant of benefits to imply a threat of reprisals.

The danger inherent in well-timed increases in benefits is the suggestion of a fist inside the velvet glove. Employees are not likely to miss the inference that the source of benefits now conferred is also the source from which future benefits must flow and which may dry up if it is not obliged.[74]

---

[71] *Id.* at 1436–1437 (footnote omitted). *Accord* Bata Shoe Co., 116 NLRB 1239, 1241–1242 (1956); Lake Superior District Power Co., 88 NLRB 1946, 1948 (1950). As the quoted language indicates, the Board has never distinguished promises of benefits and the grant of benefits, nor has it distinguished promises of benefits contingent upon a union defeat and promises made in absolute terms. Indeed, even if the employer decides upon the grant of benefits in advance of the campaign for reasons having nothing to do with unionization, their announcement during the campaign will generally constitute an unfair labor practice. Hineline's Meat Plant, Inc., 193 NLRB 867 (1971).

[72] International Harvester Co., 179 NLRB 753, 753–754 (1969). See also Texaco, Inc., 178 NLRB 434 (1969), enf'd, 436 F.2d 520 (7th Cir. 1971), in which a bargaining order was predicated on an employer's solicitation and adjustment of grievances.

[73] 365 U.S. 405 (1964).

[74] *Id.* at 409 (footnote omitted).

The Board, at times, has suggested a wholly different explanation for treating grants and promises of benefits as illegal. In *Texas Transport & Terminal Co.*,[75] the employer threatened reprisals and granted wage increases to discourage union support. The Board commented: "The threats were the stick, the grant of wage increases the carrot."[76] The Board's theory in this case appears to be that by granting benefits the employer is attempting to win favor among employees and to persuade them that they will receive satisfactory wages and working conditions without the assistance of the union.[77]

The vice of a last-minute grant of benefits that attempts to demonstrate that employees do not need a union to assure favorable treatment is by no means clear. One theory on which such conduct might be held unlawful is suggested by the court's statement in *Exchange Parts*, that "the beneficence of an employer is likely to be ephemeral if prompted by a threat of unionization which is subsequently removed."[78] A last-minute grant of benefits for the purpose of discouraging union activity may represent only the employer's response to the immediate prospect of unionization rather than a long-range policy of maintaining a high level of benefits. Because of their assumed lack of sophistication, the employees will be unaware of the ephemeral nature of the last-minute grant of benefits and will be misled into believing that unionization is necessary to secure future benefits.[79]

While only those grants of benefit that the employer intends to influence employee voting choice are unlawful, the employer's intent need not be communicated to the employees in order for the grant to be unlawful. The Board apparently assumes that the employees will make the connection on their own.[80]

---

[75] 187 NLRB 466 (1970).

[76] *Id.* at 468.

[77] See also Bok, *supra* note 22, at 113.

[78] 375 U.S. at 410. This statement was triggered by the Court of Appeals' suggestion that enforcement of the Board's order would have the "ironic" result of "discouraging benefits for labor." 304 F.2d 368, 376 (5th Cir. 1963).

[79] See Bok, *supra* note 22, at 114. This analysis would be inapplicable to cases such as Hineline's Meat Plant, Inc., 193 NLRB 867 (1971), in which the Board relied on *Exchange Parts* in finding unlawful a last-minute announcement of new benefits which the employer had previously decided to grant for reasons other than to thwart unionism. While the employer was found to have timed the announcement of the new benefits to achieve maximum impact on employee voting behavior, there was little reason to suppose, regardless of the timing of the announcement, that benefits granted for reasons unrelated to the threat of unionization would not survive the employees' decision with respect to unionization.

[80] See Texas Transport & Terminal Co., 187 NLRB 466 (1970); Hineline's Meat Plant, Inc., 193 NLRB 867 (1971).

Other Reminders of Employer Power

The fragility of rational decision making in the Board's view is further demonstrated by cases holding that certain forms of employer campaigning are so potent that they are inconsistent with freedom of choice regardless of the content of the statements made. In *General Shoe Corp.*,[81] the company's general manager and the personnel manager met with small groups of employees in their offices and urged them to vote against the union. Their statements were found to be moderate in tone, but the Board still set the election aside because they were made in the "locus of final authority."[82]

Home visits by the employer for the purpose of campaigning against the union are also prohibited. In *Peoria Plastics Co.*,[83] the Board equated such visits with calling employees into the employer's office individually and concluded that they interfered with free choice regardless of whether the employer's remarks were coercive.[84]

Interference with Free Choice Unrelated to Employer Power

Employee free choice is thought to be vulnerable to a variety of campaign tactics that do not trade upon the employer's economic power over the employees, but which nonetheless prevent employees from acting in a rational and non-emotional fashion. All campaign speeches during working time to massed assemblies of employees within twenty-four hours of the election are prohibited because such speeches "have an unwholesome and unsettling effect and tend to interfere with . . . sober and thoughtful choice."[85]

Appeals to racial prejudice, when regarded by the Board as inflam-

---

[81] 97 NLRB 499 (1951).

[82] *Id.* at 502. "When rank-and-file employees are brought to the company offices in small groups, they do not deal in 'arms length' relationship with the company officials they are directed to see. Anti-union opinions, and the suggestion that the employees reject the union, when uttered in that locus of final authority in the plant, take on a meaning and significance they do not possess under other circumstances." *Id.* See Peoples Drug Stores, Inc., 119 NLRB 634, 635–636 (1957). But see NVF Co., 210 NLRB 663 (1974). The Board also assumes that the impact of the employer's statements will be greater when there are few employees present to hear his statements than when there are many, presumably because they will feel more isolated. Tuttle & Kift, 122 NLRB 848, 849 (1959).

[83] 117 NLRB 545, 547 (1957).

[84] Home visits by unions are permissible because the union does not have control over tenure of employment and working conditions. Plant City Welding & Tank Co., 119 NLRB 131, 133–134 (1957). The right to engage in home visits for unions is also deemed important because "unions often do not have the opportunity to address employees in assembled or informal groups. . . ." *Id.* at 133.

[85] Peerless Plywood Co., 107 NLRB 427, 429 (1953).

matory, are proscribed because "[t]hey create conditions which make impossible a sober, informed exercise of the franchise."[86] Similarly, linking the trade union movement to communism may be a basis for setting aside an election.[87] Even statements made by outside parties unrelated to the employer or the union may provide a basis for setting aside an election if the Board concludes that these statements created an atmosphere in which rational decision making could not take place.[88]

Elections may also be set aside for infractions of a variety of rules that are designed to protect the impartial atmosphere of Board elections rather than employee freedom of choice. Thus, in *Athbro Precision Engineering Corp.*,[89] a Board agent was seen drinking beer with a union representative in a tavern about a mile from the plant during the interim between two polling periods. Conceding that the Board agent's conduct did not affect the votes of the employees, the Board nonetheless set aside the election in order to "maintain and protect the integrity and neutrality of its procedures."[90]

Some rules appear to be based both on the Board's desire to protect its processes and its assumption of the fragility of free choice. The distribution of a facsimile of an official ballot marked in a way that suggests that the Board endorses a particular choice is grounds for setting aside an election,[91] as is the addition of a partisan message to an official Board notice entitled "Rights of Employees."[92] Sustained conversation between representatives of the parties and prospective voters waiting to cast their ballots is prohibited so as to maintain order

---

[86] Sewell Mfg. Co., 138 NLRB 66, 71 (1962). A racial message that is truthful, germane, and noninflammatory will be allowed. *Id.* at 70–71.

[87] Universal Mfg. Corp., 156 NLRB 1459, 1466 (1966).

[88] In Universal Mfg. Corp., *id.,* an election was set aside on the basis of newspaper ads, editorials, a cartoon, and a handbill reproduction of that cartoon. The Board stated: "By appealing to the employees' sentiments as civic-minded individuals, injecting the fear of personal economic loss, and playing on racial prejudice, the full-page ads, the editorials, the cartoon, and the handbill were calculated to convince the employees that a vote for the union meant betrayal of the community's best interests. Faced with pressure of this sort, the employees in our opinion were inhibited from freely exercising their choice in the election." *Id.* See Automotive Controls Corp., 165 NLRB 450, 462 (1967); Monarch Rubber Co., 121 NLRB 81, 83 (1958). Cf. P.D. Gwaltney Jr. & Co., 74 NLRB 371, 378 (1947).

[89] 166 NLRB 966 (1967). Compare IUE v. NLRB, ——— F. Supp. ———, 67 LRRM 2361 (D. D.C. 1968) and NLRB v. Athbro Precision Engineering Co., 423 F.2d 573 (1st Cir. 1970). See also Austill Waxed Paper Co., 169 NLRB 1109 (1968), in which the Board set aside an election because a Board agent left the ballot box unsealed and unattended for two to five minutes.

[90] 166 NLRB at 966.

[91] Allied Electric Products, Inc., 109 NLRB 1270, 1271–1272 (1954).

[92] Rebmar, Inc., 173 NLRB 1434 (1968).

in the polling area and prevent last-minute distraction and pressures on employees in order that they may "consult their consciences without interference."[93]

Assumptions about Campaigning on Company Premises

Proceeding from its assumption that the campaign affects voting behavior, the Board has sought to insure that the union has an adequate opportunity to reach employees with its campaign.[94]

It was settled quite early in the administration of the Act that providing the union with an adequate opportunity to communicate requires that employees be free to solicit on behalf of the union during nonworking time on company premises.[95] It has been more difficult to resolve whether adequacy of union communication requires that (1) nonemployee organizers be allowed to solicit on company premises and (2) the union be allowed an opportunity to respond on company time and premises to anti-union speeches delivered by the employer on company time and premises (known as "captive audience" speeches).

Decisions of the Supreme Court indicate that the appropriate tests as to the latter are whether the employer's refusal to allow union communication on his premises "truly diminish(es) the ability of the labor organizations involved to carry their messages to the employees" or creates an "imbalance in the opportunities for organizational communication."[96] With respect to whether non-employee union organizers must be allowed to solicit on company premises absent captive audience speeches, the Supreme Court has stated the test to be whether their exclusion places employees "beyond the reach of reasonable union efforts to communicate with them. . . ."[97]

The Board treats the Court's tests as essentially the same. As far as the Board is concerned, a union does not have an adequate opportunity to communicate when there exists an imbalance in opportunities for organizational communication. The key question, then, is whether the union's opportunity to communicate with employees is approximately the same as that possessed by the employer.[98].

The Board has rarely found the union to be at an impermissible

---

[93] Milchem, Inc., 170 NLRB 362, 363 (1970).

[94] The employer, through his ability to communicate with employees during working hours, is assumed to possess this opportunity without the need for Board intervention.

[95] Republic Aviation Corp., 51 NLRB 1186, 1195 (1943), enf'd, 142 F.2d 193 (2d Cir. 1944), aff'd, 324 U.S. 793 (1945).

[96] NLRB v. United Steelworkers of America (Nutone, Inc.), 357 U.S. 357, 362–363 (1958).

[97] NLRB v. Babcock & Wilcox, *supra* note 21, at 113.

[98] See The May Company, 136 NLRB 797, 801–812 (1962).

disadvantage. Except in unusual circumstances, such as when the employees are isolated because they work on a ship, an inaccessible island, or a resort hotel,[99] the Board has rejected union demands for access by non-employee organizers to company premises, whether to solicit generally or to respond to an anti-union speech.[100] The Board assumes that unions generally have adequate opportunity to present their views to employees by means of employee solicitation on company premises combined with traditional off-premise channels of communication, such as letters, telephone calls, and union meetings.[101]

Assumptions about Authorization Card-signing as an Indication of Employee Choice

If the union collects authorization cards signed by a majority of employees, it may, under certain circumstances, obtain an order directing the employer to bargain without an election or even after losing an election.[102] The Board issues comparatively few such orders, preferring to rely on elections as the prime determinant of employee desires with respect to unionization.[103] Indeed, an employer who commits no unfair labor practices need not recognize a union that possesses authorization cards signed by a majority of his employees, but may insist on an election.[104]

The Board's treatment of authorization cards compared to elections as an indication of employee choice is based on the following as-

[99] Sioux City & New Orleans Barge Lines, Inc., 193 NLRB 382, enf'mnt den., 472 F.2d 753 (8th Cir. 1973) (ship); Alaska Barite Co., 197 NLRB 1023 (1972) (isolated island); S & H Grossinger's Inc., 156 NLRB 233 (1965) (resort hotel).

[100] See R. WILLLAMS, P. JANUS & K. HUHN, *supra* note 19, at 287–290. Such access has been allowed when the employer maintains an unlawfully broad no-solicitation rule, Montgomery Ward & Co., 145 NLRB 846, 849 (1964), or a broad, but privileged, rule, May Dept. Stores Co., 136 NLRB 797 (1962).

[101] This assumption was reaffirmed in Excelsior Underwear, Inc., 156 NLRB 1236, 1240–1242 (1966), in which the Board ordered employers to provide unions with the names and addresses of employees eligible to vote in pending elections so that the union could communicate with those employees off company premises, and in General Electric Co., 156 NLRB 1247 (1966), where the Board refused to reconsider its policy of denying equal time for union responses to captive audience speeches, stating that it preferred to wait "until after the effects of Excelsior become known." *Id.* at 1251. The Board did not state how, in the absence of any procedure for gathering data, it proposed to determine the effects of Excelsior, nor has it since announced its findings as to those effects.

[102] See note 16 *supra* and accompanying text. The Board will issue a bargaining order based on a card majority when it finds the employer to have engaged in unfair labor practices of sufficient magnitude that a free and fair election cannot thereafter be held. See generally NLRB v. Gissel Packing Co., 395 U.S. 575, 591–592 (1969).

[103] See NLRB v. Gissel Packing Co., 395 U.S. 575, 596 (1969).

[104] Linden Lumber Div., Summer & Co., 190 NLRB 718 (1971), aff'd., 419 U.S. 301 (1974).

sumptions: (1) an employee who signs a union authorization card does so because he wishes union representation, unless the solicitor of his signature represents either expressedly or impliedly that the sole purpose of the card is to obtain an election;[105] (2) the decision to sign an authorization card does not involve the same careful, informed consideration as the voting decision;[106] (3) an employee who does not sign an authorization card does not wish union representation or is uncommitted.[107]

THE BOARD'S INCONSISTENT APPLICATION OF ITS ASSUMPTIONS

The Board does not always apply its behavioral assumptions consistently. For example, the assumption that employees will infer threats or promises from ambiguous statements has, at times, been given great weight. At other times, less sensitivity has been attributed to employees.[108] Thus, in *Birdsall Construction Co.*,[109] the employer stated that if the union won the election and insisted on a contract that increased costs "we are certainly as businessmen going to have to consider very strongly the necessity of moving our operations."[110] The Board held that this would not be interpreted as a threat to move the plant if the union won the election, but as a prediction of what might happen if the union won.[111]

At times, a majority of the Board, wholly as a matter of speculation and with no more factual data than that possessed by a previous majority, has rejected a rule based upon one assumption in favor of

---

[105] See Cumberland Shoe Corp., 144 NLRB 1268, 1269 (1963); Englewood Lumber Co., 130 NLRB 394, 394–395 (1961); Note, *Union Authorization Cards*, 75 YALE L.J. 805, 824 (1966).

[106] This conclusion is implicit in the decision to permit an employer who does not commit unfair labor practices to insist upon an election. Cf. Carson, *The Gissel Doctrine: When a Bargaining Order Will Issue*, 41 FORDHAM L. REV. 85, 88–91 (1972). This assumption may, to some extent, be premised upon a Board feeling that authorization cards are more readily procured by coercion or fraud than are votes. See Note, *Union Authorization Cards, supra* note 105, at 824–825.

[107] The Board has never issued a bargaining order where the union has not had an authorization card majority. The Board thus treats only card-signers as counting toward the union's majority status.

[108] See Swift, *NLRB Overkill: Predictions of Plant Relocation and Closure and Employer Free Speech*, 8 GA. L. REV. 77, 96–98 (1973); C. MORRIS, THE DEVELOPING LABOR LAW, 75 (1971).

[109] 198 NLRB 163 (1972).

[110] *Id.* at 7.

[111] The employer's statements here certainly seem no less threatening than those made by the employer in Thomas Products Co., 167 NLRB 732 (1967), *supra* note 43. On occasion, the Board has also rejected the assumption that discussion of possible future benefits will be interpreted by employees as a promise of benefits in exchange for voting against the union. In Coverall Rental Service,

a rule based upon a contrary assumption. For example, the Board held at one time that captive audience speeches, absent a union opportunity to reply, were unlawful because "printed materials and individual solicitations do not approach the persuasive power of the employer's oral presentation."[112] In *Livingston Shirt Co.*,[113] it reversed itself, concluding that unions were not unduly hindered in their organizational activities, despite being limited to printed materials and individual solicitations while the employer used captive audience speeches. Changing direction again in *May Department Stores*,[114] the Board stressed the powerful effect of a captive audience speech, dismissing all methods open to the union as "catch-as-catch can."[115]

Another example of a reversal in Board law, explained by a changed behavioral assumption, dealt with the legality of a union's offer to waive initiation fees for those employees who sign union authorization cards before an election. The Board originally took the position that such waivers interfered with employee free choice on the theory that an employee who had received a waiver would be constrained to vote for the union, so as to receive the financial benefits of the waiver, even if he did not want union representation.[116] Subsequently, in *DIT-MCO*,[117] the Board reversed itself, concluding that a waiver of initiation fees would not constrain an employee to vote contrary to his desires.[118]

Inc., 205 NLRB 880, 881 (1973), the employer made the following statement with respect to profit-sharing plans: "Your Board of Directors has been considering several of those. . . . However, as you probably understand, any improvement or promise of improvement in our profit-sharing plan at this time might be misunderstood to be an unfair labor practice. . . ." The Board, in disagreement with its regional director, found that the statement did not constitute an implied promise of benefits.

[112] Metropolitan Auto Parts, Inc., 102 NLRB 1634, 1636 (1953).

[113] 107 NLRB 400, 406 (1953).

[114] 136 NLRB 797 (1962).

[115] *Id.* at 801. Technically, *May Department Stores* was not a reversal of *Livingston Shirt Co.*, inasmuch as the former dealt with a department store, for which the Board has long had special rules, while the latter involved a manufacturing concern. Nonetheless, the emphasis of the Board's opinion in *May* was clearly contrary to that in *Livingston.*

[116] LoBue Bros., 109 NLRB 1182, 1183 (1954).

[117] 163 NLRB 1019, 1021–1022 (1967).

[118] The Board also reversed itself in Litho Press of San Antonio, 211 NLRB 1014 (1974) holding that showing of the film "And Women Must Weep" is neither an unfair labor practice nor a sufficient basis for setting aside an election. The film, which vividly portrays strike violence, had been held unlawful in a series of cases beginning with Plochman & Harrison—Cherry Lane Foods, Inc., 140 NLRB 130, 132–133 (1962). *Accord* Spartus Corp., 195 NLRB 134 (1972); Hawthorn Co., 166 NLRB 251 (1967); Carl T. Mason Co., 142 NLRB 480, 483 (1963). The theory on which the Board originally viewed the film as interfering with employee free choice, stated briefly in *Plochman & Harrison, supra,* was set out in

The Board's inconsistent application of its behavioral assumptions may, in large measure, be due to its lack of information. For example, the frequent changes in the law relating to captive audience speeches may reflect different assumptions of new Board members as to the impact of such speeches. Absent empirical data, Board members whose beliefs as to the impact of particular conduct differ from those of their predecessors are free to assert their beliefs as fact.

More likely, however, the changes have been due to the different views of new members as to the desirability of employer freedom to campaign against unionization. Those who value highly the employer's freedom to campaign state that employer speech has a limited impact and that unions have ample opportunity to respond; those who view the employer as an intruder in employee resolution of the question of union representation, or who place a high value on union representation, state the opposite. The behavioral assumptions, then, are frequently rationalizations for conclusions reached on other grounds. They can easily be used in this fashion, because they do not rest on empirical data.[119]

---

detail in Chairman McCulloch's concurring opinion in *Carl T. Mason Co., supra,* at 485–486 (footnotes omitted): "The use of professionally scripted and acted motion pictures in Board elections is a new tactical device of enormous potential and influence. The motion picture is a much more powerful instrument than the printed or spoken word in arousing emotions and influencing attitudes. Not only is its initial impact greater, it also has a more lasting effect. From their experience in political elections and their reading of newspapers, most people have learned to treat charges, statements, and promises made in political campaigns with a measure of skepticism. They have learned that exaggerations, misstatements, and appeals to prejudice are an inevitable part of such campaigns, and this experience is a help in evaluating propaganda used in Board elections.

"However, the case of motion pictures used as propaganda in electoral campaigns attendant upon Board elections is different. There is no body of similar experience available to the ordinary voter to permit him to evaluate such presentations. Few individuals are able to see behind the impression of authenticity that a skilled director may create by the use of characters, dialogue, and situation. A sophisticated person would probably recognize a film such as 'And Women Must Weep', for what it is, propaganda intended to create anti-union feeling, and will appropriately weigh or discount its one-sided and distorted message. But such films are not meant for sophisticated audiences. I have no doubt that among audiences of working men and women, as well as others, 'And Women Must Weep' is emotionally overpowering."

In overruling *Carl T. Mason Co.,* as well as all other decisions holding "And Women Must Weep" to constitute improper interference with employee free choice, the Board did not discuss Chairman McCulloch's behavioral analysis.

[119] The instability of Board rules controlling campaigning is also a function of the broad language of the statute, which permits Board members to read their own views into the law, and the political nature of the appointive process, which tends to produce Board members ideologically committed to the interests of labor or management. See Bok, *supra* note 22, at 39–42. For an interesting defense of politically motivated changes in Board rules, see Bernstein, *supra* note 11, at 574, n.10.

THE ROLE OF THE COURTS

The courts have tended to defer to the Board's judgment regarding the impact of campaign tactics on employee voting behavior. For example, the Board's assumption that ambiguous statements are likely to be perceived as threats was supported by Judge Learned Hand in *NLRB* v. *Federbush Co.*[120]

> Words are not pebbles in alien juxtaposition; they have only a communal existence; and not only does the meaning of each interpenetrate the other, but all in their aggregate take their purport from the setting in which they are used, of which the relation between the speaker and the hearer is perhaps the most important part. What to an outsider will be no more than the vigorous presentation of a conviction, to an employee may be the manifestation of a determination which it is not safe to thwart. The Board must decide how far the second aspect obliterates the first.[121]

On occasion the courts have taken the metaphor of laboratory conditions more seriously than has the Board, holding that the Board should have set aside elections when it has not. This tendency has been particularly pronounced in cases involving alleged union misrepresentations.[122] In *Allis-Chalmers Mfg. Co.* v. *NLRB*, [123] the union claimed that nine benefits granted to white collar employees were due to those benefits having been negotiated by the union on behalf of production workers. The union's claim was at least arguably true as to eight of these. The Board held that the union's propaganda was "virtually accurate," but the court held otherwise.

> Even if we were to assume that the first eight items were, as a matter of fact, negotiated for the production and maintenance workers by the union and passed ... along to the draftsmen ... item nine did not go through that process. ... If truth is diluted it is no longer truth. A glass of pure water is no longer pure if one-ninth part is contaminated. There cannot be "virtually" the truth any more than there can be "virtually" a virgin.[124]

---

[120] 121 F.2d 954 (2nd Cir. 1941).

[121] *Id.* at 957.

[122] R. WILLIAMS, P. JANUS & K. HUHN, *supra* note 19, at 23, attribute this close judicial scrutiny of alleged union misrepresentations to a belief that the Board has treated unions more favorably than employers in applying the "laboratory conditions" standard.

[123] 261 F.2d 613 (7th Cir. 1958).

[124] *Id.* at 616. In Cross Baking Co. v. NLRB, 453 F.2d 1346 (1st Cir. 1971), the union claimed that a competitor's employees had obtained a $.75 an hour increase under a union contract, when in fact the increase was approximately $.60 spread over three years. The Board found no substantial misrepresentation; the court

On other occasions the courts have viewed the Board as attributing too great an impact to employer actions. For instance, the Board has held that interrogation as to union sympathies is necessarily coercive unless the employer utilizes various safeguards.[125] While courts have accepted the Board's basic premise, they have been more willing to find exceptions in particular cases, with some courts treating failure to abide by the Board's safeguards merely as evidence that the interrogation may have had a coercive impact.[126]

In its decisions with respect to union authorization cards, the Supreme Court has accepted some of the Board's assumptions, rejected others, and added assumptions of its own. In *NLRB* v. *Gissel Packing Co.*,[127] the Court accepted the Board's basic assumptions about the validity of authorization cards as an indication of employee choice.[128] The court also made two additional assumptions: (1) the employer will have an opportunity to present his side of the unionization issue to employees before they sign cards because the union will inform the employer of its organizing drive early in the campaign;[129] (2) card-signers are under no greater group pressure to sign and not revoke an authorization card than are other employees to state and not vary from a voting intent, because elections are most often held in small units in which virtually every voter's sentiments can be carefully and individually canvassed both before and after the election. All employees in such elections are subject to pressures to disclose their voting intent and to vote in accord with that intent.[130]

Additional assumptions relating to union authorization cards were set forth in *NLRB* v. *Savair Mfg. Co.*,[131] in which the Supreme Court held that a union's offer to waive initiation fees for all employees who sign cards before an election interferes with employee free choice. The Court assumed: (1) some employees who do not wish union repre-

---

reversed. In Walled Lake Door Co. v. NLRB., 472 F.2d 1010 (5th Cir. 1973), the union claimed to represent employees at four of the employer's plants when in fact it represented them at two. The Board dismissed the employer's objection; the court reversed.

[125] See notes 50–51 *supra* and accompanying text.

[126] NLRB v. Lorben Corp., 345 F.2d 346, 347 (2d Cir. 1965); Bourne v. NLRB, 332 F.2d 47, 48 (2d Cir. 1964).

[127] 395 U.S. 575 (1969).

[128] *Id.* at 602–603.

[129] The Court predicated this assumption on the union's desire to subject the employer to the unfair labor practice provisions of the Act. "[T]he union must be able to show the employer's awareness of the drive in order to prove that his contemporaneous conduct constituted unfair labor practices on which a bargaining order can be based if the drive is ultimately successful." *Id.* at 603.

[130] *Id.* at 604.

[131] 414 U.S. 270 (1973).

sentation will sign cards to avoid the initiation fee in the event the union wins the election;[132] (2) these card-signers will then feel obligated to vote for the union, even though they oppose union representation;[133] (3) authorization cards help the union win the election because employees will interpret the cards as an indication of the union's support; if actual union support is not accurately reflected by the cards, employees may be misled into voting for the union;[134] (4) the fist-in-the-velvet-glove theory of *Exchange Parts*[135] applies to the waiver of initiation fees, because "the failure to sign a recognition slip may well seem ominous to non-unionists who fear that if they do not sign they will face a wrathful regime should the union win."[136]

SUMMARY OF THE BOARD'S ASSUMPTIONS

The Board's basic assumptions about employee voting behavior, to the extent that they can be discerned from a somewhat inconsistent course of decisions, result from the view that the employee voter, like the political voter, acts on the basis of an informed and reasoned judgment, voting to further his own best interests. He is attentive to the campaign, from which he receives most of his information about union-management relationships, and by which he is powerfully influenced. Indeed, the employee voter's susceptibility to campaign influence is even greater than that of the political voter, primarily because of his economic dependence on the employer. As a result of this dependence, he is likely to interpret the employer's statements, if ambiguous, as containing implied promises of benefit if he rejects the union or threats of reprisal if he does not. Even if he previously favored union representation, he will react to those promises or threats, or to their effectuation, by voting against the union. In view of the employee voter's susceptibility to the employer's economic power, the Board must intervene to prevent the employer from trading on his position. The Board also must prevent both employer and union from utilizing those emotional appeals deemed capable of interfering with the employee's ability to make a free and reasoned choice.[137]

---

[132] *Id.* at 275.

[133] *Id.* at 277–278.

[134] *Id.* at 277.

[135] NLRB v. Exchange Parts Co., 375 U.S. 405 (1964).

[136] NLRB v. Savair Mfg. Co., 414 U.S. 270, 281 (1973).

[137] In fairness to the Board, it surely does not assume that all employees are affected by the campaign, but that a sufficient number may be to change the outcome of a substantial number of elections. The question, then, is whether campaigning of the sort regulated by the Board does have a sufficient impact to justify the costs of that regulation.

POLITICAL VOTER STUDIES AND ATTITUDE CHANGE RESEARCH

The Board's assumptions about the influence of campaigning on voting behavior in representation elections are not wholly consistent with the findings of social scientists studying the effects of influence attempts in other settings. Indeed, the Board's central assumption—that the employee voter in weighing the merits of union representation will attend to and be significantly influenced by the campaigns of the parties—is contrary to the findings of political voter studies.[138] Most voters in political elections make their final voting decision in advance of the election campaign. In their study of the 1960 presidential campaign, Lazarsfeld, Berelson, and Gaudet found that 50 percent of the voters had made up their minds six months before the election and 75 percent had done so shortly after the candidates were chosen.[139] Furthermore, the political vote is not generally determined by reasoned choice carefully calculated from the candidates' stands on the issues in the immediate campaign, but primarily by ethnic, class, and family influences that predate and transcend the campaign.[140] The implicit model of the omnicompetent citizen who attends to the campaign and carefully weighs the alternatives in the process of making a voting decision is thus not an accurate characterization of the political voter.[141]

The empirical studies of political behavior have demonstrated overwhelmingly that people not only have well-formed political predispositions, but that the campaigns are for the most part not effective in influencing people to vote contrary to those predispositions. The political campaign appears to have two primary effects. For those people who make up their minds early, the campaign may provide a rationale for their decisions. For those who delay their voting decision, the campaign appears primarily to activate latent predispositions.[142] Since most political voters make early and firm decisions, investigations of campaign effectiveness have focussed on those voters who report themselves to be undecided or who switch from supporting one candidate to another during the course of the campaign. The model of the open-minded voter is not even an appropriate characterization of the undecided voters. They have fewer opinions on issues and are

---

[138] See Bok, *supra* note 22, at 48.

[139] P. F. LAZARSFELD, B. BERELSON & H. GAUDET, THE PEOPLE'S CHOICE 54 (Colum. U. Press Paperback ed. 1968).

[140] Cf. A. CAMPBELL, P. CONVERSE, W. MILLER & D. STOKES, THE AMERICAN VOTER 86–87, 184–209 (1964).

[141] See Sears, *supra* note 28, at 324–337.

[142] P. F LAZARSFELD, B. BERELSON & H. GAUDET, *supra* note 139, at 83.

less likely to participate in election events or expose themselves to political communications than voters whose decisions are made early.[143] The switchers are "the least interested in the election, the least concerned about its outcome, the least attentive to political material in the formal media of communication, the last to settle upon a vote decision, and the most likely to be persuaded, finally, by a personal contact, not an 'issue' of the election."[144]

To be sure, results from the political studies may not generalize to union representation elections. The employee voter may have a less powerful predisposition for or against union representation than the political voter has for or against the major political parties, a factor that might increase the proportion of initially undecided voters. On the other hand, it is unlikely that employees have no well-formed attitudes regarding their wages, hours, and working conditions. Very intense attitudes are formed by direct experience, and the experience of working for the employer who is a party in the election should be highly salient to the employee's vote predisposition. It is also possible that many employees have well-formed attitudes toward unions resulting from union membership in previous jobs or information about unions acquired from family members, friends, and the mass media.

Another respect in which union representation elections may be thought to differ from political elections is that the direct relevance of the representation election to the employee's terms and conditions of employment may increase the saliency of the representation election. Political studies have found that voters become more involved when the issues of the campaign are economic and personally salient.[145] The unexpectedly high political involvement of farmers in the 1956 presidential election has been interpreted as a reaction to economic conditions.[146] If the saliency of economic issues leads to increased involvement one should expect, as is true, higher voting rates in union representation elections than political elections.[147] But, drawing the

---

[143] *Id.* at 56.

[144] *Id.* at 59. Key has asserted that the switchers are not uninterested in the election, describing them as "persons whose peculiarity is not lack of interest, but agreement on broad political issues with the stand-patters toward whom they shift." V. O. KEY, JR., THE RESPONSIBLE ELECTORATE 104 (1966). Key did not, however, assert that switching is a product of the campaign. Rather, he concluded that switchers, as other voters, "respond most assuredly to what they have seen, heard, experienced. Forecasts, promises, predicted disaster, or pie in the sky may be less moving." *Id.* at 52.

[145] See S. VERBA and N. NIE, PARTICIPATION IN AMERICA: POLITICAL DEMOCRACY AND SOCIAL EQUALITY 113 (1972), ". . . on matters of the politics of everyday life, citizens know what they want."

[146] A. CAMPBELL, P. CONVERSE, W. MILLER & D. STOKES, *supra* note 140, at 220.

[147] In fiscal 1975, votes were cast by 88 percent of all eligible employees in NLRB elections. 40 NLRB ANN. REP. 241 (1975).

parallel further, those people who demonstrate high interest levels form stable political vote intentions.[148] They may be more attentive to the campaign, but their high intake of campaign propaganda serves to insulate them from switching, not influence them to switch. It is thus unlikely that the greater salience of the issues to the voters in a union representation election makes the pre-election campaign a more significant element in influencing voters to switch than in a political election.

The primary distinction between political elections and union representation elections has long been thought to lie in the employees' economic dependence on their employer in the latter.[149] The employer's power to administer sanctions, whether positive or negative, is assumed to provide him with an effective source of influence. The Board assumes that if an employer invokes his economic power, employees initially favoring union representation will switch and vote against the union. The empirical research on communicator power and the effectiveness of influence attempts, however, indicates that achieving behavior change is not always so simple.

An influence attempt may be ineffective for any of several reasons. Selective exposure is one of the most widely accepted explanations for the frequent failure of persuasive communications to change attitudes and affect behavior. Thus, employees who are opposed to unionization may anticipate that a union letter or meeting will attempt to influence them to support the union. Such an influence attempt is likely to be avoided altogether.[150] If the employees are

---

[148] P. F. LAZARSFELD, B. BERELSON & H. GAUDET, *supra* note 139, at 53, 67.

[149] Dean Theodore J. St. Antoine has stated: "[E]mployee fear . . . takes this whole question completely outside the area with which we are used to dealing in political elections. . . . Think of a man whose whole livelihood is dependent upon a particular job. That is the loss he faces. This factor may vary. I can imagine that in the city of Pittsburgh an employer could make a certain kind of speech, using the language a lawyer has taken out of a book as being approved in past NLRB elections. He might not cause the least bit of fear in the employees listening to that speech. . . . But there are other places in our country where the identical speech would have a totally different impact. Out on the Great Plains, for example, you can get into a little town where one proprietary employer holds sway as economic emperor. In that little town the banker, the newspaper, the sheriff, and the entire community dance to the tune that the employer calls. There, fear can be pervasive. . . ." Southwestern Legal Foundation, Proceedings of Eleventh Annual Institute on Labor Law 244–245 (1965). See also NLRB v. Gissel Packing Co., 395 U.S. 575, 612 (1969).

[150] There is, according to Triandis, clear evidence of *de facto* selectivity, although empirical studies of preferences indicate that selectivity is not a general psychological phenomenon. H. C. TRIANDIS, ATTITUDE AND ATTITUDE CHANGE (1971). Selective exposure does not, however, account for all instances of the failure of persuasive communications to persuade. Sears & Freedman, *Selective Exposure to Information: A Critical Review,* 31 PUBLIC OPINION QUARTERLY 194–213 (1967).

exposed to the influence attempt, they may still insulate themselves from its effect by misperceiving, suppressing, or forgetting the information.[151]

The research on perceptual distortion also indicates that when a person is exposed to a communication that is discrepant from his own position on an issue, he is likely to see that communication as even more discrepant than it is.[152] Thus a union supporter might very well interpret an employer's ambiguous statements as implied threats or promises. But the Board's assumption that the union supporter will react to a threat or promise with a vote switch is inconsistent with the studies finding that if a communication is perceived as very discrepant, people tend to respond by rejecting the source rather than changing their own positions.[153] For instance, employer threats of reprisal may be calculated to arouse fear and thus inhibit employees from participating in union activities. But the threat may not be intimidating if the employee rejects the likelihood that the employer will carry out the threat, either because the employer's threat is unlawful—he cannot do that—or the employer is seen as making idle threats—he will not do that.

Even if the communication does arouse a very high level of fear, it does not necessarily follow that the influence attempt will be successful. Some scholars have claimed that there is a positive relationship between fear and persuasion.[154] On the other hand there is evidence that the relationship between fear arousal and behavior change may be shaped like an inverted U.[155] The greatest amount of behavior change may occur with moderate levels of fear. Under conditions of low fear, the pro-union employee may be unaffected by the employer's influence attempt. Under conditions of high fear, the employee may conclude that he needs the union for protection. A discriminatorily discharged employee may become a martyr.[156] Employees with strong pro-union attitudes may experience some fear following an employer threat, but still be able to interpret the communication with respect to their currently held opinions—"we need a union to control the employer's ability to act unilaterally."

---

[151] H. C. TRIANDIS, *supra* note 150, at 156.

[152] McGuire, *The Nature of Attitudes and Attitude Change* in G. LINDZEY & E. ARONSON (eds.) HANDBOOK OF SOCIAL PSYCHOLOGY, vol. 3, 222 (2d ed. 1969).

[153] *Id.* at 223.

[154] Higbee, *Fifteen Years of Fear Arousal: Research on Threat Appeals: 1953–1968,* 72 PSYCHOLOGICAL BULL. 426 (1968).

[155] H. C. TRIANDIS, *supra* note 150, at 191–192.

[156] See Bok, *supra* note 22, at 41; Arbie Mineral Feed Co. v. NLRB, 438 F.2d 940, 944 (8th Cir. 1971); NLRB v. Crystal Tire Co., 410 F.2d 916, 920 (8th Cir. 1969).

One condition that might affect the impact of an employer's influence attempt is the degree to which employees are aware of the employer's intent. Union supporters are likely to be sensitive to the employer's anti-union sentiments. The union may also warn employees that the employer's speech or behavior is calculated to frighten them or buy them off. While employee sensitivity to the employer's intent may heighten perception of the influence attempt, it may also serve to minimize its impact.[157]

The effectiveness of the promised or granted reward should also vary with its value to the employee, the degree to which it is related to the reason for union activity, and, in the instance of a promise, the perceived likelihood of fulfillment. An employee may interpret a promise in light of previous unfulfilled employer promises and not be influenced.[158] Or, he may distort the intent of the promise or grant to support his prior opinion, thinking that if the employer will promise or grant this kind of benefit when a union is only a threat, he would be likely to grant even greater benefits if union representation became a reality.[159]

Still another factor relevant to the effect of an employer influence attempt is the degree to which the employer can and does monitor compliance.[160] Scrutiny of overt union organizational activity is not difficult, and the employer may seek no more: if overt union activity ceases, union supporters may view the union as ineffective and vote against it. The employer's ultimate goal, however, is to influence vote and that occurs under circumstances most difficult to scrutinize—a secret ballot election conducted by a government agency. The employer's power to bring about the behavior he desires may be significantly lessened by the employees' belief in the secrecy of the ballot, if, that is, they believe the ballot to be secret.

On the other hand, the secrecy of the ballot, even if accepted by the employees, may not insulate them against the employer's efforts

---

[157] See McGuire, *supra* note 152, at 185. In the case where the appropriate behavior change is ambiguous or unclear, however, prewarning may clarify what behaviors are appropriate and actually increase the degree of change.

[158] See *Id.* at 182, 195.

[159] One union representative has so stated: "In an effort to defeat the union in organizational campaigns, the companies have given wage increases prior to the representation election. Instead of buying the vote of the youth, it has served only to whet his appetite. He votes for the union more readily, for he is convinced with the power of the union he can do at least twice as well no later than the first week following the election." Speech by M. C. Weston, Jr., director of United Steelworkers District 35, *Labor Relations Problems Created by the Expectations of Young Workers,* 75 LRR 281, 282 (1970).

[160] See McGuire, *supra* note 152, at 194.

to influence their vote. Empirical research indicates that group pressure for compliance will increase when rewards or sanctions are defined so that all members of the group share a common fate.[161] If employees believe that the employer will reward or sanction the group as a whole based on the election outcome, they may influence each other to vote against union representation.[162]

SUMMARY

The Board assumes that employees are likely to attend to and be significantly influenced by the pre-election campaign in deciding whether or not to vote for union representation. The political voter studies and the attitude change research indicate, however, that persuasive communications are not generally effective in changing attitudes or behavior. The purpose of this study was to test the validity of the Board's assumptions in light of the political voter studies and attitude change research.

---

[161] *Id.* at 195.
[162] *Id.* at 195.

CHAPTER 2

Methodology

The purpose of this study was to measure the effect of the pre-election campaign, particularly unlawful campaigning, on employee predispositions to vote for or against union representation. In order to accomplish this objective, it was necessary to determine how employees intended to vote before the campaign began and how they ultimately voted. It was also necessary to determine which campaign issues employees remembered. Our assumption was that employees were less likely to have been influenced by campaign issues they did not remember than by those they did remember.

We used a two-wave panel design, interviewing the same employees at different stages of the election campaign.[1] Employees were interviewed as soon as possible after the direction of election and again immediately after the election.[2]

The primary purpose of the Wave I interview was to assess employees' pre-campaign sentiments about union representation. Employees were asked how they felt about their working conditions and about unions in general. They were also asked whether or not they had signed a union authorization card and how they would vote if the election were to be held the next day. In the Wave II interview, employees were asked to recall the content of the campaign and to disclose how they had voted and why.

We studied thirty-one elections during the period from February 1972 through September 1973. Of these, the unions won eight and lost twenty-three. Of the approximately 1,300 employees who were contacted, 1,239 completed two full interviews. Another six elections

---

[1] Panel designs are typically used to study voting behavior in political elections. See, e.g., B. R. BERELSON, P. F. LAZARSFELD & W. N. MCPHEE, VOTING: A STUDY OF OPINION FORMATION IN A PRESIDENTIAL CAMPAIGN (1954); P. F. LAZARSFELD, B. R. BERELSON, & H. GAUDET, THE PEOPLE'S CHOICE (3d ed. 1969); A. CAMPBELL, P. E. CONVERSE, W. E. MILLER & D. E. STOKES, THE AMERICAN VOTER (Abridged ed. 1964).

[2] Initially, we interviewed the voters three times before the election. This approach was dropped after the first pre-test, primarily because the campaign was compressed into such a brief period that repeated questioning elicited too little additional information to warrant the cost of frequent interviews.

were studied during the pretest stage, which took place from July 1968 through January 1972.[3]

ELECTIONS

Screening Criteria

Since it was not economically feasible to collect data throughout the country, we limited the study to those states under the jurisdiction of the NLRB regional offices in Chicago, Peoria, Cincinnati, Indianapolis, and St. Louis. We were notified of the approximately 1,600 elections that were scheduled in these regions from January 1972 to September 1973. Elections in which there was not sufficient time to conduct the first wave of interviews at least ten days prior to the election were screened out. The risk that a major portion of the campaign would already have taken place was too great and the likelihood of any subsequent campaign having a measurable impact too small to make these elections appropriate for testing hypotheses as to campaign impact. We also screened out elections involving more than one union, so that the effect of employer and union campaigning would not be confounded by inter-union campaigning.

Selection Criteria

Since we wanted to test the effect of the campaign, particularly unlawful campaigning, on voting behavior, the primary consideration in selecting elections was the likelihood of vigorous, possible unlawful campaigning. In order to maximize the generalizability of our findings, we also sought to include a variety of businesses, unions, unit sizes, and communities.

Predicting which elections would have vigorous campaigning was difficult, since the choice of elections to be studied had to be made quite early in the election process. In determining which elections might be hotly contested with a high potential for illegal behavior, we considered: (1) the strength of the employer's opposition to unionization; (2) whether the law firm representing the employer had a reputation for representing employers who campaigned strongly and sometimes unlawfully; (3) whether the employer had engaged in unlawful practices in prior elections; (4) whether the employer appeared willing to abide by counsel's advice in conducting the campaign; (5)

---

[3] All data reported here were collected in the final thirty-one elections. The pre-test results are discussed in Getman, Goldberg & Herman, *The NLRB Voting Study: A Preliminary Report,* 1 JOURNAL OF LEGAL STUDIES 223 (1972).

the views of employer and union representatives as to the likely nature of the campaign.

We were quite successful in identifying elections in which there was vigorous campaigning by both parties. In twenty-eight of the thirty-one elections in the sample, at least one party engaged in substantial campaigning by distributing written materials, holding meetings, and personally contacting employees during the period between Wave I and the election. In twenty elections, both parties campaigned vigorously after the Wave I interview. Unlawful campaigning occurred in twenty-two elections.

The thirty-one elections represented a broad range of business operations. Employers in eighteen elections were involved in some type of manufacturing operation. The eligible voters in seventeen of these units were production and maintenance employees; the other unit was composed of clerical employees. There were three automobile dealerships in which the voters were mechanics. The other operations (and eligible voters) were: two retail stores (sales and stockroom employees); two warehouses (warehouse employees); two health care facilities (nurses's aides, kitchen, laundry, housekeeping, and maintenance employees); one motel (maids, housemen, bellmen, and maintenance employees); one multiple line insurance company (salesmen); one manufacturer and distributor of food products (driver-salesmen); one trucking company (truck drivers and dock employees).

The International Brotherhood of Teamsters participated in ten of the elections (32 percent of the sample). The remaining elections involved fourteen different unions; the only ones represented more than once were the Auto Workers (3), Steelworkers (3), Machinists (3), and Retail Clerks (2).[4]

The number of voters in the units studied ranged from four to just under four hundred. The average was ninety-six. These units tended to be larger than those in most NLRB elections. While only 13 percent of all NLRB elections conducted during fiscal 1973 were in units of more than one hundred employees, 45 percent of the elections we studied during that period were in units with more than one hundred employees.[5] We chose to concentrate on the larger units in order to get a statistically stable estimate of campaign impact.

We studied elections in Illinois, Indiana, Iowa, Missouri, and Kentucky. They were located in communities ranging in size from Chicago

---

[4] Teamsters are the most frequent participants in NLRB elections on a nationwide basis. In fiscal 1973, Teamsters were involved in 34 percent of all NLRB elections. 38 NLRB ANN. REP. 231 (1973).

[5] 38 NLRB ANN. REP. 246–247 (1973).

and St. Louis to Chatsworth, Illinois (pop. 1,255) and Morgantown, Kentucky (pop. 1,394). Local unemployment rates ranged from a high of 10.1 percent to a low of 2.6 percent, with the average at 4 percent. Some communities were heavily trade union organized, others were not. There were 1,551 union locals in the Chicago area, none in Butler County, Kentucky, and an average of sixty-one in the standard metropolitan statistical area or county in which the election was held.[6]

The demographic characteristics of the units varied widely. Most were comprised primarily of white males (nineteen elections), but there were also units with a majority of white females (ten elections) and black females (two elections). In fifteen units the largest group of employees was less than 24 years old; in one unit the employees were mostly older than 55. Most of the employees had finished high school in fifteen units, but in seven units a majority of employees had attended only grade school. The most frequently reported hourly rates ranged from under $2.00 (six elections) to in excess of $5.00 (two elections).[7]

EMPLOYEES

Names and Addresses

In order to interview employees eligible to vote in an NLRB election, we needed their names and addresses. The direction of election defines the eligible voters in general terms, e.g. all production and maintenance employees, but does not identify those employees. The NLRB does, however, require that seven days after the direction of election the employer must provide it with a list of names and addresses of employees in the election unit for transmittal to the union.[8] While we might have been able to obtain a copy of this list from the employer or union, we were concerned that to do so might discredit the independence of the study and adversely affect employee cooperation.

On October 28, 1969, we requested the Board to make employee names and addresses available to us in those elections we wished to study. The Board refused, contending that the study represented an

---

[6] Treating the extent of organization as related to the size of the civilian labor force 16 years or older, the most heavily organized area in the sample was McCracken County, Kentucky (2.04 union locals per thousand); the least organized was Butler County, Kentucky (0); and the median was .70 locals per thousand.

[7] The demographic characteristics of the sample are set out in Appendix A.

[8] See Excelsior Underwear, Inc., 156 NLRB 1236 (1966); NLRB v. Wyman-Gordon Co., 394 U.S. 759 (1969).

unwarranted invasion of employee privacy, that it might upset the "laboratory conditions" under which the Board seeks to conduct elections, and that, at very least, the study would lead to the filing of objections that would delay the Board in processing the election.

On August 6, 1970, we filed suit against the Board in the United States District Court for the District of Columbia, asserting that we were entitled to the list of employee names and addresses under the Freedom of Information Act.[9] The district court ordered the Board to make the lists available to us and its decision was affirmed by the Court of Appeals for the District of Columbia Circuit.[10] On August 31, 1971, nearly two years after we had requested the Board to provide us with the lists of employee names and addresses, it was ordered to do so.[11]

Sampling Design

The sampling design called for interviewing all employees in units of twenty-five or fewer employees. In units of more than twenty-five employees, we interviewed a one-third randomly selected sample with a minimum sample size of twenty-five and a maximum of one hundred.

This design was a compromise between our desires to study as many elections as possible and to interview as many employees as possible in the elections studied. We concluded that the marginal utility of interviewing more than one-third or one hundred of the employees in large units was less than that of including additional elections in the sample.

Obtaining the Interview

Our study design required that we interview employees in the midst of a heated campaign and inquire about their union sympathies. It was possible that employees, particularly those who supported unionization,

---

[9] Act of July 4, 1966, Pub. L. No. 89–487, 80 Stat. 250, amending Administrative Procedure Act, Ch. 324, 3, 60 Stat. 238 (1946). Although Pub. L. No. 89–487 was repealed, its substantive provisions were enacted into the United States Code by Act of June 5, 1967, Pub. L. No. 90–23, 81 Stat. 54, U.S.C. 552 (1970).

[10] Getman v. NLRB, 450 F. 2d 670 (1971). The Board requested the Supreme Court to stay the district court's order, but its request was denied by Mr. Justice Black. NLRB v. Getman, 404 U.S. 1204 (1971).

[11] Some of the lists, once received, proved to be inaccurate. Of the thirty-one lists, we estimated that the addresses were 30–39 percent inaccurate on two, 20–29 percent inaccurate on nine, 10–19 percent inaccurate on eleven, 0–9 percent inaccurate on nine. These figures err in the direction of indicating a higher proportion of correct addresses than was actually the case. Most of the interviewing was done by telephone and the correctness of the address was not usually verified unless the employee could not be reached by telephone.

Table 2-1

Eligibility, Contact, Refusal, and Completion Rates

Election Number	Sample Size	Wave I					Wave II				
		Number Interviewed	Eligibility Rate	Contact Rate	Refusal Rate	Completion Rate	Number Interviewed	Eligibility Rate	Contact Rate	Refusal Rate	Completion Rate
1	136	110	99.3%	91.8%	11.3%	81.5%	106	99.1%	99.1%	1.8%	97.2%
2	32	22	96.9	87.1	18.5	71.0	20	100	100	9.9	90.9
3	38	34	97.4	91.9	0	91.9	33	100	100	2.9	97.1
4	81	63	100	83.9	7.4	77.8	58	100	98.4	6.5	92.1
5	56	43	96.4	85.2	6.5	79.6	37	97.7	100	11.9	88.1
6	60	53	95.0	94.7	1.8	92.9	53	100	100	0	100
8	59	50	100	98.3	13.8	84.7	49	100	100	2.0	98.0
9	52	43	100	86.5	4.4	82.7	38	100	85.3	7.3	34.4
10	135	115	95.6	92.2	3.4	88.4	103	95.7	97.3	3.7	93.6
11	19	18	94.7	100	0	100	17	100	100	5.6	94.4
12	16	16	100	100	0	100	13	100	100	18.8	81.3
13	8	18	100	100	0	100	7	100	87.5	0	87.5
14	4	4	100	100	0	100	4	100	100	0	100
15	8	8	100	100	0	100	8	100	100	0	100
16	31	25	87.1	96.3	3.8	92.6	21	96.0	100	12.5	87.5
18	38	30	89.5	88.2	0	88.2	25	100	90.0	7.4	83.3
19	18	16	88.9	100	0	100	15	100	100	6.3	93.8
20	49	44	93.9	97.8	2.2	95.7	31	72.2	96.9	0	96.9
21	32	29	93.8	96.7	0	96.7	24	100	89.6	7.6	82.8

Left-hand block (rows 22–33):

	Sample	Eligibles	%	%	%	%
22	32	27	96.9	100	12.9	87.1
23	15	13	100	100	13.3	86.7
24	138	111	96.4	93.2	10.5	83.5
25	30	26	93.3	92.9	0	92.9
26	60	56	98.3	96.7	1.8	94.9
27	91	75	96.7	93.2	8.5	85.2
28	35	23	88.6	77.4[c]	4.2	74.2[c]
29	36	35	100	97.2	0	97.2
30	127	101	87.4	92.8	1.9	91.0
31	50	41	96.0	91.7	9.1	83.3
32	36	28	94.4	85.3	3.4	82.4
33	83	60	96.4	87.5	14.3	75.0
Totals	1605	1326	95.7	92.1	6.3	86.3

Right-hand block:

Eligibles	%	%	%	%
26	100	100	3.7	96.3
12	100	100	7.7	92.3
104	94.6	100	1.0	99.0
22	100	88.5	4.3	84.6
52	96.3	100	3.7	96.3
33[a]	82.9	94.9	10.8	84.6
65	97.3	98.6	9.7	89.0
43[b]	100	97.9	8.5	89.6
21	95.7	100	4.6	95.5
32	97.1	97.1	3.0	94.1
89	90.1	98.9	1.0	97.8
32	95.0	84.2	0	84.2
25	100	96.4	7.4	89.3
55	96.7	98.3	3.5	94.8
1273	91.1	97.7	4.6	93.2

[a] Control group. Interviewed at Wave II only. Sample size was 47.
[b] Control group. Interviewed at Wave II only. Sample size was 48.
[c] Interviewing prematurely terminated due to court proceedings.

$$\text{Eligibility} = \frac{\text{Eligibles}}{\text{Sample}}$$

$$\text{Refusal rate} = \frac{\text{Refusals}}{\text{Interviews} + \text{refusals}}$$

$$\text{Completion rate} = \frac{\text{Interviews}}{\text{Eligibles}}$$

$$\text{Contact rate} = \frac{\text{Interviews} + \text{refusals}}{\text{Eligibles}}$$

would refuse to cooperate with the study because of fear that we would disclose what they told us, thus exposing them to the risk of employer retaliation. It was also possible that some employees might refuse to be interviewed, or to disclose their votes, because of a desire for privacy wholly unrelated to any fear of reprisal. Field procedures were developed and modified throughout the pre-test elections in order to minimize the refusal rate.

As shown in Table 2–1, the Wave I refusal rate ranged from 0–18.5 percent, with an across-election average of 6.3 percent. At Wave II, the refusal rate ranged from 0–18.8 percent, with an average of 4.6 percent. The non-contact rate was also low, averaging 7.9 percent at Wave I and 2.3 percent at Wave II. The overall completion rate at Wave I was 86.3 percent; at Wave II, 93.2 percent.[12]

Table 2–2 shows that the non-contacts and refusals did not bias the within election samples with respect to vote. The proportion of union voters in the total across-election sample was precisely the same (45 percent) as the proportion of union voters in the total thirty-one elections. The sample results differed significantly from the election results in only two individual elections, 19 and 20. In election 20 there was a six-month delay between Wave I and the election due to an appeal from the regional director's direction of election. Substantial turnover during that period reduced the sample size from forty-four employees to thirty-one employees.

MEASURES

Predispositions

The major purpose of the Wave I interview was to determine employees' union sentiments prior to the pre-election campaign. Employees were asked about their attitudes towards working conditions and unions, whether they had signed a union authorization card, and how they planned to vote.[13]

The intent and card-sign questions were the most sensitive in the Wave I interview. We tried to minimize refusals to answer these questions by asking them late in the interview and by wording them to be as nonthreatening as possible. In addition, interviewers were trained to use two back-up questions for employees who initially refused to

---

[12] Combining these data to encompass both Waves I and II would not be meaningful as the sample sizes varied because some employees left the company between interviews. In addition, control groups were added at Wave II in elections 26 and 27.

[13] The Wave I interview schedule is set out in full in Appendix B.

state their intent. The refusal rate for the card-sign question was 2 percent; the refusal rate for the intent question was 5 percent.

The card-sign question provided a means of determining whether or not employees were answering our questions truthfully. In each election we asked the union to indicate whether or not the employees

Table 2-2

Proportion of Union Voters in the Sample as Compared to the Total Unit

Election	Proportion of Union Voters in the Sample	Sample Size	Proportion of Union Voters in the Unit	Unit Size
1	.55	97	.58	277
2	.44	16	.48	25
3	.68	31	.67	81
4	.34	50	.47	152
5	.29	24	.28	109
6	.33	45	.38	124
8	.28	42	.34	140
9	.60	30	.47	105
10	.43	89	.44	383
11	1.00	15	.76	17
12	.00	9	.08	13
13–15	.20	15	.24	17
16	.33	18	.30	43
18	.44	18	.37	67
19*	.75	12	.50	16
20*	.96	26	.74	102
21	.76	17	.72	29
22	.43	23	.43	75
23	.45	11	.40	15
24	.28	82	.37	209
25	.33	21	.36	36
26	.43	60	.47	138
27	.33	97	.37	177
28	.35	17	.17	53
29	.10	31	.16	76
30	.82	73	.72	216
31	.26	27	.26	104
32	.24	21	.16	57
33	.53	49	.53	111
Total	.45	1066	.45	2967

*$p \le .05$

whom we interviewed had signed an authorization card. Table 2–3 indicates that nearly all employees answered this sensitive question honestly. Other questions in the Wave I interview were designed to determine employees' demographic background and their previous job and union experiences.

Table 2-3

Employee Response to Card-sign Question
Compared to the Union List of Card-signers

Employee Response	Union List		Total
	Did Not Sign	*Signed*	
Did not sign	449	51	500
column %	89 %	11 %	52 %
Signed	53	383	436
column %	10 %	85 %	46 %
Cannot remember and refused	3	15	18
column %	1 %	4 %	2 %
Total	505	449	954

NOTE: Unions in three elections did not provide card-sign data.

Vote

A major purpose of the Wave II interview was finding out how employees had voted. Of the 1,239 employees who completed both interviews, 90 percent disclosed their vote. The finding, reported in Table 2–2, that the within-election samples were unbiased estimators of the election results indicates that employees answered the vote question honestly.

Campaign Familiarity

The other major purpose of the Wave II interview was to determine employees' exposure to and recollection of the campaign. Closed-end screening questions were used to determine if the employee was exposed to a particular type of campaigning, e.g., "Did you, at any time before the election, get any letters or other written material from the Company discussing the Union or the election?" Those employees who answered "yes" were then asked for their recollection of the campaign message, "What did they say?"[14]

---

[14] The Wave II interview schedule is set out in full in Appendix C.

In order to determine the content of the employer and union campaigns, we interviewed the organizer in charge of the union's campaign and the person in charge of the employer's campaign, normally the personnel manager or labor relations attorney. We asked for copies of all written materials used in the campaign, transcripts of all speeches, and a report of what was said in speeches and meetings for which transcripts were not available. Additionally, each party was questioned about the issues raised in personal efforts to persuade employees to vote for or against the union.

During the pre-test studies we developed content categories for coding campaign issues. This code allowed us to classify the issues raised in each election so that we could compare familiarity with similar issues across elections.[15]

All campaign materials collected from the parties, including the content of speeches and personal efforts to persuade, were read and coded. A campaign profile was then formed for each campaign.[16] These profiles provided a baseline for determining how familiar each employee was with the issues raised in that campaign.

Prior to coding the employees' Wave II interview schedules from a particular election, the coder would familiarize himself with the campaign profile for that election.[17] It is possible that the coders' prior knowledge of the actual campaign issues built in a bias favoring the coding of an employee's response as recognition of a campaign issue. We chose, however, to run that risk rather than possibly understating campaign familiarity.

After the initial coding was completed, a portion of the interview schedules were check-coded by one of the other coders. The proportion varied with the size of the election. If there were under thirty respondents, all interview schedules were checked. If there were thirty to seventy respondents, 50 percent were checked, and if there were more than seventy respondents, 30 percent were checked. Inter-coder reliability averaged 92 percent and in no election was it below 90 percent. All discrepancies between coders were discussed and resolved.

Union and company campaign familiarity indices were constructed for each employee. An employee's familiarity index is the proportion of issues in the campaign profile that he mentioned in the Wave II interview.

---

[15] The code is contained in Appendix D.

[16] A typical campaign profile is presented in Appendix E.

[17] All coding was done by Professor Getman, Professor Goldberg, and Ms. Barbara Farrell, a coding assistant.

Unlawful Campaigning

Most unlawful campaign tactics consist of threats or acts of reprisal or promises or grants of benefit. Two questions were included in the Wave II interview specifically to elicit reports of such unlawful campaigning. One asked whether the employer had taken or threatened harmful action against union supporters; the other asked whether the employer had given or promised benefits to employees to get them to vote against the union. If an employee answered either question affirmatively, he was asked what the employer had said or done. We determined whether or not employees perceived any unlawful reprisals or benefits by examining their responses to all Wave II open-ended questions.[18]

In order to evaluate the Board's assumptions about the effect of unlawful campaigning, it was necessary to decide whether or not unlawful campaigning had occurred. If unfair labor practice charges or objections to the election were filed and ruled upon, the official disposition of those charges was treated as determinative of the legality of the conduct involved. At times, however, charges or objections were not filed even though conduct had occurred that was arguably or even clearly unlawful. The losing party was sometimes unaware of the conduct in question or its unlawfulness or, if the election was lost by a wide margin, not interested in the possibility of obtaining a rerun election or even a bargaining order. Additionally, no winning party ever protested the loser's election practices, presumably since the only remedy in such a case would be a cease and desist order of little practical value.

When charges were not filed, we made a preliminary determination, based upon the campaign materials and what the parties told us, as to whether conduct had occurred that was arguably unlawful.[19] All arguably unlawful speech and conduct not passed upon by the Board was submitted to Melvin J. Welles, Administrative Law Judge, NLRB, who decided whether material was either unlawful or grounds on which valid objections might be based. While Judge Welles was acting in an unofficial capacity, he applied the same standards as if he were acting officially.[20]

---

[18] Unlawful campaigning codes are indicated in the master code, Appendix D.

[19] We did not attempt to resolve conflicts of testimony between employees and representatives of the parties as to what was said or done unless we had copies of the literature or speech involved. If employees reported unlawful speech or conduct not initially mentioned to us by the employer or union representative, we called the attention of the relevant party to it to see whether his failure to report it was an oversight. If he denied it, we accepted that denial.

[20] Melvin J. Welles has been an NLRB administrative law judge since 1970.

If Judge Welles found either unlawful or objectionable conduct, he decided whether the appropriate remedy was a new election, an order to cease and desist from the unlawful conduct, or a bargaining order. Conduct taking place during the campaign was coded as illegal or objectionable only on the basis of a decision by the Board, an administrative law judge in official Board proceedings, or on a finding by Judge Welles.[21]

METHOD OF INTERVIEWING AND POSSIBLE BIASES

Procedures

As soon as we decided to study an election, we notified the union and the employer. We asked that they stress our neutrality in response to any employee questions about the study and inform employees that they had no objection to their participation. Some employers and unions encouraged employees to participate in the study, but most took a hands-off position, advising employees that they were free to participate or not as they wished.

As soon as we received the list of employee names and addresses, each employee in the voting unit was sent a letter containing a brief description of the study. The letter was designed to arouse the employees' curiosity about the interviews and to inform them that they might be contacted by an interviewer in the next few days. It was sent to all employees, rather than just those in the sample, in order to prevent employee speculation as to why some had received a letter, while others had not.

We used a variety of devices to demonstrate the legitimacy of the study. The letter was sent on university stationery and contained a copy of a newspaper article describing the study. A press release was sent to local news media, and one of us appeared, whenever possible, on local radio and television.

Approximately three days after the letters were mailed, interviewing began. The average time from the beginning of interviewing to the

---

Prior to that, he had been chief counsel to Board Member Sam Zagoria (1965–70); deputy assistant general counsel, Enforcement Section, NLRB (1961–65); supervisory attorney, NLRB (1949–61); attorney, NLRB (1946–49).

[21] The only exception to this practice occurred in election 32. In that election, the regional director issued a complaint alleging employer threats of reprisal and coercive interrogation. The case was settled on the employer's agreement to post a notice that it would not engage in the complained of conduct in the future. The employer would not consent to an interview, so we had neither an admission nor a denial of the allegations in the complaint. The employee reports of the campaign, however, confirmed in some detail the truth of those allegations. Accordingly, we concluded that the allegations were valid and submitted the case to Judge Welles solely for the determination of an appropriate remedy.

election was twenty-one days.[22] Once interviewing began, it was rapidly completed. Eighty-seven percent of all Wave I interviews took place in the first four days of interviewing.

Approximately three days before the election, all employees interviewed at Wave I were sent a postcard reminding them that they would be contacted for another interview on the day and time that had been agreed upon at the conclusion of the Wave I interview. Wave II interviewing began immediately after the election. It, too, was rapidly completed, with 83 percent of all interviews being conducted within forty-eight hours of the election.

Telephone and Personal Interviews

Sixty-eight percent of the Wave I interviews and 83 percent of the Wave II interviews were conducted by telephone. An interview was conducted in person only if the employee could not be reached by telephone or would not agree to a telephone interview.[23]

The length of the interview depended not so much on whether or not the interview was conducted by telephone or in person, but on the verbal skill and gregariousness of the employee. Wave I interviews lasted from twenty to forty-five minutes, Wave II interviews from thirty minutes to an hour.

There were no significant differences between those employees interviewed by telephone and those interviewed in person with regard to the proportions of each who signed authorization cards, intended to vote for union representation, or actually voted for the union. Nor did those interviewed by telephone tend to be less truthful in their responses. A comparison of the responses of both groups to the question asking if they had signed a union authorization card shows that 90 percent (869/966) of those interviewed by telephone responded truthfully, as did 89 percent (179/201) of those interviewed in person. We were apprehensive that those interviewed by telephone might be less willing to talk at length about the campaign, but there were no significant differences between the two groups in reported familiarity with the campaign.

There were, however, significant differences in refusal rates to questions about voting intent and actual vote. Of those interviewed by telephone, 5 percent refused to disclose their vote intent and 11 per-

---

[22] This does not include election 20 in which there was a six-month delay from Wave I to the election. The employer in this election appealed to the Board the regional director's decision to hold an election.

[23] The higher proportion of interviews conducted by telephone at Wave II is due to the interviewers' success at Wave I in obtaining unlisted telephone numbers or in obtaining consent, previously withheld, to a telephone interview.

cent refused to disclose how they voted. The comparable figures for those interviewed in person were 1 percent and 6 percent. There was also a significant difference in reports of unlawful campaigning. Forty-six percent of those interviewed in person reported one or more unlawful campaign practices as compared to 36 percent of those interviewed by telephone.

The fact that most employees were interviewed at Wave II by telephone and that people interviewed by telephone were more likely than people interviewed in person to refuse to answer the vote question did not bias the within-election sample estimate of the actual election outcome. The slightly higher refusal rate on the intent and vote questions in telephone interviews was, thus, an acceptable trade-off for the savings in time and money made possible by extensive telephone interviewing.

Interviewers

A staff of forty-three interviewers was used during the approximately eighteen months of data collection. Most of the interviewers were law students, although some were graduate students in labor relations. We found in the pre-test studies that interviewers with a background in labor law or labor relations were able to question employees about the campaign better than interviewers who had no familiarity with union representation elections.

Interviewers were trained in techniques for obtaining interviews and maximizing the amount of data collected. Much of the training consisted of role-playing exercises, such as getting an interview from a reluctant employee, using nonbiasing probes to obtain additional information, controlling the pace of the interview with an effusive employee, and recording completely the responses to open-ended questions. During the pre-test studies, the principal investigators accompanied the interviewers in the field and commented on their work. Completed interview schedules were read, mistakes were pointed out, and future assignments were based on the quality of the interviewer's work.

There were ten female interviewers, three black interviewers, and three who were Spanish-speaking. The Spanish-speaking interviewers conducted all interviews with Spanish-speaking respondents. All other interviews, both personal and telephone, were assigned depending upon availability. No attempt was made to have the same interviewer call at Wave I and Wave II unless the employee requested it, or the Wave I interviewer felt that the employee would be skeptical of a new interviewer.

Those interviewers who were particularly successful in obtaining interviews were used as "trouble-shooters." Their task was to interview employees who were initially unwilling to be interviewed. There were 142 trouble-shooting attempts made at Wave I, of which 53 (37 percent) were successful; 116 attempts were made at Wave II, of which 57 (49 percent) were successful.

Although all interviewers were trained to elicit and record responses to the open-ended questions as fully as possible, some interviewers were better at this task than others. Interviewer performance was evaluated by comparing the campaign familiarity of employees interviewed by different interviewers. We found that if the best ten of the forty-three interviewers had interviewed all employees, the average employee's familiarity with the company campaign would have been increased by less than 2.5 percent; familiarity with the union campaign would have been increased by less than 2 percent. Variations in interviewer ability thus did not have a substantial effect on the measurement of campaign familiarity.[24]

The Effect of the Interview

The data collection procedures were carefully designed to avoid sensitizing employees to the campaign or influencing their voting behavior. The first interview was scheduled as early as possible in the campaign. No questions were asked relating to the campaign, and employees were given no hint that such questions would be asked in the second interview. The letter to the employees and the press release stressed the neutrality of the study and that it was being conducted independently of both union and employer. Interviewers were trained to express no opinion on the value of unionization, even if their opinions were sought (as they sometimes were) by employees.

The cost of using a control group in each election to test the success

---

[24] The following procedure was used to evaluate interviewer performance: In each election in which an interviewer worked, we averaged the familiarity with the company and union campaigns of all employees whom he interviewed. Each interviewer's within-election company and union average was subtracted from the average familiarity of all interviewers in that election. If an interviewer's average was higher than the election average, he was credited with the difference; if it was lower, the difference was charged against him. An interviewer's company and union difference scores were weighted and averaged across all elections that he worked. Interviewers were rank ordered on the basis of their cross-election averages. The average company campaign familiarity of those employees interviewed by the ten highest ranking interviewers was 2.41 percent higher than the average familiarity of employees interviewed by the other thirty-three interviewers. The average union campaign familiarity of employees interviewed by the ten highest ranking interviewers was 1.66 percent higher.

of our efforts to avoid influencing employees was prohibitive. Control groups were used in elections 26 and 27. The employees in those elections were divided randomly into two groups. Employees in the control group were interviewed only after the election, while employees in the regular sample were interviewed according to the normal two-wave procedure.

The employees in the two groups were compared on all demographic variables. No significant differences were found on any variable relevant to the study.[25] There were no significant differences in campaign familiarity, reports of unlawful campaigning, or vote between control and regular groups. These data provide substantial evidence that the study neither increased employees' sensitivity to the pre-election campaign nor affected their vote.

On two occasions, we studied a second election in a unit in which we had studied a previous election.[26] Further evidence that the study did not increase employee sensitivity to the campaign is provided by the second election data. Some employees were interviewed in both elections, others only in the second election. If any group of employees should have been sensitized by questioning, it was those who knew from past experience that the Wave II interviews would deal with the campaign. Yet those employees who were interviewed in both elections were not significantly more familiar with the campaign than those interviewed solely at the second election. Indeed, there were no significant differences in campaign familiarity between those re-interviewed and those not even employed at the time of the first election.

Refusals

It is possible that those employees who refused to be interviewed, although not biasing the sample estimates of the election results, might have biased estimates of familiarity and perception of unlawful campaigning. Some data are available for four groups of employees who can be characterized as semi-refusals: (1) those who initially refused to be interviewed at Wave I, but acquiesced at the request of a troubleshooter; (2) those who completed Wave I, refused initially at Wave II, but were interviewed by a trouble-shooter; (3) those who completed Wave I, but refused to be interviewed at Wave II; and (4) those who completed both interviews, but would not disclose their vote.

---

[25] The control group in election 26 had a significantly lower proportion of Republicans and a significantly higher proportion of independents than the regular group.

[26] Elections 4 and 24 were in the same unit, as were elections 9 and 33.

If those employees who refused to be interviewed were influenced by fear of reprisals because their union sympathies might be disclosed to the employer, there should be a disproportionately large number of union supporters in the various refusal groups. Instead, Table 2–4 shows that the proportion of employees favoring union representation at the Wave I interview in each refusal group is less than that of the comparable group of non-refusals. The distinguishing characteristic of the refusals is thus their disposition, at Wave I, to vote against union representation. It is likely that this disposition explains, in substantial measure, the reluctance of these employees to be interviewed. Being against union representation is strongly associated with satisfaction with the *status quo*. To some employees satisfied with the *status quo*,

Table 2-4

Voting Intent of Semi-Refusals
Compared to Other Employees

Type of Interview	Company	Intent Uncertain		Union		Total
Troubleshot Wave I	27		2		15	44
row %		61%		5%		34%	
Regular Wave I	439		87		522	1048
row %		42%		8%		50%	
Total	466		89		537	1092
Troubleshot Wave II	27		7		15	49
row %		55%		14%		31%	
Regular Wave II	439		81		520	1040
row %		42%		8%		50%	
Total	466		88		535	1089
Wave II refusal	23		5		14	42
row %		55%		12%		33%	
Wave II completion	468		90		545	1103
row %		43%		8%		49%	
Total	491		95		559	1145
Vote refusals	31		25		35	91
row %		34%		28%		38%	
Vote disclosers	420		63		485	968
row %		43%		7%		50%	
Total	451		88		520	1059

both the union and the study were perceived as outside agents, intruding into a satisfactory employer-employee relationship. These employees were both opposed to the union and reluctant to cooperate with the study.

The comparatively small number of employees who finally refused to be interviewed or to disclose their vote did not result in any major differences in the vote distribution in the sample as compared to the election results. Equally important, the total omission from the sample of the refusals does not appear to have biased the sample in the direction of having fewer employees coerced by employer unlawful campaigning than in the population as a whole. The refusals, who tended to be against union representation at Wave I, required no coercion to bring them into the employer's camp and were unlikely to have been the target of such tactics. Additionally, there is no evidence that these employees possessed characteristics different from the sample that would render them peculiarly susceptible to coercion.

A high refusal rate in elections characterized by substantial illegal behavior would suggest a relationship between refusals and situations conducive to fear of reprisal. There was, however, no evidence of such a relationship. The refusal rate was no higher in elections in which substantial illegal campaigning was found than in elections in which no unlawful campaigning was found.[27]

BOARD AND COURT CHALLENGES TO THE STUDY

Three employers filed post-election objections with the Board, alleging that by interviewing employees we interfered with their free choice in the election. One set of objections was withdrawn and the Board dismissed the other two.[28]

One employer instituted judicial proceedings against us on two separate occasions, seeking to enjoin us from studying elections in two different plants. The first suit, filed at a time when Finfrock Motor Sales[29] was pending before the Board, was withdrawn when we agreed not to study that election until Finfrock was decided. The second suit was settled, at a time when 90 percent of Wave I interviewing had been completed, on the basis of our promise not to interview any further until after the election and the employer's promise to provide us with all campaign materials.

[27] See Tables 5–1 and 5–2 for a description of the unlawful campaigning found in the elections studied.

[28] Finfrock Motor Sales, 203 NLRB 541 (1973); Alloy Engineering & Casting Co., Case No. 38-RC-1415 (1974) (unreported).

[29] *Supra* note 28.

CHAPTER 3

The Predispositions of Vote

Board regulation is based on the assumption that pre-campaign intent is tenuous and easily changed by the campaign. Employees, however, have been working for the employer involved and, as a result, may be expected to have stable attitudes toward their employer and their working conditions. In addition, some employees have been union members while holding previous jobs, and virtually all have been exposed to other peoples' opinions about the merits of union representation.

Since union organizing drives promote union representation as a remedy for unsatisfactory working conditions and company campaigns respond by praising working conditions and deprecating the value of unionization, employees whose opinions are initially strong may be wholly unaffected by the campaign. At the very least, prior attitudes should affect the way employees respond to the campaign issues.

Attitudes and voting intent were measured in the Wave I interviews, which occurred as soon as possible after the direction of election or consent election agreement. In nearly every election, the period between the Wave I interview and the election was marked by substantial campaigning on the part of one or both parties. If the campaign influenced employees to vote contrary to their initial predispositions, neither their attitudes towards working conditions or unions nor their vote intent should be highly related to their vote. If, on the other hand, the campaign did not cause employees to vote contrary to their initial predispositions, then pre-campaign attitudes and intent should predict vote.

ATTITUDES AND VOTE

Attitudes are abstractions that account for the relationship between a set of personal experiences and a behavior. Attitudes may exert a directive and dynamic influence on behavior.[1] We anticipated

[1] McGuire, *The Nature of Attitudes and Attitude Change* in G. LINDZEY & E. ARONSON (eds.) HANDBOOK OF SOCIAL PSYCHOLOGY, vol. 3, 147 (2d ed. 1969).

that employees' attitudes toward their working conditions and toward unions would be relevant to their decision to vote for or against union representation.

Attitudes toward Working Conditions

Job satisfaction questions emphasized those working conditions most likely to be affected by unionization. Items that correlated highly with vote in the pre-test studies were used, since attitudes were of interest as predictors of vote.[2] Seven questions dealing with specific working conditions were asked in the pre-election interview. An eighth question asked whether the employee was satisfied with the company as a place to work. Four of these items were repeated in the post-election interview, so that attitude change could be measured.

Items were scored on a three-point equal interval scale: satisfied, don't know or uncertain, and dissatisfied. An employee's responses to the eight items were summed to form an index of his satisfaction with working conditions.[3] The four attitude items in Wave I that were repeated in the Wave II interview were summed separately to make short form indices to be used in the attitude change analyses.

The reliability of the long form ($r = .78$) and both short form indices (Wave I, $r = .68$; Wave II, $r = .69$) indicates that the items measure a common psychological concept, satisfaction with working conditions.[4] This degree of internal consistency among the items justified using them together as an index.

There was a significant correlation between satisfaction with working conditions and vote ($r = -.53$).[5] This indicates that employees who were dissatisfied with working conditions were most likely to

---

[2] A correlation is a statistical index of the degree of association between two variables. It ranges from 1, indicating a perfect positive correspondence between scores on two variables, through 0, indicating no correspondence between them, to –1, a perfect negative relationship in which high scores on one variable correspond to low scores on the other.

[3] Fewer than 1 percent of the sample failed to answer any single job satisfaction question. The missing data were not systematic, and no employee failed to answer more than two of the eight questions. Missing responses were scored as uncertain or don't know, so that attitude indices could be constructed for all employees who participated in both interviews. This is a customary method of treating random missing data, since it is nonbiasing.

[4] Reliability has a technical meaning in this context. It is an index of the degree to which the questions measure a common psychological concept. There are several standard methods of estimating reliability. The one used here was based on maximum likelihood estimate of unidimensional common variance among the items. This factor analytic estimate is less conservative than split-half or coefficient alpha estimates and therefore is more appropriate for attitude change analysis.

[5] "Significance" is also a technical term indicating the likelihood that the result found by analyzing the sample data represents a non-zero relationship in the

vote for union representation. Those satisfied with working conditions
supported the company.

Figure 3–1 shows the proportion of the sample voting union at each

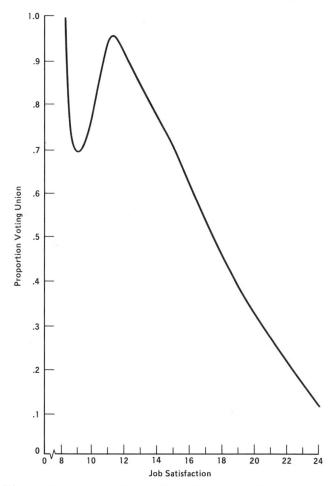

Figure 3-1. Proportion of Employees Voting Union at
Each Level of Job Satisfaction

population. We use the .01 level of significance at all times. By stating that the
correlation between satisfaction and vote ($r = -.53$) is significant at the .01 level,
we can be 99 percent confident that the relationship in the population is not zero.
With a very large sample, such as the one in this study, even low correlations will
be significantly different from zero. A more meaningful question is the power of a
relationship. The power of a correlation is its square, which indicates the proportion of the variance of one variable that can be accounted for by the other. A
correlation of .10 is significant at the .01 level if the sample is greater than 1,000,
but it may not be very meaningful because it shows that the two variables have
only 1 percent of their variance in common.

level of satisfaction. Satisfaction scores ranged from a low of 8, indicating dissatisfaction with all working conditions, to a high of 24. The average company voter scored 22, while the average union voter scored 16. Employees with a satisfaction score below 18 voted three to one (303–99) for union representation; those who scored 18 or above voted three to one (453–149) against union representation. Knowing whether an employee's satisfaction score was greater or less than 18 thus allows one to predict his final vote with 75 percent accuracy.

Table 3–1 presents the correlations between the job satisfaction items, the Wave I job satisfaction index and vote. The individual

Table 3-1

Correlations between Job Satisfaction Items, Wave I Job Satisfaction Index, and Vote

Item	Job Satisfaction Index[b]	Vote[c]
1.[a] Are you satisfied or not satisfied with your wages?	.67	−.40
2.[a] Do supervisors in this company play favorites or do they treat all employees alike?	.66	−.34
3. Are you satisfied or not satisfied with the type of work you are doing?	.34	−.14
4. Do your supervisors show appreciation when you do a good job or do they just take it for granted?	.62	−.30
5.[a] Are you satisfied or not satisfied with your fringe benefits, such as pensions, vacations, holiday pay, insurance, and sick leave?	.64	−.31
6. Do you think there is a good chance or not much chance for you to get promoted in this company?	.56	−.30
7. Are you satisfied or not satisfied with the job security at this company?	.66	−.42
8.[a] Taking everything into consideration, would you say you were satisfied or not satisfied with this company as a place to work?	.65	−.36

[a]Questions that were repeated in the Wave II interview.
[b]$p \le .01$; $r = .07$; $N = 1163$.
[c]$p \le .01$; $r = .08$; $N = 1004$.
NOTE: The negative correlations indicate that employees who were satisfied tended to vote against union representation.

satisfaction items correlating most highly with vote were job security ($r = -.42$) and wages ($r = -.40$). Employees who were not satisfied with existing job security and wages were the most likely to vote for union representation.

The only satisfaction item not substantially correlated with vote was satisfaction with the work itself ($r = -.14$). Table 3–2 shows that 94 percent of the company voters and 85 percent of the union voters reported satisfaction with the type of work they were doing.[6] Those few employees who were dissatisfied with their work were more likely to vote union than those who were satisfied. This item was not a good predictor of vote, however, since employees who were satisfied with their work, but dissatisfied with other aspects of their working conditions, tended to vote union. Unionization would seem to be especially appealing to employees who like the type of work they are doing but feel working conditions are unsatisfactory. These employees have a particular interest in attempting to change the conditions in their current situation, since they have no dissatisfaction motivating them to try to find a different type of work.

Table 3-2

Satisfaction with Type of Work and Vote

Vote		Dissatisfied	Uncertain Don't know	Satisfied	Total
Company		33	2	517	552
	row %	6%	.4%	94%	
Union		64	4	384	452
	row %	14%	1%	85%	
Total		97	6	901	1004
	row %	10%	1%	89%	

(The three data columns Dissatisfied, Uncertain Don't know, and Satisfied fall under the spanning header Satisfaction*.)*

---

[6] Excluding the don't know and uncertain answers from the percentage base, 90 percent of the employees sampled were satisfied with their work. These results agree closely with those from 1971 and 1973 surveys of working men and women. The Survey Research Center, University of Michigan, reported that 90–91 percent of workers responded satisfied when asked: "All in all, how satisfied are you with your job?" (*Job Satisfaction: Is There a Trend?* Manpower Research Monograph No. 30, U.S. Dept. of Labor, Manpower Administration, 1974).

Attitudes toward Unions

The union attitude questions focussed on employees' feelings about unions in general rather than the union involved in the election, since we could not assume that employees had firsthand experience with any union, much less the one that was a party to the election. Interviewers were also instructed to assure employees that their responses did not have to be based on personal experience.

Employees were no more likely to refuse to answer union attitude questions than job satisfaction items.[7] There were, however, more don't know and uncertain responses to union attitude questions than to job satisfaction items, probably reflecting employees' greater familiarity with their own working conditions than with unions in general. Uncertain and don't know responses ranged from 10–16 percent for most union attitude items, compared to 1–5 percent for the job satisfaction items. Twenty-eight percent of the employees expressed no opinion in response to the question asking whether or not union dues were too high, probably because this question appeared to require more specific information than the other questions.

Union attitudes were measured on a scale of agree, don't know or uncertain, and disagree. The item analysis of the pre-test data indicated that employees who answered uncertain or don't know to questions about unions were more likely to vote against the union than for it. On the basis of the pre-test results, we scored uncertain or don't know responses as slightly unfavorable instead of neutral.[8]

The short and long form union attitude indices, like the job satisfaction indices, were highly reliable (Wave I long form, $r = .81$, Wave I short form, $r = .72$, Wave II short form, $r = .74$). Employee responses to the union attitude items were for the most part internally consistent, indicating that using the items to form an index was justified.

The correlation between union attitudes and vote was .62. Favorable attitudes toward unions in general create a strong predisposition to vote for union representation. Figure 3–2 shows that the percentage of employees voting for union representation increases at each level of greater favorability towards unions. Union attitude indices ranged from a low score of 8 to a high score of 32. The average union voter's score was 26; the average company voter scored 15. Figure 3–2 shows that employees who had a union attitude index of 22 or higher favored union representation by approximately three to one (381–

---

[7] Fewer than 1 percent of the sample failed to answer any single question. Missing data were scored as if the employee's response had been don't know.

[8] Agree was scored as 4; uncertain or don't know as 2; disagree as 1.

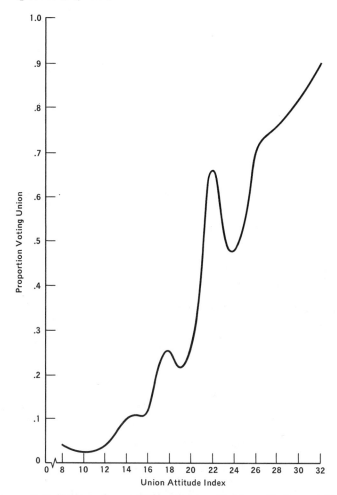

**Figure 3-2. Proportion of Employees Voting Union at Each
Level of Favorability Toward Unions in General**

138); those with an index below 22 were opposed more than four to
one (414–71). Knowing whether an employee's union attitude score
was greater or less than 22 enables one to predict his vote with 79
percent accuracy.

Table 3–3 represents the correlations between the union attitude
items, the Wave I index, and vote. All the individual items correlated highly with vote, the one relating to overall attitude toward
unions at .60. The weakest correlation, not surprisingly, is between
vote and the belief that unions are a major cause of high prices. The
likelihood that unionization of their employer would contribute to

Table 3-3

Correlations between Union Attitude Items,
Wave I Union Attitude Index, and Vote

Item	Union Attitude Index[b]	Vote[c]
1. Unions are becoming too strong. Do you agree or disagree?	.66	.40
2.[a] Unions make sure that employees are treated fairly by supervisors. Do you agree or disagree?	.65	.39
3.[a] Unions help working men and women to get better wages and hours. Do you agree or disagree?	.60	.38
4.[a] Unions interfere with good relations between companies and workers. Do you agree or disagree?	.62	.37
5. Union dues are too high. Do you agree or disagree?	.64	.45
6. When a strike is called, it is generally for a good reason. Do you agree or disagree?	.66	.44
7. Unions are a major cause of high prices. Do you agree or disagree?	.58	.26
8.[a] Taking everything into consideration, would you describe your overall attitude toward unions as favorable or not favorable?	.80	.60

[a]Questions that were repeated in the Wave II interview.
[b]$p \leq .01$; $r = .07$; $N = 1163$.
[c]$p \leq .01$; $r = .08$; $N = 1004$.

inflation was probably less salient to most employees than the potential immediate economic gains of unionization. Many employees who thought that unions in general were a major cause of high prices nevertheless voted for union representation.

Predicting Vote from Attitudes

Whether or not an employee favors union representation in dealing with his employer is likely to be a function of his views as to the desirability of union representation in general as well as his satisfaction with his current working conditions. The union attitude and job satisfaction indices were designed to measure the contribution of each type of predisposition to the vote decision. An employee who is dissatisfied with his current working conditions but very unfavorable toward unions would be much less likely to vote for union representation than one who is also dissatisfied and has a generally favorable attitude toward unions. Similarly, an employee who is generally favorable toward unions but satisfied with his working conditions might not wish to risk a change in those conditions that might occur if a union were voted in.

In order to utilize both types of predisposition to predict vote, the union attitude and job satisfaction indices were combined in a multiple linear regression equation.[9] As shown in Table 3–4 the cross validated correlation predicting vote from the two attitude indices was .67.[10] Employee attitudes, measured prior to intense pre-election campaigning, thus form strong and stable predispositions to vote for or against union representation.

Table 3-4

Multiple Linear Regression of Attitudes to Predict Vote in Two Samples

	Sample 1 *N = 501*	*Sample 2* *N = 503*
Standardized beta weights		
Union attitudes	.46	.49
Job attitudes	−.34	−.23
Multiple correlation	.70*	.64*
Cross validated correlation	.67*	.67*

*$p \leq .01$

The regression equation may be used to predict how each individual

[9] Multiple regression is a procedure for determining the maximum linear relationship between a criterion, here vote, and a combination of predictors. M. M. TATSUOKA, VALIDATION STUDIES (Inst. for Personality & Ability Testing, Champaign, Ill. Selected Topics in Advanced Statistics No. 5, 1969).

[10] Because a multiple correlation is based on the particular characteristics of a sample, it is an overestimate of the relationship between predictor and criterion variables in the population from which the sample is drawn. In order to estimate the relationship in the relevant populations (voters in these thirty-one elections as well as voters in union representation elections generally), the following standard procedure was used. The sample within each election was randomly split into two groups. The within-election groups were used to form two across-election subsamples. As shown in Table 3–4, each group was analyzed separately. The predictor weights from each subsample were then applied to the other to determine the cross-validated multiple correlation.

employee will vote. The prediction is based on a Bayesian estimate of the likelihood that each employee is a union or company voter in view of his attitudes, the average union and company voter's attitudes and the actual proportion of union and company voters in the sample.[11] A 50 percent likelihood of voting for or against the union was used as the criterion for classifying employees as potential union or company voters.

As shown in Table 3–5, the attitudes of 83 percent of the company voters and 78 percent of the union voters correctly predicted their vote. Overall, we could correctly predict 81 percent of the employees' votes from their pre-campaign attitudes.[12]

Table 3-5

Comparison of Predicted Votes, Based on Pre-Campaign Attitudes, with Actual Votes

		Predicted Vote		
Actual Vote		*Company*	*Union*	*Total*
Company		460	92	552
	row %	83%	17%	
Union		100	352	452
	row %	22%	78%	
Total		560	444	1004
	row %	56%	44%	

The 81 percent prediction rate achieved by using both job and union attitudes is not substantially higher than the 75 percent achieved by using job satisfaction alone or the 79 percent using union attitudes alone. Although attitudes toward unions in general and satisfaction with current working conditions are different psychological concepts, in the context of a union representation election they are highly related $(r = -.51)$. The employees who were most favorable toward unions in general were also the ones least satisfied with their current working conditions.

Figure 3–3 shows that at Wave I attitudes were already broadly polarized in the direction of the employees' final vote. The distribu-

[11] See W. W. COOLEY & P. R. LOHNES, MULTIVARIATE PROCEDURES FOR THE BEHAVIORAL SCIENCES (1962).

[12] Attitudinal data collected prior to the 1956 presidential election correctly predicted the vote of 86 percent of the electorate. A. CAMPBELL, P. E. CONVERSE, W. E. MILLER & D. E. STOKES, THE AMERICAN VOTER 37–38 (Abridged ed. 1964).

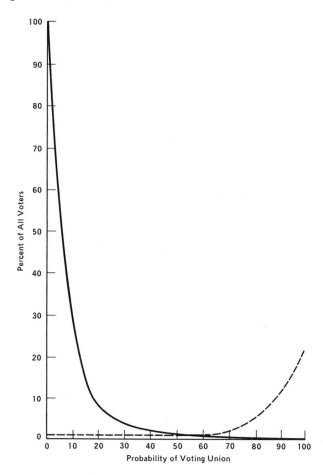

Figure 3-3. Distribution of Union and Company Voters by the Probability of Voting for the Union

tion, which peaks to the left, shows the probability of actual company voters voting against the union. Sixty-six percent of the company voters fall in the interval from 0 to 19 percent probability of a union vote based on their pre-campaign attitudes. The distribution that peaks to the right represents actual union voters. Fifty-three percent of the union voters fall in the interval from 80 to 100 percent probability of voting for the union. Not only were attitudes stable throughout the subsequent campaigning by both parties, but they had polarized prior to the beginning of intensive campaigning. Changing attitudes enough to cause a behavior change is never easy, but it is particularly difficult when attitudes toward that behavior are clearly favorable or unfavorable. Under these circumstances, attitudes may moderate substantially without causing a change in behavior.

Prediction errors are indicated by the overlap of the two distributions at the .50 value. Seventeen percent of the actual company voters were predicted to be union voters; 22 percent of the union voters were predicted to be company voters. The tails of both distributions are remarkably flat. The prediction was in error for about 2 percent of the sample across the entire range of attitudes. That is, we incorrectly predicted the votes of about 2 percent of the employees who had been very positive toward unionization, 2 percent who had been very negative, and about the same proportion whose attitudes were in the middle of the range. Prediction errors among employees with very strong attitudes may in part be due to some of those employees erroneously reporting their actual vote.

Predicting Vote from Intent

Intent was the single best predictor of vote ($r = .73$). Table 3–6 shows that 94 percent of the employees intending to vote for the company did so, as did 82 percent of those intending to vote for the union. Of the 905 employees who reported a firm intent for or against the union, 87 percent voted in accordance with that intent. By using intent to predict vote, we correctly predicted the outcome of twenty-nine of the thirty-one elections.[13]

Intent is a function of attitudes. The cross-validated multiple correlation between union attitudes and job satisfaction and intent was .75 (see Table 3–7). Employees whose job satisfaction was low relative to others in their unit and who at the same time had favorable attitudes toward unions intended to vote for union representation. Similarly, most employees who were satisfied with working conditions and generally unfavorable toward unions at no time intended to vote for union representation. The .67 correlation between attitudes and vote indicates that to a large extent employees acted on their attitudes.

---

[13] We were wrong in elections 25 and 33. Attitudes also predicted the outcome of all but two elections, missing in elections 1 and 22. See Appendix F. Elections 13–15 were treated as one election for this and some other analyses, because there were so few employees in each unit—three in 13, four in 14, eight in 15. Each unit was composed of mechanics employed by a different auto dealer in the same small town, the same union was involved in each, the same lawyer directed each company campaign, and the elections were held on successive days.

Table 3-6

Comparison of Vote Intent
Prior to the Campaign and Actual Vote

Vote	Intent Company	Undecided	Intent Union	Refused	Total
Company	393	43	88	28	552
column %	94%	68%	18%	78%	55%
Union	27	20	397	8	452
column %	6%	32%	82%	22%	45%
Total	420	63	485	36	1004
row %	42%	6%	48%	4%	

Table 3-7

Multiple Correlation between Attitudes and Intent

	Sample 1 N = 488	Sample 2 N = 480
Standardized beta weights		
Union attitudes	.53	.54
Job attitudes	−.33	−.31
Multiple correlation	.76*	.75*
Cross validated correlation	.76*	.75*

*$p \leq .01$

The powerful correlation between attitudes and vote, as well as that between intent and vote, is contrary to the Board's assumption that pre-campaign intent is tenuous and easily altered by the campaign. The relationship between predispositions and vote is not only powerful but broadly general. Attitudes and intent predicted vote in midwestern farm communities, urban ghettos, and rural Kentucky towns, among employees working in factories, warehouses, retail stores, nursing homes, and offices, in units ranging from four to nearly four hundred employees. Attitudes and intent predicted vote for males and females, whites, blacks, and Spanish-speaking, old and young, well and poorly educated. They predicted vote when local unemployment was 2 percent and when it was 10 percent. There is no reason to suppose that a similarly powerful relationship between predispositions and vote would not exist in other union representation elections. Admittedly, the relationship has not been established empirically in regions outside the midwest and upper south. The diversity of the situations in which predispositions do predict vote, however, suggests that the relationship would be nullified only in truly extraordinary circumstances.

DETERMINANTS OF PREDISPOSITIONS

This study was designed to determine the effects of campaigning on employees' predispositions to vote for or against union representation. It was not designed to identify the determinants of those predispositions. Nevertheless, we were able to consider two possible sources of influence on predispositions to vote for or against union representation.

Demographic Characteristics and Job Experiences

If employees who have similar demographic characteristics or job experiences have similar attitudes toward unions or their working conditions, the determinants of those attitudes may be traced to experiences that those employees have in common. If one were to find, for example, that black employees tended to vote union, the psychological explanation would not be in race *per se* but in those experiences common to black men and women that lead to attitudes favorable to union representation.[14]

The correlations between demographic and job experience characteristics, predispositions, and vote in Table 3–8 indicate that across elections there were only slight tendencies for employees with similar characteristics and experiences to have similar predispositions. While many of the correlations in Table 3–8 are statistically significant, none is very powerful.

Although the Board has assumed that employees are generally unsophisticated about union-management relations,[15] 43 percent of the employees we interviewed had been union members on other jobs. Seventy-five percent reported that a member of their immediate family (father, mother, or spouse) had been a union member. Thirty percent of the sample had even voted in a previous NLRB election. These

---

[14] Herman, Dunham & Hulin, *Organizational Structure, Demographic Characteristics and Employee Responses,* 13 ORGANIZATIONAL BEHAVIOR AND HUMAN PERFORMANCE 206–232 (1975).

[15] See, e.g., Boaz Spinning Co., Inc., 177 NLRB 788 (1971); Bausch & Lomb, Inc., 185 NLRB 262 (1970).

Table 3-8

Demographic Characteristics, Job Experiences,
Predispositions, and Vote

		Union Attitude Index[a]	Job Attitude Index[a]	Intent[b]	Vote[b]	Scoring Key: Low Score Responses[c]
Age		−.14*	.13*	−.11*	−.11*	24 years or less
	N	1160	1160	1101	1065	
Sex		−.02	.03	.01	.06	Male
	N	1159	1159	1101	1066	
Race		−.10*	−.03	−.10*	−.11*	Minority
	N	1100	1100	1044	1010	
Education level		.02	−.06	−.02	−.01	1–4 years of school
	N	1158	1158	1099	1063	
Political preference		.13*	−.06	.07	.09	Other than Democratic
	N	1162	1162	1103	1067	
Marital status		−.04	.02	−.04	−.05	Not married
	N	1162	1162	1103	1067	
Tenure		−.15*	.00	−.10*	−.09*	Less than 1 year
	N	1162	1162	1103	1067	
Hours		−.03	.00	−.03	−.05	Less than 25 hours per week
	N	1159	1159	1100	1064	
Wage rate		−.12*	.06	−.12*	−.13*	Under $2 per hour
	N	1136	1136	1085	1042	
Previous union member		.02	.00	−.01	−.02	No
	N	944	944	891	868	
Family union member		.03	−.03	.02	.03	No
	N	1162	1162	1103	1067	
Voted for union in previous NLRB election		.55*	−.41*	.50*	.48*	Voted against the union
	N	351	351	343	338	

*p ≤ .01
[a]Attitude indices scored such that a high score indicates favorable attitudes.
[b]Intent and vote scored such that a high score indicates a union supporter.
[c]See also Wave I interview schedule, Appendix C.

facts cast doubt on the Board's assumption that employees are generally unsophisticated with respect to union-management relations.

Favorable attitudes toward unions in general are slightly more characteristic of minority group members $(r = .10)$, younger employees $(r = -.14)$, and supporters of the Democratic party $(r = -.13)$. Prior union membership is not associated with more favorable attitudes toward unions, suggesting that many employees who had been union members elsewhere had not been wholly satisfied with union representation. Similarly, the union membership of family members did not predispose employees to be favorable to unions. Only previous experience that reflects attitudes favorable to unions is strongly associated with current attitudes toward unions. Employees who had voted for union representation in a previous NLRB election were more favorable toward unions in general $(r = .55)$, suggesting that favorable attitudes toward unions remain consistent.

Significantly higher satisfaction with working conditions was characteristic of only one demographic group. Older employees were slightly more satisfied than younger employees $(r = .13)$. While the older employees in our sample may have held better jobs, a more likely explanation is that their previous work experience made current working conditions more acceptable. Long-tenured employees were not significantly more satisfied with working conditions than junior employees, and tenure, more than age, is normally associated with better jobs and higher wages.[16]

The relationships of demographic and job experience characteristics to intent and vote are similar to their relationships to attitudes. Age, race, wage rate, and tenure correlate significantly, though not strongly.

The significant but low-powered relationships between demographic characteristics, job experiences, predispositions, and vote may be due to powerful trends in some elections being nullified by contrary trends in other elections. Although the number of employees in a particular election was often too small for minor trends to reach significance, we analyzed the association in each election between demographic characteristics, job experience, predispositions, and vote. The only contrary trends found were with respect to race. In all elections but 18 and 31 a higher proportion of black employees than white employees were in favor of union representation.[17]

---

[16] See Gibson & Klein, *Employee Attitudes as a Function of Age and Length of Service: A Reconceptualization,* 13 ACADEMY OF MANAGEMENT JOURNAL 411–426 (1974). The correlation between age and tenure in our sample was .50.

[17] In election 18, one of the employer's campaign themes was that the union was anti-black.

In sum, employees' strong predispositions to vote for or against union representation cannot be wholly attributed to these common demographic characteristics or job experiences.

Pre-Wave I Campaigning

It is possible that employee predispositions to vote for or against union representation were stimulated, fixed, or changed by campaigning that occurred before the Wave I interview. There was little campaigning between the card-signing drive and the direction of election. Some campaigning did, however, take place in the period between the direction of election and the Wave I interview.[18] If the campaigning that occurred prior to Wave I served to fix predispositions, the relationship between predispositions and vote should be significantly stronger in elections in which there was substantial campaigning before Wave I than in elections in which there was not.

In order to test this hypothesis, elections were divided into two groups: those in which neither party conducted a substantial campaign prior to Wave I and those in which one or both did so. (A substantial campaign was defined for purposes of this analysis as one in which at least one meeting was conducted.) Table 3–9 shows that pre-interview campaigning did not affect the relationship between predispositions and vote. Voting was as predictable when there had been no substantial campaigning prior to Wave I as when there had been campaigning. There is thus no evidence that pre-Wave I campaigning had the effect of fixing attitudes or intent.

There was, in any event, sufficient campaigning after Wave I to enable us to test the Board's hypothesis that voting intent is easily altered by the campaign. Indeed, most of the campaign, particularly that conducted by the employer, took place after Wave I. Across all elections, 74 percent (45/61) of the company meetings were held and 77 percent (120/156) of the company written materials were distributed after the Wave I interview. The unions held 51 percent (55/108) of their meetings and distributed 64 percent (96/150) of their written materials after Wave I.

The campaigning that took place after Wave I could not have changed many employees' voting intent. Eighty-seven percent of those

---

[18] Wave I interviewing began an average of eleven days after the direction of election. We were unable to conduct the Wave I interviews earlier, because the list of employee names and addresses that the employer is required to furnish the Board (Excelsior Underwear, Inc., 156 NLRB 1236 (1956)) and that the Board was required to give us (NLRB v. Getman, 450 F.2d 670 (D.C. Cir. 1971)) was not due until seven days after the direction of the election.

Table 3-9

Relationship between Predispositions and Vote in Elections with Substantial Pre-Wave I Campaigning Compared to Elections without Substantial Pre-Wave I Campaigning

	Correlations with Vote		
Campaign Group[a]	Union Attitude Index	Job Attitude Index	Intent
No substantial campaigning	.64*	−.49*	.73*
N	137	137	136
Substantial campaigning	.63*	−.53*	.73*
N	834	834	802

	Test for the Difference between Correlations		
	Union Attitude Index	Job Attitude Index	Intent
Z[b]	.25	.58	.05

*$p \leq .01$

[a]Elections 12, 18, 20, 25, 26, and 31 had no substantial campaigning prior to the Wave I interview. Elections 19 and 32 could not be classified, since we were unable to determine the extent of pre-Wave I campaigning. They were excluded from this analysis.

[b]Z is the test for the difference between correlations in two independent samples. Z must be greater than 2.33 to be significant at the .01 level.

employees who stated an intent at Wave I voted consistently with that intent. It is possible that the absence of substantial switching between Wave I and the election is due to the fact that most of the employees who could be influenced by the campaign had switched before the Wave I interview. To accept this hypothesis, one must assume that the limited campaigning which took place prior to Wave I had a greater effect than the more substantial campaigning after Wave I.

WHEN PREDISPOSITIONS DO NOT PREDICT VOTE

Predispositions failed to predict vote accurately for 19 percent of the employees interviewed.[19] Neither demographic nor job experience

---

[19] This percentage is appropriate for both the attitudinal and intentional predictions. Attitude data were available on all employees, but some employees were undecided at Wave I or refused to answer the intent question. Because the two

characteristics distinguished the attitude errors or switchers from those who voted in accord with their pre-campaign attitudes or intent. Switchers and attitude errors who voted company resembled other company voters; those who voted union resembled other union voters.

Employees who switched or were attitude errors did experience significantly greater attitude change than employees who voted in accord with their predispositions. Table 3–10 shows that the job satisfaction of employees who intended to vote union or whose attitudes predicted they would do so, but who voted company, increased more than that of union supporters who voted union ($r = .44$; $.45$). Their attitudes had become much less favorable toward unions generally than the attitudes of union voters ($r = -.59$; $-.63$). The union attitudes of company supporters who switched to the union became significantly more favorable than those of company supporters who voted for the company ($r = .31$; $.51$). Their satisfaction with working conditions also decreased significantly more than that of company voters ($r = -.25$; $-.33$).[20]

Since attitudes were measured for the second time after employees voted, it is impossible to determine whether attitude change preceded vote switch. It is, however, possible that employees switched because something in the campaign caused them to reevaluate their opinions, thus precipitating attitude change and vote switch. In Chapter 4 we turn to the influence of the campaign on switching.

The finding that switch is associated with attitude change might indicate that employees who switched from a union intent to a company vote were not coerced by unlawful employer campaigning. If they had been coerced, their attitudes should still resemble those of union voters, even though they voted against the union. The research on

predispositional measures were so highly correlated ($r = .75$), those employees who were switchers (their intent did not correctly predict their vote) were also likely to be prediction errors (their attitudes did not correctly predict their vote). There was no gain in vote predictability by adding intent to attitudes in the multiple regression equation as most of the switchers were still erroneously classified. Using attitudes alone in the regression equation resulted in a lower level of prediction, but not all switchers were prediction errors, so that a somewhat different and larger group of employees, the prediction errors, was identified.

[20] The attitude change scores used in this analysis are known as true residual gain or true independent change scores. See Tucker, Damarin, & Messick, *A Base-free Measure of Change*, 31 PSYCHOMETRIKA 457–473 (1966) and Cronbach & Furby, *How Should We Measure "Change"—or Should We?* 74 PSYCHOLOGICAL BULL. 68–80 (1970). True change scores are used because raw change scores are systematically related to errors of measurement. Residual gain or independent change scores represent attitude change that is uncorrelated with initial attitudes.

Table 3-10

Correlations between Vote and Attitude
Change within Predisposition Groups

Predisposition	Correlation between Vote and Union Attitude Change	Correlation between Vote and Job Attitude Change	N
Intent union	−.59*	.44*	485
Attitudes predict union vote	−.63*	.45*	444
Intent company	.31*	.25*	420
Attitudes predict company vote	.51*	−.33*	560

*$p \leq .01$

attitude change, however, indicates that behavior inconsistent with attitudes stimulates attitudes to change to be consistent with that behavior.[21] A union supporter who was coerced into voting against the union thus might have changed his attitudes to be consistent with his vote. In Chapter 5, we consider the effect of unlawful campaigning on vote.

SUMMARY

Board regulation of the campaign rests on the assumption that the pre-campaign intent of most employees is tenuous and easily changed by the campaign. The data indicate, however, that employees have strong and stable predispositions to vote for or against union representation. The typical union voter is dissatisfied with his current working conditions, though not necessarily with the work itself, and generally favorable toward unions. The votes of 81 percent of the employees could be predicted from their pre-campaign attitudes and intent. Employees who switched or whose attitudes did not predict their vote experienced significantly more attitude change than employees who voted in accord with their predispositions. For the great majority of the employees, then, the data are inconsistent with the Board's assumption.

---

[21] McGuire, *A Syllogistic Analysis of Cognitive Relationships* in M. J. ROSEN-BERG, C. I. HOVLAND, W. J. McGUIRE, R. P. ABELSON & J. W. BREHM (eds.), AT-TITUDE ORGANIZATION AND CHANGE (1960).

CHAPTER 4

The Campaign and Vote

Since 81 percent of the employees voted in accord with their pre-campaign attitudes and intent, the Board's model of the employee whose vote is easily changed by the campaign is descriptive of at most 19 percent of the voters. Whatever effect the campaign may have had on other employees, it was not sufficient to cause them to vote contrary to their initial predispositions. Our discussion of the effect of the campaign considers the relationships between predispositions, campaign familiarity, and vote for all employees, as well as the relationship between the campaign and vote for those employees whose predispositions did not predict vote.

The Board assumes that many employees are influenced by the campaign to vote differently than they intend because their pre-campaign intent is tenuous, they attend closely to the issues raised in the campaign and make their final decision based on those issues. In order to determine the extent to which employees were attentive to the campaign, we compared the issues reported by each employee as having been raised in the campaign with the actual campaign issues set out in written materials, speeches, and personal contacts. An employee's Union Familiarity Index (UFI) is the proportion of union campaign issues he recalled. The Company Familiarity Index (CFI) is similarly constructed.

Both indices were constructed in a manner designed to maximize the employee's familiarity score. An employee was treated as recalling any campaign issue mentioned in response to any open-ended question, including those asking his and other employees' reasons for vote. It was unnecessary for an employee to report any details of a campaign issue to be credited with having recalled that issue. For example, one employee answered questions about the content of a union letter as follows.

> Said they'd make it better (x) pay (x) stop bosses playing favorites (x) retirement plan (x) don't know, just get us one (x) that's all.[1]

---

[1] An (x) indicates that at this point the interviewer asked the employee either to explain the previous response or to state what else was in the letter.

This answer was coded as recalling the union's claims that it would improve wages, obtain a retirement plan, and prevent supervisors from treating employees unfairly. While the employee furnished no details about the union's claims, he did remember the issues that had been raised.

FAMILIARITY LEVELS

General

Table 4–1 shows that the number of campaign issues varied widely from election to election. The average company campaign contained approximately thirty issues; the average union campaign approximately twenty-five issues. We used the percentage of issues an employee recognized in determining his familiarity index, rather than the number of issues recognized, in order to compensate for the different number of issues introduced in different campaigns.[2]

Table 4–1 suggests the existence of a relationship between the number of issues in a campaign and familiarity with that campaign. The significant negative correlations between number of company issues and familiarity ($r = -.55$) and number of union issues and familiarity ($r = -.56$) implies that employees recalled more about campaigns in which there were fewer issues. That conclusion is spurious because an employee who mentioned four issues in a forty-issue campaign would have a familiarity index of 10, while an employee who mentioned four issues in a ten-issue campaign would have a familiarity index of 40. The data actually indicate that regardless of how many issues were

---

[2] Although using percent of issues recognized to create the familiarity indices compensated for the differing number of issues in the campaigns, it built in a dependency between the election mean and variance (an index of spread or dispersion of the observed indices around the mean). The result was that in elections in which the mean familiarity was low, so was the variance, while high means were associated with high variance (CFI $r = .86$; UFI $r = .82$). This dependency was undesirable since it artificially emphasized differences among elections. Our primary form of analysis was to group employees by campaign exposure or elections by type of campaign and test for differential familiarity. The relationship between election mean and variance was likely to inflate the variability within groups, artificially depressing what would otherwise be significant between-group differences. In situations such as this, transformations are commonly used. We transformed each employee's familiarity index by taking the square root prior to further analyses. This transformation reduced the correlation between election means and variances (CFI $r = .12$; UFI $r = .12$) without affecting the primary characteristic of the familiarity index as a representation of the proportion of issues recalled. The means presented in the tables have been re-transformed by squaring. We would like to acknowledge the assistance of Dr. Charles Lewis, Department of Psychology, University of Illinois at Urbana-Champaign, in determining the proper transformation.

Table 4-1

Number of Campaign Issues and Average Campaign
Familiarity by Election

Election Number	Number of Company Issues	Average Company Familiarity	Number of Union Issues	Average Union Familiarity
1	19	21.16	11	15.21
2	23	16.73	21	10.30
3	20	17.22	14	17.64
4	28	13.62	23	6.10
5	17	12.04	22	4.45
6	34	8.53	30	5.90
8	37	8.76	33	4.41
9	31	6.76	35	4.54
10	29	8.12	47	4.49
11	46	6.92	34	10.63
12	35	6.40	17	6.55
13	8	6.10	12	16.73
14	8	11.36	12	5.06
15	8	11.42	12	11.90
16	28	6.71	18	8.70
18	35	8.41	21	7.51
19	*	*	28	8.70
20	36	5.87	19	4.28
21	25	11.83	32	8.70
22	28	11.02	31	9.42
23	21	5.66	14	3.03
24	49	4.93	*	*
25	35	9.49	18	6.55
26	34	5.95	26	6.45
27	34	9.55	29	8.58
28	48	9.24	33	9.18
29	43	13.32	29	4.54
30	38	7.08	35	7.24
31	21	21.16	33	6.35
32	36	6.86	20	8.35
33	41	6.71	28	6.30
Average	29.79	9.60	24.57	7.44

*All analyses of company familiarity exclude fourteen employees in election 19. The employer in this election would neither provide copies of campaign material nor discuss the campaign with us. All analyses of union familiarity exclude 102 employees in election 24, since the union did not campaign in this election.

emphasized in the campaign, employees recalled an average of three company issues and between two and three union issues.

There were an average of thirty issues in the company campaigns and twenty-five issues in the union campaigns. Most employees, when asked to recall what the employer had said in letters, meetings, or personal contacts, could recall only 10 percent of the company campaign issues (CFI = 9.60). When asked the same questions about the union campaign, employees on the average reported approximately 7 percent of the issues (UFI = 7.44).[3] This low level of familiarity with the campaigns of both parties contradicts the Board's assumption that employees are attentive to the campaign. Either the employees largely ignored the campaign or they quickly forgot the issues. In either event, they cannot meaningfully be described as having been attentive to the campaign.[4]

Familiarity with Particular Campaign Issues

One might anticipate that even if most employees recalled comparatively few issues, nearly all employees would recall those issues that were central to the campaign. This was not the case.

Table 4–2 shows that no company issue was reported by more than 40 percent of the total number of employees in the elections in which it was raised.[5] Only six company campaign issues were reported by 30 percent or more of the employees: improvements do not depend on unionization (310); new company or management has recently taken over (511); plant closing or moving may follow unionization, though not as retaliation for unionization (131); the financial costs of unionization outweigh its gains (410); the union is an outsider and will both interfere with the efficient operation of the business and harm employer-employee relationships (341); unionization may be followed

---

[3] The low level of campaign familiarity was not due to a substantial time lag between the end of the campaign and the Wave II interview. Eighty-four percent (1059/1264) of all Wave II interviews took place within two days of the election, 92 percent (1163/1264) within four days. The correlation between the number of days after the election the Wave II interview took place and CFI was −.05, the correlation with UFI was .02, neither of which were significantly different from zero.

[4] Voters in political elections have been found similarly inattentive to the campaign. Only 16 percent of the voters in the 1948 Presidential election knew the correct stands of both candidates on two major issues of the campaign. Over one-third knew one stand correctly or none at all. B. BERELSON, P. LAZARSFELD & W. McPHEE, VOTING 227 (1954).

[5] For inclusion in Table 4–2 or 4–3 an issue had to be emphasized in at least one election and raised in at least four others.

by the loss of some existing benefits, though not as a result of employer retaliation (111).[6]

Table 4-3 shows that the union themes that it would improve wages (810) and that it would prevent unfairness (820) were recalled by many more employees, 71 percent and 64 percent respectively, than any company theme. These themes correspond to opinions held by many employees prior to the campaign. The frequency with which they were repeated thus may be due to their salience. Alternatively, it may be due to an awareness that unions typically claim the ability to improve wages and insure fair treatment. Recall of other themes was substantially lower with only one other issue—union will improve working conditions generally (829)—reported by more than 30 percent of the voters.

While the campaign issues most frequently used tended to be those most highly recognized when they were used, there are some interesting exceptions. The company assertion that the costs of unionization (dues, etc.) outweighed its gains (410) was an issue frequently raised and well remembered, but the union's power to fine employees (412) and its alleged lack of concern for employee welfare (420), also frequently used, were much less frequently reported. The risk of strikes attendant upon unionization (210) was regularly used and recognized, but the possibility of losing wages (232) or jobs (220) in the event of a strike, equally used, was rarely reported. Lost wages may be so inherent in a strike as not to be mentioned separately from the strike issue, but the possibility of job loss would not appear to fall in this category.

Some company issues that were not often used received a high degree of recognition when they were. Included in this category are the statements that the company involved had a new management that should be given a chance to prove itself (511) or was too small to warrant unionization (510). The assertion that discharges or layoffs might take place after a union victory (151) was also rarely used, but frequently reported.

Union issues most frequently used also tended to be those most frequently reported, again with some exceptions. Issues touching upon union democracy, whether involving the choice of union leaders (860), the decision to call a strike (960), or union decision-making processes generally (861) received little recognition. Recognition of those union themes minimizing the financial costs of unionization—dues, initiation

---

[6] The number in parentheses following each issue is the code number for that issue. The entire code appears in Appendix D.

Table 4-2

Recognition of Company Campaign Issues

Issue Code	Number of Elections in Which Issue Was Used	Number of Employees in Elections in Which Issue Was Used	Percent of Employees Reporting Issue in Elections in Which Issue Was Used	Issue Content
310	28	1055	40	Improvements not dependent on unionization
511	7	338	37	New company/management recently taken over
131	14	590	35	Plant closing/moving may follow unionization (non-retaliatory)
410	26	943	33	Financial costs of union dues, etc. outweigh gains
341	26	1001	32	Union is outsider. Will interfere with efficiency, harm employer-employee relations
111	22	857	30	Loss of benefits may follow unionization (non-retaliatory)
300	27	1010	27	Wages good, equal to/better than under union contracts
151	9	264	25	Discharges/layoffs may follow unionization (non-retaliatory)
302	12	450	20	Pensions/profit-sharing good, equal to/better than under union contracts
315	10	470	20	Wages/working conditions will/may improve
210	23	810	19	If union wins, strike may follow
360	20	756	19	Employer has treated employees fairly/well/equally
510	7	256	19	Company too small to need union

640	25	995	19	Get facts before deciding. Employer will provide facts, accept employee decision
432	7	286	15	Union corruption
412	15	645	13	Union may fine employees
361	6	230	12	Named individual has treated employees fairly/well/equally
516	5	69	11	Company will fight union as hard as legally possible
656	6	263	11	No retaliation if union wins
232	22	918	10	Strikers will lose wages, lose more than gain
304	16	604	10	Sick leave/insurance good, equal to/better than under union contracts
371	8	302	10	Phase II prevents wage increase greater than employer would/has raised
303	12	533	9	Holidays/vacations good, equal to/better than under union contracts
306	15	550	8	Miscellaneous specific working conditions good, equal to/better than under union contracts
420	22	906	8	Unions not concerned with employee welfare
622	18	699	8	Employees should be certain to vote
651	14	503	8	No retaliation against union supporters if union loses
220	21	833	7	Strike may lead to loss of jobs
654	5	178	7	Good points of unionization
213	6	247	6	This union involved in strikes elsewhere
422	9	299	5	Union may be arbitrary/unresponsive
424	6	225	5	Union can/has/will cause employees to be discharged
460	8	322	3	Unions use violence as a tactic
464	6	273	2	Union has engaged in unlawful conduct (non-violent)
521	11	367	2	Union easy to get in, difficult to get out

Table 4-3

Recognition of Union Campaign Issues

Issue Code	Number of Elections in Which Issue Was Used	Number of Employees in Elections in Which Issue Was Used	Percent of Employees Reporting Issue in Elections in Which Issue Was Used	Issue Content
810	26	865	71	Wages unsatisfactory; union will improve
820	27	976	64	Union will prevent unfairness, set up grievance procedure/seniority system
829	17	583	36	Working conditions in general unsatisfactory; union will improve
814	21	772	28	Sick leave/insurance unsatisfactory; union will improve
876	23	848	26	Union has obtained gains elsewhere
813	20	578	23	Holidays/vacations unsatisfactory; union will improve
812	20	693	19	Pensions unsatisfactory; union will improve
830	26	910	17	Union strength will provide employees with voice in wages, working conditions
816	7	378	11	Safety conditions unsatisfactory; union will improve

Statement			Code
Union not outsider, bargains for what employees want	10	910	24	861
Personal criticism of employer	10	213	6	982
Employer promises/good treatment may not continue without union	7	752	20	877
Employees choose union leaders	6	696	18	860
Employer tried to deceive employees	6	488	12	950
Employer will seek to persuade/frighten employees to vote against union	6	677	18	955
Production requirements unsatisfactory; union will improve	6	239	5	818
Dues/initiation fees reasonable	5	744	21	970
Union will require job classification	5	395	9	819
Company fears union strength	4	485	14	831
Employees have legal right to engage in union activity	3	635	17	923
Strikes are not called unnecessarily	3	449	12	961
No initiation fees for present employees	3	342	12	971
This is appropriate union for this company/industry	2	234	6	832
Union does not fine/assess members	2	436	11	972
No dues until contract signed/ratified	1	443	13	973
No strike without vote	1	763	18	960
Employer unconcerned with employee welfare	1	245	6	886
Authorization cards confidential	0	228	5	925

fees, and fines (970–973)—was also low. In sum, employees appeared interested in the union's assertions as to the positive, job-related aspects of unionization rather than its costs or the internal structure of the union.

In order to test whether important issues are recalled in precise detail, we asked about union campaign statements as to wages obtained elsewhere. Such statements are central to many campaigns and when deemed significantly inaccurate have been the basis for setting aside elections. The Board has stated that wages obtained elsewhere are "a subject of utmost concern to the employees."[7]

There were twenty-two elections in which the union campaign included a statement about wages it obtained elsewhere.[8] Employees in each of those elections were asked if the union had made such a statement. Only 50 percent (367/733) were aware that it had. Only 22 percent were able to recall the amount of the claim within 10 percent.[9] Few employees recall even wage claims with the precision assumed by the Board.

Precision of recall was unrelated to vote. There were no more union voters among those who recalled the union's wage claims within 10 percent than among those whose recall was not within 10 percent or those who remembered that the union had made wage claims, but had no recollection of the amount of the claim.

Familiarity in Particular Elections

Some issues were particularly salient in certain elections. When an employer or union emphasized a theme that was relevant to the specific situation, recognition was high.

In election 1, for example, the employer was known to be in serious financial straits and had recently been close to bankruptcy. Extensive layoffs had taken place in which supervisors had been allowed to displace employees without regard to seniority. The relevance of the themes with unusually high recognition is obvious: 313 (company in bad financial condition—89 percent); 310 (improvements not depend-

---

[7] See, e.g., Western Health Facilities, 208 NLRB 56 (1974). The courts, too, regard assertions about wages as crucial to the decision whether or not to unionize. See NLRB v. Houston Chronicle Publishing Co., 300 F.2d 273, 280 (5th Cir. 1962).

[8] None of these statements was challenged before the Board as being inaccurate, nor did we have access to data that would determine their accuracy.

[9] Any employee response arguably accurate within 10 percent was so categorized. In elections 30 and 31, for example, the union published salary ranges for a number of different job classifications; a response within 10 percent of any range was coded as accurate.

ent on unionization—67 percent); 820 (job security, seniority system —69 percent).[10]

Shortly before the campaign in election 6, new management had taken control. During the campaign the employer closed a unionized plant about fifty miles away. The closing was reported in the local newspaper and on the plant bulletin board. Once again, the salience of the highly recognized themes is evident: 111 (benefits lost elsewhere after union victory—60 percent), 151 (layoffs have taken place elsewhere after union victory—60 percent), 511 (new management should be given a chance—53 percent).

In election 5, theme 300 (wages equal to/better than under union contracts) was recognized by 63 percent of the voters, more than twice the recognition of any other company issue. The union had organized a nearby employer in the same business; many employees believed that its contract provided terms and conditions of employment inferior to their own.

Some instances of unusually high recognition of a specific theme are not so easily explained. In election 31, the employer raised the issue of union corruption (432) by distributing a *Reader's Digest* article, "Time to Root Out Labor Racketeers," that discussed primarily Teamsters, the union involved in that election. Only 19 percent of the voters reported that union corruption had been a campaign theme. The same article was distributed in election 4, also involving Teamsters, but here the union corruption issue was reported by 68 percent of the voters.

Familiarity and Demographic and Job Experience Characteristics

The correlations between demographic and job experience characteristics and familiarity in Table 4-4 show that the campaigns were slightly more salient to certain groups of employees than others. Employees who had greater familiarity with the company campaign were likely to be male ($r = -.21$), married ($r = .12$), long tenured ($r = .18$), well-paid ($r = .28$), and better educated ($r = .16$). Those who were more familiar with the union campaign likewise were male ($r = -.16$), better educated ($r = -.16$), and better paid ($r = .14$). Union campaign familiarity was correlated with age ($r = -.12$), not tenure, probably because the younger employees in the sample had somewhat

---

[10] Theme 313 was omitted from Table 4-2 because it appeared in only three elections. It had an average recognition factor of 43 percent (89 percent, 26 percent, 14 percent).

Table 4-4

Correlations between Demographic Characteristics, Job Experiences, and Familiarity with Company and Union Campaigns

Demographic Characteristics Job Experiences		Company Familiarity		Union Familiarity	
Age		−.02		−.12*	
	N		1223		1135
Sex		−.21*		−.16*	
	N		1222		1134
Race		−.06		−.07	
	N		1161		1073
Education level		.16*		−.16*	
	N		1221		1132
Political preference		−.03		.00	
	N		1225		1137
Marital status		.12*		.07	
	N		1225		1137
Tenure		.18*		.05	
	N		1225		1137
Hours		−.02		.01	
	N		1222		1134
Wage rate		.28*		.14*	
	N		1190		1106

*$p \geq .01$
NOTE: Items scored as presented in Table 3-8.

more favorable attitudes toward unions, predisposing them to be more attentive to the union campaign. The relationship between education and familiarity may be due to the ability of better educated people to comprehend and articulate public issues more readily than those less well educated. Alternatively, the better educated employees may have been more interested in the campaign.

The better informed employee in our sample fits a profile of male heads of households, who are older or more permanent employees with relatively well-paying jobs. This profile is similar to that of the political voter who pays the most attention to the campaign.[11] Employees who fit this profile thus appear generally attentive to current issues.

---

[11] See B. BERELSON, P. LAZARSFELD & W. MCPHEE, *supra* note 4, at 241. P. LAZARSFELD, B. BERELSON & H. GAUDET, THE PEOPLE'S CHOICE (Colum. U. Press paperback ed. 1968).

PREDISPOSITIONS, FAMILIARITY, AND VOTE

Our finding that employees generally are not familiar with the campaign suggests one reason why most employees vote in accord with their predispositions: they are unaware of the campaign issues and therefore largely unaffected by them. Another explanation for the seeming inability of the campaign to change votes might be due to selective exposure.[12] This theory would suggest that the campaigns are ineffective because union supporters attend only to the union campaign and company supporters attend only to the company campaign. This could take place if, for example, company supporters neither attend union meetings nor read union literature. Alternatively, they might ignore the message. In either event, we would expect union voters to know more than company voters about the union campaign and company voters to know more than union voters about the company campaign.

Familiarity

There was no significant difference between company and union voters' familiarity with the employer's campaign. Figure 4–1 shows that both company and union voters recalled approximately 10 percent of the company campaign issues. Union voters, however, were significantly more familiar with the union campaign than were company voters. Union voters reported an average of 13 percent of the union campaign issues, while company voters reported less than 5 percent of the union campaign issues.

The same pattern characterizes company and union voters recall of specific campaign issues. Union and company voters reported company issues in about equal proportions. A substantially higher proportion of union voters than company voters reported specific union campaign issues.

Company supporters' lesser familiarity with the union campaign and their tendency to vote in accord with their predispositions may be due to selective exposure. Union voters, however, know as much about the company campaign as do company voters. Selective exposure thus cannot account for the general failure of the campaign to cause union supporters to switch to the company.

A possible explanation for the union supporters' general imperviousness to company influence attempts may lie in perceptual distortion.[13]

[12] McGuire, *The Nature of Attitudes and Attitude Change* in G. LINDSEY and E. ARONSON (eds.), HANDBOOK OF SOCIAL PSYCHOLOGY, vol. 3, 218 (2d ed. 1969).
[13] *Id.* at 258.

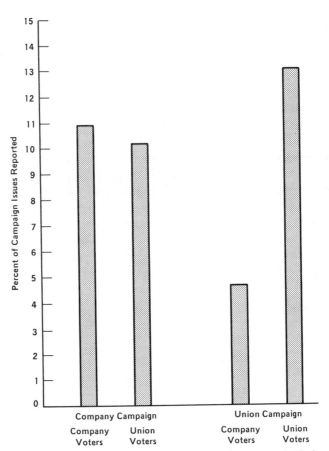

Figure 4-1. Campaign Familiarity of Company and Union Voters

For example, union supporters probably expect the employer to be anti-union. This expectation may lead them to perceive the employer's words and acts as more threatening to union supporters or critical of the union than do company supporters. These same expectations, however, may insulate the union supporters from being affected by the employer's campaign. When they perceive the employer as behaving in the negative manner that they anticipate, they are confirmed in their view that they need a union.

This explanation is supported by the fact that union voters were more sensitive to employer criticisms of the union than were company supporters. For example, 29 percent of the union voters reported that the employer made statements about union corruption, compared to 18 percent of the company voters. Employer allegations of union corruption did not, however, appear to influence employees to vote against the union. This issue was raised in eleven elections, but only nine employees mentioned it as a reason for voting against the union.[14]

The campaign perceptions of company supporters may also have been influenced by their expectations. The sole union campaign theme reported by more company voters than union voters was personal criticism of the employer, suggesting their expectation of union hostility toward the employer. The only company themes reported by substantially more company voters than union voters were that the employer has treated employees well and that new management deserves a chance to prove itself without a union. This suggests that company supporters had a favorable view of the employer and were sensitive to campaign issues consistent with that view.

Fear of Job Loss

We were particularly interested in the perception of employer campaign themes raising the possibility that a union victory might result in employees losing their jobs due to plant closing, strikes, discharges, or layoffs. If employees who vote against union representation are motivated by a fear of job loss contingent on a union victory, they should be highly sensitive to company campaign themes raising that possibility. In fact, as indicated in Table 4-5, significantly fewer com-

Table 4-5

Report of Job Loss Themes by Company and Union Voters

| Vote | Job Loss Themes | | Total |
	Not Reported	Reported	
Company	446	144	590
row %	76%	24%	
Union	254	223	477
row %	53%	47%	
Total	700	367	1067
row %	66%	34%	

---

[14] The union won five of the eleven elections in which the union corruption issue was raised.

pany voters (24 percent) than union voters (47 percent) reported any job loss theme ($r = .23$). [15]

Perception of job loss themes was unaffected by job security. Elections were divided into three groups, those in which the size of the employer's work force had decreased within the year preceding the election (5 elections), those in which it had increased (10 elections), and those in which it had remained stable (11 elections). Employees in elections characterized by a decreasing work force, in which job security would be low, reported no more job loss themes than did employees in either of the other two groups.

Nor was sensitivity to job loss themes affected by area unemployment levels. Elections were divided into two groups, those in which the county or Standard Metropolitan Statistical Area unemployment rate at the time of the election was below 3.7 percent (14 elections) and those in which it was above 3.7 percent (15 elections). There was no significant difference in report of job loss themes in the two groups, suggesting that voting against the union because of job loss fear is not related to the area unemployment rate. [16] Moreover, employees who believed it would be difficult to find another job as good as their current one were not significantly more likely to report a job loss theme than employees who thought it would be easy to do so.

In sum, perception of company campaign themes raising the possibility that a union victory would lead to job loss was significantly related only to vote. The relationship, however, was counter to that hypothesized. Union voters reported this issue significantly more often than company voters.

These data provide further evidence for the suggestion that union supporters believe the employer to be opposed to their choice and construe his campaign statements in light of that belief. They expect his opposition to manifest itself in threats of job loss; thus they interpret his remarks to contain such threats. If this is the explanation for union voters' greater recall of job loss themes, one would not expect those themes to result in switching against the union. An employee who anticipates that the employer will forecast dire prospects in the event of a union victory is likely to have discounted such forecasts in making his initial decision to vote union. Whether this is true can best be determined by analyzing the campaign perceptions of the switchers, a subject to be treated later in this chapter.

---

[15] The job themes used in this analysis were code numbers 130, 131, 150, 151, 220, 221, 710, and 711.

[16] The highest unemployment rate in any community studied was 10.1 percent, the lowest was 2.6 percent.

Familiarity and Campaign Exposure

The different familiarity of company and union voters with the union campaign suggests that company voters may be selectively exposing themselves to the campaign. If so, predispositions should be related to exposure to the union campaign and exposure should be related to familiarity. There is no significant difference between company and union voters' familiarity with the company campaign. Hence there should be no relationship between predispositions and exposure to the company campaign. Exposure to the company campaign may, nonetheless, be related to familiarity.

Written Material

Exposure to the written campaign was significantly associated with familiarity with both the company campaign ($r = .22$) and the union campaign ($r = .20$). As shown in Table 4–6, employees who received

Table 4-6

Campaign Familiarity of Employees Who Received Written Materials Compared to Those Who Did Not

Written Material	Received Average Familiarity	N	Not Received Average Familiarity	N	r	p
Company	11.36	851	5.76	104	.22	.01
Union	8.97	742	4.50	146	.20	.01

letters or other written material from the employer reported significantly more company issues (CFI = 11.36) than those who did not (CFI = 5.76).[17] Union written material had the same effect. Those who received letters or other written material from the union had a

---

[17] The sample used in Tables 4–6, 4–8, and 4–10 includes those employees for whom there were complete data about intent, vote, written materials, meetings, and personal contact. Employees in election 19 are excluded from the company campaign analyses; employees in election 24 are excluded from union campaign analyses (see note to Table 4–1). Employees in elections in which no written materials were used or in which no meetings were held are included in Tables 4–6 and 4–8 respectively, because we wanted to test the relationship between exposure and familiarity. For this purpose it made no difference why an employee did not receive written materials or attend meetings.

mean Union Familiarity Index of 8.97, compared to 4.50 for those who did not.[18]

Neither party experienced substantial difficulty in reaching the employees with written material. Letters or other written material were distributed by the employer in twenty-six elections, by the union in twenty-five elections.[19] Of the employees in these elections, 92 percent (969/1058) received some or all of the employer's material, and 85 percent (871/1021) received some or all of the union's material. The Board's requirement that the employer provide the union with the names and addresses of all employees eligible to vote[20] thus seems reasonably successful in enabling the union to reach nearly as many employees with written material as the employer.

The receipt of union written material was not limited to union supporters. Table 4–7 shows that 86 percent of those employees intending to vote company reported the receipt of union written material compared to 84 percent of those intending to vote union. Similarly 95 percent of those intending to vote union reported the receipt of company written material compared to 89 percent of those intending to vote company.[21]

Meetings

The use of meetings as a method of campaigning was more common than the use of written material. There were only three elections in

---

[18] It is possible, but not likely, that this effect, as well as those related to the other types of campaigning, is inflated by the way the interview was structured. For example, employees who reported that they had not received union letters were not asked further questions about the content of the union letters. At the pre-test stage we found that asking employees about the contents of letters they had not received or meetings they had not attended netted a negligible amount of data and inspired some animosity. In the final data collection stage, each employee was asked a battery of questions in addition to the speech and letter questions, all of which were aimed at giving him full opportunity to tell as much about the campaign as he knew. (See Appendix C, Employee Interview Schedule, Wave II Questions 1, 2, 3, 5, 7, 8, 9, 10, 14, 16, 18, and 19.) Additionally, interviewers were instructed to probe and record each employee's campaign familiarity to the maximum possible extent. It is thus unlikely that an employee who knew what was contained in the speeches or letters of the parties did not have ample opportunity to communicate that knowledge.

[19] Written materials were not distributed by the employer in elections 13–15, 16, and 23, and by the union in elections 13–15, 20, 23, and 32.

[20] Excelsior Underwear, Inc., 156 NLRB 1236 (1966).

[21] The sample used in Table 4–7 excludes employees in elections in which no written materials were sent. Table 4–9 excludes employees in elections in which no meetings were held. Since we wanted to test whether a party which used a particular campaign technique tended to reach only its own supporters, it made no sense to include elections in which that technique was not used.

which the employer did not hold a meeting (12, 13, 31); the union also held no meetings in three elections (12, 16, 31). The employer's meetings were on company time and premises; the union's meetings were held off company premises during non-work hours.

Table 4–8 shows that attending meetings is more strongly related to familiarity than is receipt of written material (company, $r = .33$; union, $r = .43$). The mean Company Familiarity Index of employees attending company meetings was 12.09, significantly greater than that of employees who did not (5.25). The mean Union Familiarity Index of employees attending union meetings was 14.15, also significantly greater than that of employees who did not (5.28).

Table 4-7

Proportion of Employees Intending to Vote Company and Union Who Received Written Campaign Materials

Intent	Received Company[a] Written Materials	Total	Received Union Written Materials	Total
Company	402	451	384	447
row %	89%		86%	
Uncertain	67	81	69	80
row %	83%		86%	
Union	500	526	418	494
row %	95%		84%	

[a]$r = .10$; $p \leq .01$

Table 4-8

Campaign Familiarity of Employees Who Attended at Least One Meeting Compared to Those Who Did Not

Meetings	Attended Average Familiarity	N	Did Not Attend Average Familiarity	N	r	p
Company	12.09	784	5.25	171	.33	.01
Union	14.15	340	5.23	548	.43	.01

The employer was substantially more successful in getting employees to attend meetings than was the union. In the elections in which company meetings were held, 83 percent (886/1068) of the employees reported that they had attended one or more company meetings, compared to 36 percent (374/1045) attending union meetings in the elections in which they were held. Furthermore, most of those employees attending union meetings were already union supporters. As shown by Table 4–9, of those employees intending to vote union, 54 percent attended one or more union meetings; of those employees intending to vote company, only 14 percent did so. There was no such difference in the audience for company meetings: 85 percent of those intending to vote union attended one or more company meetings as did 83 percent of those intending to vote company.

The significant correlation between familiarity with the union campaign and attending union meetings ($r = .43$) is not due to the fact that many of those attending union meetings were already union supporters ($r = .40$). The correlation between attending meetings and union familiarity is still significant ($r = .37$) after controlling for the effect of predisposition. Regardless of their voting intent, employees who attend union meetings are more familiar with the union campaign than those who do not.

Why do not more employees attend union meetings? The most common reasons for not attending were: held at an inconvenient time or place (40 percent), not interested in the union (29 percent), did not know about the meeting (9 percent). Nearly all employees know about union meetings, but many are reluctant to attend such meetings off company premises after working hours.[22]

The relationship between exposure to campaign materials and campaign familiarity was not affected by the number of meetings or letters. The number of employer letters ranged from one to sixteen, the number of meetings from one to five. The number of union letters ranged from one to fifteen, the number of meetings from one to eleven. The across election correlations between the number of employer speeches and letters and mean company familiarity ($r = .02$) and between the number of union speeches and letters and mean union familiarity ($r = -.27$) were not statistically significant. It is not the amount of campaigning *per se*, but exposure to the campaign that is related to familiarity.

---

[22] Those employees who said they had not attended union meetings because they were held at an inconvenient time or place were not likely to have been stating this as a subterfuge for lack of interest in the union as 48 percent were union voters.

Table 4-9

Proportion of Employees Intending to Vote
Company and Union Who Attended at Least One Meeting
Compared to Those Who Did Not

Intent	*Attended*[a] Company Meetings	Total	*Attended*[b] Union Meetings	Total
Company	379	458	63	437
row %	83 %		14 %	
Uncertain	63	87	25	83
row %	72 %		30 %	
Union	444	523	286	525
row %	85 %		54 %	

[a] $r = .11$; $p \leq .01$
[b] $r = .40$; $p \leq .01$

Personal Contact

Both parties used individual personal contact, as well as group meetings, to communicate with employees. Solicitation on behalf of the employer was typically undertaken by low-level supervisors, occasionally by those higher in management. Union solicitation was engaged in by employees favorable to the union and non-employee union organizers.

Table 4–10 shows that employees who had been spoken to alone or in a small group by a representative of the company had significantly greater familiarity with the employer's campaign (CFI = 15.13) than those who had not (CFI = 9.98). Similarly, employees who had personal contact with a union representative had a mean Union Familiarity Index of 12.49, significantly greater than the 6.75 mean of those who did not have such contact. Personal contact was, however, less highly related to familiarity than was attending meetings (company, $r = .19$; union, $r = .25$).

Of those employees contacted individually or in a small group by a union representative, 48 percent were company supporters. Sixty-eight percent of those contacted in this manner by the company were union supporters (Table 4–11). The employer, then, focussed its personal contacts on those whom it hoped to win over.

Neither party made extensive use of personal campaigning. Only 24 percent (268/1101) of the voters were contacted by a union rep-

resentative; 14 percent (157/1102) by a company representative.
Many employers had a policy of discouraging personal solicitation,
because they had less control over what was said than in formal meetings or written communications. Union organizers' explanations as to
why more employees were not personally contacted were varied. According to some, solicitation on plant premises was constrained by legal
limitations restricting oral solicitation to the non-working time of both
solicitor and solicitee. Employees whose work day was not sharply
divided into work time and rest time were said to be in doubt as to
when they were free to solicit. Other union organizers stated that off-
premise contacts were limited by employees' tendency, increased by
the interstate highway system, to live scattered over a wide area, as

Table 4-10

Campaign Familiarity of Employees
Who Were Personally Contacted
Compared to Those Who Were Not

| Personal Contact | Contacted | | Not Contacted | | | |
	Average Familiarity	N	Average Familiarity	N	r	p
Company	15.13	138	9.98	817	.19	.01
Union	12.49	240	6.75	648	.25	.01

Table 4-11

Proportion of Employees Personally Contacted
Who Intended to Vote Company and Union

| Personal Contact | Intent | | | |
	Company	Uncertain	Union	Total
Contacted by company	45	6	106	157
row %	29%	4%	68%	
Contacted by union	129	18	121	268
row %	48%	7%	45%	

well as by the difficulty of competing with a wide range of after-work activities.

The Importance of Meetings

As shown by Tables 4–12 and 4–13, individual differences in familiarity related to campaign exposure are largely accounted for by attendance at meetings. Employees who attended company meetings were significantly more familiar with the company campaign than those who did not ($r = .33$); employees who attended union meetings

Table 4-12

Correlations between Exposure to and Familiarity with the Company Campaign, Intent, and Vote

Company Familiarity	Letters	Meetings	Personal Contact	Intent	Vote
1. 1.00					
2. .22	1.00				
3. .33	.21	1.00			
4. .19	.07	.01	1.00		
5. −.03	.09	.03	.14	1.00	
6. −.04	.09	.04	.15	.73	1.00

NOTE: $r = .08$; $p \leq .01$; $N = 955$.

Table 4-13

Correlations between Exposure to and Familiarity with the Union Campaign, Intent, and Vote

Union Familiarity	Letters	Meetings	Personal Contact	Intent	Vote
1. 1.00					
2. .20	1.00				
3. .43	−.08	1.00			
4. .25	.11	−.02	1.00		
5. .35	−.10	.40	−.08	1.00	
6. .44	−.09	.46	−.08	.73	1.00

NOTE: $r = .09$; $p \leq .01$, $N = 888$.

were significantly more familiar with the union campaign than those who did not ($r = .43$).

A far larger proportion of employees attend company meetings (83 percent) than attend union meetings (36 percent). Furthermore, those who attend union meetings tend to be union supporters ($r = .40$). This is not true of company meetings ($r = -.03$). Regardless of intent, attendance at meetings is significantly related to familiarity. The company, then, has a particular advantage in communicating with the undecided and those not already committed to it.

In sum, when the employer can hold campaign meetings on working time and premises and the union cannot, the union is at a substantial disadvantage in achieving meaningful communication with employees, even when all other means of campaigning are taken into account. This disadvantage explains why company voters are less familiar than union voters with the union campaign; it also explains why union voters are as familiar with the company campaign as company voters.

In *NLRB* v. *United Steelworkers of America (Nutone, Inc.)*, the Supreme Court asked whether an employer's use of company time and premises for anti-union campaigning, combined with a refusal to allow the union to engage in similar campaigning, created an "imbalance in opportunities for organizational communication."[23] The Board has held that except in unusual circumstances, such as when the employees involved work on a ship or are otherwise isolated, such conduct on the part of the employer does not create an imbalance.[24] The data suggest that the Board's answer has been incorrect: when an employer uses company time and premises for antiunion campaigning and the union must campaign off company premises, the union is at a substantial disadvantage in communicating with the voters.

Summary: Predispositions, Campaigning, and Vote

The data on campaign familiarity, predispositions, and exposure provide some insight as to why few employees vote contrary to their initial predispositions despite intense campaigning by both parties. Many employees have strongly held opinions and attitudes about union representation prior to the campaigning that immediately precedes the election. In order for a campaign issue to affect vote, it must convince employees that their prior attitudes and beliefs were wrong. Yet, neither company nor union supporters pay particularly close

---

[23] 357 U.S. 357, 362–363 (1958).

[24] See cases cited in Chapter 1, notes 99–101.

attention to the campaign. Their voting decision is based on attitudes that antedate the campaign. Having made that decision, they feel little need to pay attention to the details of the campaign. They know and report those few campaign issues that are salient to their initial decision and little more. Furthermore, prior attitudes provide a mechanism for dealing with all types of influence attempts.

Company supporters screen out the union campaign primarily by not attending union meetings. Union supporters, in contrast, do not avoid the employer's campaign. Yet, their predispositions tend to insulate them from the effect of that campaign. They view the employer in a negative manner because he has provided unsatisfactory working conditions and been unresponsive to their grievances. They are sensitive to employer campaign themes that are critical of the union or threatening to union supporters, but discount such themes as merely confirming their view that they need a union to deal with their employer. Similarly, they disbelieve the employer's assurances that a union is unnecessary to bring about satisfactory working conditions.

THE CAMPAIGN AND REASONS FOR VOTE

Campaign Issues

Table 4–14 lists all reasons for vote relied upon by 1 percent or more of the company voters. Table 4–15 presents the same data for union voters. There was a high correspondence between reasons for vote and campaign issues. Eighty-four percent of the reasons for vote given by union voters and 71 percent of the reasons given by company voters were issues in the campaign preceding the election in which they voted.

The relationship between campaign themes and reasons for vote does not establish that the campaign influenced employees' votes by raising issues that caused them to switch. The general predictability of vote from attitudes and intent, regardless of the nature of the subsequent campaign, suggests that the campaigns touched on issues already salient to the voters in view of their existing predispositions. Its effect was to awaken or strengthen those predispositions.

The high correspondence between campaign themes and reasons for vote appears to have been the result of a scatter-gun approach to campaigning, rather than to any prescience about the concerns of the employees. The number of themes in the average campaign was approximately twenty-five and recall of most issues quite low. Nonetheless, the parties did succeed in addressing themselves to those themes salient to most of the voters.

The switchers' reasons for vote were analyzed separately in an effort to determine if particular campaign themes might have influenced their vote switch. The effort proved fruitless. Those employees who reported a company vote intent, but who switched to the union, did not differ substantially in their reasons for vote from those employees who voted in accord with their original intent. The same was true of those employees who switched from a union intent to a company vote.

Table 4-14

Reasons for Voting against Union Representation

Issue Code	*Percent of Employees Reporting Issue as Reason for Vote*	*Issue Content*
511	24	New company/management recently taken over
310	13	Improvements not dependent on unionization
410	12	Financial costs of union dues, etc. outweigh gains
341	12	Union is outsider. Will interfere with efficiency, harm employer-employee relations
360	9	Employer has treated employees fairly/well/ equally
510	6	Company too small to need union
210	6	If union wins, strike may follow
111	6	Loss of benefits may follow unionization (non-retaliatory)
300	4	Wages good, equal to/better than under union contracts
361	4	Named individual has treated employees fairly/well/equal
432	3	Union corruption
131	3	Plant closing/moving may follow unionization (non-retaliatory)
315	1	Wages/working conditions will/may improve
371	1	Phase II prevents wage increase greater than employer would/has raised

Table 4-15

Reasons for Voting for Union Representation

Issue Code	Percent of Employees Reporting Issue as Reason for Vote	Issue Content
810	54	Wages unsatisfactory; union will improve
820	44	Union will prevent unfairness, set up grievance procedure/seniority system
829	17	Working conditions in general unsatisfactory; union will improve
830	10	Union strength will provide employees with voice in wages/working conditions
812	9	Pensions unsatisfactory; union will improve
814	6	Sick leave/insurance unsatisfactory; union will improve
813	6	Holidays/vacations unsatisfactory; union will improve
816	6	Safety conditions unsatisfactory; union will improve
818	3	Production requirements unsatisfactory; union will improve
819	1	Union will require job classification
877	1	Employer promises/good treatment may not continue without union

Reasons for Vote Unrelated to Campaign Issues

Analysis of reasons for vote reveals little about the influence of those issues that appeared in the campaign. It does, however, provide some insight into the importance of those reasons for vote that did not appear as campaign issues. One reason for vote necessarily unrelated to the campaign was the employee's personal experience with union representation. Seventy-eight employees relied upon prior union experience as a reason for vote. Of those, nearly three-fourths (72 percent) voted against union representation, giving unfavorable experience with unions as one of their reasons for doing so. Prior unfavorable experience as a reason for voting against the union was thus much more influential than favorable experience as a reason for voting for the union.

Admittedly, unorganized employees may not be a representative sample of previous union members. Some of these employees may have voluntarily left their former jobs because of dissatisfaction with working conditions and held the union partially responsible. Alternatively, they may have left involuntarily and are bitter that the union was unable to protect their jobs. In either event, they would be expected to be less favorable toward unions than employees currently represented by a union.

Another common reason for vote not directly related to campaign themes was the employee's personal criticism of the type of campaigning used by the parties. Forty-three employees stated they voted against union representation because some aspect of the union's campaign was improper—most frequently that the union tried to deceive employees, made promises it could not keep, or did not campaign hard enough. Only one employee voted for union representation because of dissatisfaction with the company campaign. These responses, as is true of other reasons for vote, may be solely rationalizations for a vote resting on existing attitudes. Nonetheless, the number of criticisms of the union campaign that were given as reasons for voting against union representation is striking in view of the almost total absence of criticism of the company campaign as a reason for voting for union representation.[25]

"SUCCESSFUL" CAMPAIGNS

Company

The pre-election campaigns that were most successful were examined for the presence of campaign themes or styles of campaigning that might explain their success. Successful company campaigns were defined as those in which there was the greatest loss in union support from the card-signing campaign to vote or from intent to vote. (Union supporters at the card-signing stage were defined as those employees who signed cards.) The average loss in union support from card-sign to vote was 4 percent; for the five most successful company campaigns (2, 6, 12, 13–15, 29), the average loss was 35 percent. The average loss

---

[25] While the employee's own criticisms of the campaign were coded separately from his reports that the employer or union had engaged in such criticisms, criticisms by the employer or union may have stimulated employee criticisms. Unions, however, criticized employer campaigns in twenty elections, while employers criticized union campaigns in only seven elections. To the extent, then, that employee criticisms are a function of party comments, criticisms of the union campaign appear to have been far more salient than criticisms of the employer campaign.

in union support from intent to vote was also 4 percent; for the five most successful company campaigns (6, 13–15, 25, 27, 31), the average loss was 15 percent.

In each of these elections, many employees who had signed a card or stated an intent to vote union ultimately voted company; almost no employees who had not signed cards or stated an intent to vote for the union voted union. Across all elections, an average of 72 percent of the card-signers and 21 percent of the non-signers voted union; in these elections, only 37 percent of the card-signers and 4 percent of the non-signers did so (Table 4–16). Of those intending to vote union in all elections, an average of 82 percent did so, as did 10 percent of those

Table 4-16

**Change in Union Support from Card-sign to Vote
in Successful Company Campaigns
and Successful Union Campaigns
Compared to All Elections**

Card-sign	All Elections		Successful Company Campaigns		Successful Union Campaigns	
	Employees Voting Union	Total	Employees Voting Union	Total	Employees Voting Union	Total
Signed	351	489	25	68	183	208
row %	72%		37%		88%	
Did not sign	120	568	2	45	56	142
row %	21%		4%		39%	

intending to vote company or uncertain how they would vote; in these elections, only 50 percent of those intending to vote union and 7 percent of those intending to vote company or uncertain how they would vote ultimately voted union (Table 4–17).

We could find no characteristics that served to distinguish the successful employer campaigns from those less successful. The proportion of written material to oral campaigning was not substantially different, nor was there a different style of campaigning. The issues stressed in the successful employers' campaign materials were generally similar to those relied upon in other campaigns.[26]

---

[26] There was no significant relationship between successful employer campaigning and the employer's use of unlawful campaign tactics. The relationship between unlawful campaigning and vote is considered in Chapter 5.

Table 4-17

Change in Union Support from Intent to Vote in Successful Company Campaigns and Successful Union Campaigns Compared to All Elections

Intent	All Elections		Successful Company Campaigns		Successful Union Campaigns	
	Employees Voting Union	Total	Employees Voting Union	Total	Employees Voting Union	Total
Company or uncertain	47	483	6	83	15	101
row %	10%		7%		15%	
Union	397	485	78	156	219	238
row %	82%		50%		92%	

There was, however, one successful employer campaign that contained a unique campaign theme. In election 27, the employer asserted that some of the past and present leaders of the union involved—United Electrical, Radio and Machine Workers—had been linked to the Communist movement. It is difficult to know whether the employer's effort to discredit the union as Communist-affiliated affected employee voting behavior. As was common with employer campaign themes criticizing the union, this issue was reported by a higher proportion of union voters (44 percent) than company voters (29 percent). Seven company voters (11 percent) referred to the union's Communist ties as one of their reasons for voting against union representation, but six of those intended to vote against the union even before the company's campaign. For these voters, then, the communism theme can only have served to reinforce their pre-campaign vote intent.

In any event, with the possible exception of the communism issue in election 27, there were no campaign-related characteristics that might explain why some company campaigns were followed by a substantially greater loss in union support than others.

Union

Since the union won only eight of the elections studied, a successful union campaign was defined as one followed by a union victory. In all these elections except 9, a majority of employees signed union authorization cards.[27] The average gain in union support from card-sign to vote in these elections was 10 percent; 88 percent of the card-signers and 39 percent of the non-signers voted union (Table 4–16). The union vote in these elections averaged less than 1 percent below the proportion of those intending to vote union. Of those intending to vote union, 92 percent did so; of those uncertain or planning to vote company, 15 percent voted union (Table 4–17). The union victories, then, were marked by the union's ability to hold on to slightly more of its initial supporters than usual while picking up a slightly higher proportion of those not originally intending to vote union.

The successful union campaigns, as the successful company campaigns, were not marked by any characteristics of style or content that set them apart from those less successful. There was no evidence that the union did something right in these campaigns that, if done more generally, would have led to a higher proportion of union victories.

THE CAMPAIGN, THE SWITCHERS, AND THE UNDECIDED

Switchers to the Union

While the great majority of the employees voted in accord with their pre-campaign intent, some were initially undecided (6 percent) and others voted contrary to their original intent (13 percent). These two groups of voters were few in number, both within and across elections, but their votes were necessary for victory in nine elections.[28] In each of these elections, if some or all of the switchers or initially undecided employees who voted for the winner had instead voted for the loser, the election result would have been different.

If the undecided employees who voted for each party are more familiar with that party's campaign than the undecided who voted for the other party, that is some indication that they relied on the campaign in reaching their voting decision. Table 4–18 shows that the undecided who voted union were, indeed, significantly more familiar with the union campaign than those who voted company ($r = .34$). Those who voted company were, however, no more familiar with the company campaign than those who voted union ($r = -.02$).

A similar pattern appears among the switchers. Employees who switched from a company intent to a union vote reported significantly more about the union campaign than employees whose company intent

---

[27] Election 9, in which the union had a majority of the votes in the sample, though not in the unit, has been treated as a successful campaign for purposes of this analysis.

[28] See elections 6, 9, 10, 18, 23, 25, 28, 31, and 33 in Appendix F.

Table 4-18

Campaign Familiarity of Undecided Who Voted Union Compared to Those Who Voted Company

Campaign	Undecided Intent Company Vote		Undecided Intent Union Vote			
	Average Familiarity	N	Average Familiarity	N	r	p
Company	7.51	42	7.13	20	−.02	NS
Union	3.74	38	9.79	18	.34	.01

Table 4-19

Union Campaign Familiarity of Employees Who Voted as They Intended Compared to Those Who Switched

Campaign	Company Intent Union Vote		Company Intent Company Vote			
	Average Familiarity	N	Average Familiarity	N	r	p
Union	11.06	25	4.55	346	.19	.01

remained firm through vote ($r = .19$). (See Table 4–19.) Those who switched from a union intent to a company vote were not significantly more familiar with the company campaign than those whose union intent held firm ($r = -.02$). (See Table 4–20.)[29]

The apparent reason why the switchers and the undecided who voted union knew significantly more about the union campaign was that they attended union meetings more frequently. Table 4–21 shows

---

[29] All analyses described in this section were performed also on those employees who voted differently than their attitudes or card-signing behavior predicted. In no case were the results different from those found for the undecided and the switchers.

that 78 percent of the undecided who voted union had attended one or more union meetings compared to 16 percent of the undecided who voted company ($r = .60$). Similarly, 48 percent of those who intended to vote company but switched to the union attended a union meeting, compared to 12 percent of those who did not switch ($r = .23$). (See Table 4–22.)

The correlations between attendance at union meetings, familiarity with the union campaign, and switching to the union suggest a causal relationship. But since we could not measure the temporal relationships between switch, familiarity, and attendance at union meetings,

Table 4-20

Company Campaign Familiarity of Employees Who Voted as They Intended Compared to Those Who Switched

Campaign	Union Intent Company Vote		Union Intent Union Vote			
	Average Familiarity	N	Average Familiarity	N	r	p
Company	11.02	87	10.43	389	−.02	NS

Table 4-21

Attendance at Union Meetings of Undecided Who Voted Union Compared to Those Who Voted Company

Intent and Vote	Attended	Did Not Attend	Total
Undecided intent, company vote	6	32	38
row %	16%	84%	
Undecided intent, union vote	14	4	18
row %	78%	22%	
Total	20	36	56

Table 4-22

**Attendance at Union Meetings of Employees Who Intended
to Vote Company and Did Compared to Those Who Switched
to the Union**

Intent and Vote	Attended	Did Not Attend	Total
Intent company, vote company	48	298	346
row %	14%	86%	
Intent company, vote union	12	13	25
row %	48%	52%	
Total	60	311	371

we cannot sort out the psychological cause and effect. It is possible, however, to speculate.

It is unlikely that there are many employees who switch from a company intent to a union vote prior to obtaining some new information about the union. Admittedly, a switch to the union could be the result of re-thinking existing information or obtaining new information about the employer. However, an intent to vote against union representation is the product of attitudes that have been some time in forming. A change in those attitudes during the brief campaign period without some new information about the union seems unlikely.

It is also unlikely that the new information that stimulates the undecided and switchers to reevaluate their feelings about union representation comes initially from attending a union meeting. Union meetings are held after work, away from the employer's premises, during the employees' leisure hours. Not many employees are likely to be motivated to attend such meetings out of sheer curiosity or desire to maximize their information about both parties.

It seems likely that the relationship between campaign familiarity, attendance at union meetings, and switch to the union is this: some employees, particularly those who have had no direct experience with union representation, may, as they learn about unions, see in unionization a possible means of improving their working conditions. This could lead to an interest in unions and attendance at union meetings, which in turn would lead to further information, which could provide a basis for attitude change and a decision to vote for the union. This decision may either precede or follow attendance at a union meeting. In either event, the switchers and the undecided who vote union, particularly those who attend union meetings, would be expected to show, as they do, greater familiarity with the union campaign than those employees who originally had the same intent or were undecided, but voted company.

Even if exposure to and familiarity with the union's campaign influences some employees who are initially undecided or intend to vote company to switch (and indeed switch may precede exposure and familiarity), the influence is not strong. Neither the undecided nor the switchers were very familiar with the campaign of either party. Those who voted union were no more familiar with the union campaign than those who intended to vote union and did; those who voted company were no more familiar with the company campaign than those who intended to vote company and did.[30] Furthermore, a substantial majority of both switchers (76 percent) and undecided (68 percent) voted company. The union campaign may be influencing some employees, but not enough to make a difference in many elections.[31]

Switchers to the Company

The tendency of the switchers and the uncommitted to vote company, despite evidence that they are not particularly familiar with the company campaign, is explicable in terms of the timing and function of the employer and union campaigns. Typically, it is the union campaign that comes first. A group of employees, dissatisfied with working conditions, contacts a union organizer. The organizer and these employees then seek to enlist the support of other employees by representing unionization as a solution to both current and past grievances. The union campaign serves to stimulate favorable attitudes toward unions and inform those employees who have had little direct experience with unions about the merits of union representation. The employer may make some response to the union organizing

[30] These data are entirely consistent with the political voter studies that show the switchers and the undecided are less attentive to political communications than those voters who make early and firm vote decisions. See, e.g., P. LAZARSFELD, B. BERELSON & H. GAUDET, *supra* note 11, at 56, 59.

[31] In only two of the eight elections won by the union (9 and 33) was the union's victory due, in part, to the votes of the switchers or the undecided. In neither of those elections, however, did the union have a majority of these employees. In election 9, they split 3–3; in election 33, they voted against the union, 6–4.

drive, but frequently many employees have signed cards before the employer is aware of the organization attempt.

Under these circumstances the union may gain the support of some employees despite the fact that their dissatisfaction with working conditions is not deep-seated and their attitudes toward unions not wholly favorable. The imminence of an actual election, when their choice is to be made final, combined with the employer's campaign, may cause these employees and those initially undecided to vote against union representation.

Union supporters who switch to the company do not appear to be influenced by the particular issues raised in the company campaign. That campaign, however, may encourage employees to reconsider their initial decision to support the union. Employees who sign a union authorization card because of their dissatisfaction with particular aspects of the job may be reminded that on the whole working conditions are not too bad and that they cannot really know what will happen if the union gets in. Employees who switch to the company may display little familiarity with company campaign issues because that campaign is not providing them with information, but stimulating favorable attitudes toward working conditions and uncertainty about the effects of unionization.

The employer's campaign may also serve to demonstrate that he is aware of the dissatisfaction that led to the union organizing drive. Once he has demonstrated that awareness and indicated an interest in remedying the causes of employee dissatisfaction, some employees who originally favored union representation may be willing to allow him an opportunity to do so.[32] The employer's success in persuading employees that he should be given a chance to improve working conditions need not be reflected in a high degree of employee familiarity with his campaign, since what the employer says may be less important than his ability to convince his employees that he is interested in remedying the causes of their dissatisfaction. Successful communication of that interest can be accomplished even though the employer makes no statements about improvements and the employees do not attend closely to the particular issues the employer does raise. The undecided and the switchers who vote company thus may be influenced by the employer's campaign, yet not demonstrate a high level of familiarity with that campaign.

---

[32] This tendency is particularly noticeable when there has been a change in management or ownership. The most frequent reason for voting against union representation was that new management should be allowed an opportunity, free of the union, to improve working conditions.

SUMMARY

The Board assumes that employees are attentive to the campaign and that the campaign changes votes. The average employee, however, could remember only 10 percent of the company campaign issues and 7 percent of the union issues.

No company issue and only two union issues were reported by more than 40 percent of the total number of employees in the elections in which they were raised. Union voters were significantly more familiar with the union campaign than company voters. This difference in familiarity was associated with attendance at union meetings. There was no significant difference between union and company voters' familiarity with the company campaign. There were, however, differences between company and union voters' familiarity with specific themes of the company campaign. Union voters were more likely than company voters to report criticism of the union and job loss themes.

There was no evidence that any individual campaign issue was particularly effective in influencing employees to vote for the party raising that issue. Nor could we find any characteristics that served to distinguish successful campaigns from those less successful.

Employees who switched to the union were more familiar with the union campaign and more likely to have attended a union meeting than those who did not. Employees who switched to the company were not more familiar with the company campaign than those who did not.

CHAPTER 5

Unlawful Campaigning and Vote

The assumption underlying most Board decisions finding particular campaign tactics to be unlawful is that those tactics may coerce union supporters into voting against the union. On the basis of this assumption, the Board will set aside the results of an election in which the employer has sought to influence employee choice by threats or acts of reprisal (hereafter "reprisals") or promises or grants of benefit (hereafter "benefits"). If the Board believes the effect of the employer's unlawful conduct to be particularly great, it will order the employer to bargain with the union involved, even though a majority of the employees voted against union representation.[1] The assumption that unlawful campaign tactics are likely to have a substantial impact on vote is inconsistent with the findings discussed in Chapters 3 and 4. Vote is closely related to pre-campaign attitudes and intent; recollection of campaign issues is generally low; and switching to the company is unrelated to familiarity with the company campaign.

Nonetheless, a substantial majority of both the switchers (76 percent) and the undecided (68 percent) voted company. It is necessary to consider the possibility that these employees were affected by unlawful campaigning. Unlawful campaigning may also have had an impact on other voters that was not evident in considering the campaign as a whole.

We used two methods to determine whether unlawful campaigning occurred. If unfair labor practice charges or objections to the election were filed, we relied on the Board's disposition of those charges. When charges or objections were not filed, all arguably unlawful speech and conduct was submitted on an informal basis to an NLRB administrative law judge. The judge reviewed this speech and conduct as he would have done if they had been submitted to him in his official capacity. He decided if the campaigning had been unlawful and, if so, the appropriate remedy.

Of the thirty-one elections studied, the employer was found to have

---

[1] NLRB v. Gissel Packing Co., 395 U.S. 675 (1959). This assumes that there is only one union in the election and that it has an authorization card majority.

Table 5-1

Unlawful Campaign Tactics Resulting in a Bargaining Order

Election	Campaign Tactics
2	Promises of benefit (improved wages and working conditions) Formation and domination of employee representation committee Interrogation
11	Threats of reprisal (termination of existing pension plan if union wins) Promises of benefit (improved working conditions) Grants of benefit (wages increased at non-union store to discourage unionization at this store) Interrogation
16	Discharge, hiring on basis of union sympathies (union supporters discharged, replaced by employees opposed to unionization) Threats of reprisal (close plant if union wins) Tightened up work rules in retaliation for union activity Interrogation
21	Threats of reprisal (discharge union supporters, take away benefits) Promises of benefit (improved wages and working conditions) Interrogation
24	Grants of benefit (wages and fringe benefits improved, employees treated better) Hiring on basis of suspected union sympathies (refused to hire women whose husbands worked in union plants) Interrogation
25	Threats of reprisal (tighten up if union wins) Promises of benefit (improved wages and fringes) Grants of benefit (gave raises, built lunchroom, cleaned work area, treated employees better) Interrogation
28	Threats of reprisal (close plant, discharge union supporters, no overtime or promotion for union supporters, terminate profit-sharing and education programs) Promises of benefit (improved working conditions) Attempted surveillance of union activities Interrogation

Table 5-1 *(cont'd)*

Election	Campaign Tactics
29	Grants of benefit (wages and hours improved, disliked supervisor, transferred) Promises of benefit (improved wages) Interrogation
32	Threats of reprisal (close plant, discharge union supporters, take away benefits) Interrogation

engaged in unlawful campaigning in twenty-two. Campaign violations serious enough to warrant a bargaining order were found in nine elections.[2] As shown by Table 5-1, the unlawful campaign tactics resulting in bargaining orders included reprisals, benefits, interrogation, formation and domination of an employee representation committee, and attempted surveillance of union activities. Similar conduct, albeit to a lesser extent, was found in the remaining thirteen unlawful elections. (See Table 5-2.)[3]

TYPE OF CAMPAIGN AND VOTE

Since the Board reserves the bargaining order remedy for elections in which it finds egregiously unlawful campaigning, the impact of campaigning on vote should be greatest in these elections. Less serious violations of the Act are believed by the Board to have a significant, though less powerful impact on vote. In order to test these assumptions, elections were divided into three categories: (1) those with unlawful campaigning resulting in a bargaining order; (2) those with unlawful campaigning in which no bargaining order was issued; (3)

[2] More bargaining orders were recommended than is normal in Board cases since the administrative law judge was directed not to consider whether the union had an authorization card majority or whether it won the election. We were interested in whether the campaign tactics involved were sufficiently serious to warrant a bargaining order, assuming other conditions for such an order were met. Had bargaining orders been limited to cases in which the union had a card majority, but lost the election, only two such orders would have been issued. This is not an unusually high proportion of bargaining orders in a group of thirty-one elections chosen for their hard-fought nature and the likelihood of their containing serious unlawful practices.

[3] The union was found to have engaged in unlawful campaigning in one election by misrepresenting its power to cause employees to be discharged.

Table 5-2

Unlawful Campaign Tactics
Not Resulting in a Bargaining Order

Election	Campaign Tactics
1	Threats of reprisal (close plant) Promises of benefit (improved wages and working conditions)
4	Interrogation Statements indicating the futility of selecting a bargaining representative
6	Promises of benefit (improved wages and working conditions) Interrogation Surveillance of union meetings
13–15	Promises of benefit Interrogation
18	Interrogation
22	Establishment of employee communication program
23	Interrogation
27	Threats of reprisal (discharge union supporters) Promises of benefit (improved wages and working conditions) Interrogation Dealing with employee committee while election pending
30	Threats of reprisal (move plant)
33	Threats of reprisal (eliminate individual discussions with employees)

NOTE: The nature of the unlawful campaign tactics in election 19 are not set out in this table as the employer refused to provide campaign information. The employer and union agreed, however, that the election should be set aside because each may have engaged in conduct "which had a tendency to interfere with the holding of a free and fair election."

those with no unlawful campaigning (sometimes referred to as "clean").

Employees were classified on the basis of their predispositions and vote. Potential union voters are those who had either: (1) signed a union authorization card; (2) been predicted to vote union based on their attitudes; (3) stated that their intent was to vote union; or (4) stated that they were undecided how to vote. If unlawful campaigning has the effect assumed by the Board, fewer potential union voters should actually vote union in unlawful elections than lawful elections. The loss of potential union supporters should be greatest in bargaining order elections.[4]

Table 5-3

Proportion of Potential Union Voters
Who Voted against Union Representation
in Clean, Unlawful, and Bargaining Order Elections

| Type of Potential Union Voter | Type of Campaign | | | | | | | |
| | Clean | | Unlawful | | Bargaining Order | | | |
	Percent Voting Company	N	Percent Voting Company	N	Percent Voting Company	N	F^a	p
Intent undecided	.60	15	.65	26	.79	19	.77	NS
Intent union	.07	284	.10	436	.09	224	.66	NS
Attitude predicted union vote	.08	291	.10	451	.09	238	.31	NS
Card-signer	.09	311	.16	487	.11	235	4.45	.01

NOTE: Election 5 was not included in any Chapter 5 analyses dealing with the effect of a Board finding of unlawful compaigning. No charges or objections were filed, and we had insufficient data on which to judge the legality of the employer's campaign.

[a]F is a statistic useful for determining whether there are significant differences in responses or behaviors between groups. It is appropriate to think of the F statistic as a ratio of the variability of responses or behaviors between groups compared to the variability within groups.

The data on voting behavior do not support the Board's assumptions. There was no group of potential union voters in which a significantly greater proportion voted against union representation in bargaining order elections than in clean elections or in elections characterized by lesser unlawful campaigning. Table 5–3 shows no

---

[4] Many of the same employees are identified as potential union voters by each of the four methods used. In order to test the Board's assumptions as broadly as possible, we examined the effect of unlawful campaigning on each of these four groups separately. The data were analyzed by one-way analyses of variance. This technique enabled us to determine whether there were any significant differences between groups in the proportion of employees voting company.

significant differences at all except that card-signers voted against union representation significantly more often in unlawful elections than in clean elections. There was, however, no difference in the proportion of card-signers voting against the union in unlawful and bargaining order elections combined than in clean elections.[5]

In sum, there is little evidence of the validity of the Board's assumptions regarding the impact of unlawful campaign tactics on voting behavior. There is also no evidence to support the Supreme Court's assumption that the Board is capable of distinguishing between those unlawful tactics that have a substantial impact on predispositions to vote union, thus warranting a bargaining order, and those that have a lesser impact.[6]

Only thirty-five of the reasons given for voting against union representation related to unlawful employer campaign tactics. Employees who referred to unlawful campaign tactics as a reason for voting against union representation were distributed evenly among clean, unlawful, and bargaining order elections. It is possible that employees who voted against the union because of unlawful campaign tactics were reluctant to admit this either to themselves or to our interviewers. Such reluctance should not, however, deter them from reporting that other employees had voted against the union because of these tactics. Those who gave reasons other than unlawful campaigning for their own vote did not, however, attribute the anti-union votes of others to unlawful campaign tactics.[7]

PERCEPTION OF UNLAWFUL CAMPAIGNING

There are at least two possible reasons why campaigning viewed by the Board as potentially coercive, and thus unlawful, is not associated with loss of union support. It may be that no more employees perceive unlawful campaigning in elections in which the Board finds it has occurred than in those elections in which the Board does not find it has occurred. Alternatively, more employees may perceive unlawful campaigning when the Board finds it has occurred, but not be influenced to vote against union representation.

---

[5] Significant effects were tested by Scheffé *post hoc* comparisons of the differences between each of the three types of elections, as well as the difference between clean elections and unlawful and bargaining order elections combined.

[6] See NLRB v. Gissel Packing Co., 395 U.S. 575 (1969). It was not possible to test the effect of specific types of unlawful campaigning, interrogation and surveillance of union activities, promises and grants of benefits, threats and acts of reprisal, on voting behavior, since several types of unlawful campaigning occurred in the same elections.

[7] See Appendix C, question 16.

Our measure of perception of unlawful campaign tactics is the extent to which such tactics are remembered. Accordingly, each employee was asked about the content of the employer's campaign, his own reason for vote, other employees' reasons for vote, and whether the employer had threatened or taken reprisals against union supporters or promised or granted benefits as a reward for rejecting union representation. Employees who mentioned unlawful tactics in response to any of these questions were treated as having perceived those tactics in the employer's campaign.[8]

Bargaining Order Elections

Across all elections, approximately one-third of the employees reported that the employer had used one or more unlawful campaign tactics. Such reports, however, were not significantly more frequent in bargaining order elections than in clean elections or those with other unlawful tactics.

It is possible that the method of interviewing or coding affected the measure of perception of unlawful tactics, particularly in elections in which the employer engaged in such tactics. For example, an employee who reported that the employer said layoffs might follow a union victory may have meant that the employer had threatened layoffs in reprisal for a union victory. Alternatively, he may have meant that the employer discussed the possibility that a union victory would lead to higher wages, higher prices for the employer's product, a lesser demand for that product, and consequent layoffs. The former statement would be unlawful, the latter would not. While interviewers were trained to probe ambiguous statements of this type, it is possible that the probes were not always successful in obtaining unambiguous statements. In addition, coders treated ambiguous responses as reports of lawful tactics. Some employee reports of employer statements thus may have been coded as lawful, when the employee actually perceived the employer as making an unlawful statement.

In order to be sure that our results were not distorted, a secondary analysis was performed, using employee responses that might, under probing, have revealed an unlawful reprisal or benefit. Such responses, characterized as "quasi-unlawful" tactics, included all reports of pos-

---

[8] Employees interviewed by telephone were significantly less likely to report unlawful campaigning than employees interviewed in person. It is unlikely, however, that telephone interviewing biased the findings related to perception of unlawful campaigning. There were no more telephone interviews in elections in which unlawful campaigning was found than in those in which it was not. Those interviewed by telephone were no more or less likely to be union voters than those interviewed in person.

sible harmful effects of a union victory and beneficial effects of a union loss.[9]

Adding reports of quasi-unlawful tactics to reports of what were unquestionably unlawful tactics increased the proportion of employees reporting one or more unlawful tactics from one-third to two-thirds. It did not, however, result in any change in the relative frequency of such reports in bargaining order elections as compared to other unlawful elections or clean elections. Employees in elections in which any unlawful campaigning was found were no more likely than employees in clean elections to report that unlawful campaigning had occurred.[10]

Threats and Acts of Reprisal

The effect of threats and acts of reprisal on reports of such campaigning was analyzed by grouping elections into three categories: (1) those with no unlawful campaign tactics; (2) those with unlawful tactics other than a threat or act of reprisal; (3) those containing threats or acts of reprisal.[11] Approximately 20 percent of the employees reported that the employer had either threatened or taken reprisals against union supporters. The frequency of such reports did not, however, increase significantly in elections in which such conduct actually occurred. Awareness of the employer's economic power and his ability to use it against union supporters appears to exist apart from those employer actions assumed by the Board to remind employees of that power.

Promises and Grants of Benefit

For purposes of analyzing the effect of promises and grants of benefit on perception, elections were divided according to the same procedure used for analyzing other effects: (1) no unlawful tactics; (2) unlawful tactics other than promises or grants of benefit; (3) promises or grants of benefit.[12] The proportion of employees reporting

---

[9] See the code in Appendix D. Codes falling in the quasi-unlawful category are: 111, 131, 151, 220, 316, 711, 722, 732, 742, and 752.

[10] All analyses of the perception of unlawful campaign tactics were followed by a secondary analysis including quasi-unlawful tactics. There was no instance in which the inclusion of quasi-unlawful tactics led to results that supported the Board's assumption when the original analysis had not. Accordingly, no further results of quasi-unlawful tactic analysis are reported.

[11] Reprisal codes were 110, 130, 150, 221, 330, 340, 343, 610, 710, 721, 750, 751, 761, 763, 771, 774, 776, 780, 782, and 787.

[12] Benefit codes were 315, 613, 660, 730, 731, 733, 734, 740, and 741.

unlawful promises or grants of benefit averaged 25 percent with no significant difference whether or not such conduct occurred. Board findings that illegal benefits were promised or granted were unrelated to employee reports of such behavior.

The Supreme Court has stated that the "danger inherent in well-timed increases in benefits is the suggestion of a fist inside the velvet glove."[13] The Court assumes that employees will infer from a grant of benefits designed to encourage them to vote against union representation that the employer is threatening reprisals if they choose union representation. If the Court is right, employees should report more threats of reprisal in elections in which the employer has granted or promised benefits than in clean elections.

It was not possible to test the Supreme Court's theory directly, since most elections in which unlawful benefits were found also included unlawful threats or acts of reprisal. However, any straightforward explanation of the data indicates that the Court's theory is in error. A Board finding that a threat or act of reprisal had occurred was not associated with greater employee perception of threats or acts of reprisal. Moreover, there was no greater perception of reprisals in elections in which benefits occurred together with reprisals than in elections in which no unlawful campaigning was found. The promise or grant of benefits, even in conjunction with reprisals, does not increase the perception of reprisals. There is thus no reason to suppose that a promise or grant of benefits standing alone would lead employees to infer a threat of reprisal if they choose union representation.

Conclusion

There is no evidence that a greater proportion of employees perceive unlawful campaigning when the Board finds it has occurred than when the Board does not. This may explain why campaigning viewed by the Board as potentially coercive, and thus unlawful, is not associated with a loss of union support. If there is no relationship between employee perceptions of unlawful campaigning and Board findings of unlawful campaigning, there is no reason to expect a relationship between employee behavior and Board findings.

The difference between Board findings and employee perceptions of unlawful campaigning may be due to the constraints placed on the Board by Section 8(c) of the Act and the First Amendment to the Constitution. An employer is generally free to state facts about the effects of unionization, as long as he does not threaten employees

---

[13] NLRB v. Exchange Parts Co., 375 U.S. 405, 409 (1964).

with reprisals if they unionize or promise them benefits if they do not unionize. An employer may state that other plants have closed or moved because of union wage demands, if that is true and the employer does not imply that he would close or move as a retaliatory measure if his employees vote for union representation.[14]

There is a fine line between an employer's speech that accurately describes the harmful economic consequences of unionization elsewhere and one that implicitly threatens economic reprisal if his employees choose a union. The Board must respect that line, but employees need not. They are free to infer from the employer's statement that other plants have closed or moved because of union wage demands that he will close or move his plant if the union wins the election. They are equally free to infer threats or promises from other statements that the Board cannot find unlawful. If any sizeable number of employees perceive threats or promises in speech the Board cannot find unlawful, there will be, as the data show, no relationship between Board findings and employee perceptions of unlawful campaigning.

The difference between Board findings and employee perceptions of unlawful campaigning may also be due, in part, to limitations on the Board's power to find unlawful employer conduct that has the effect of discouraging unionization. Assume, for example, that during the pre-election period, the employer discharges a prominent union supporter. Unless the Board can prove that the reason for the discharge was the employee's union activities, it cannot find the discharge unlawful.[15] Many employees may believe, regardless of the Board's finding, that the employee involved was discharged because he was a union supporter. This, too, would result in a discrepancy between Board findings and employee reports of unlawful campaigning.[16]

PERCEPTION OF UNLAWFUL CAMPAIGNING AND SWITCH

Even though Board findings and employee perceptions of unlawful campaigning differ, it is still possible that potential union voters who perceive unlawful campaigning will switch and vote against the union. If unlawful campaigning does have this effect, more potential union

---

[14] NLRB v. Gissel Packing Co., 395 U.S. 575, 618 (1969); The Louis-Allis Co., 182 NLRB 433 (1970).

[15] Radio Officers' Union v. NLRB, 347 U.S. 17 (1954).

[16] The difference between Board findings and employee perceptions of unlawful campaigning may also be caused by perceptual distortion. See pp. 144–145 *infra*.

voters who vote against union representation than those who vote for union representation should perceive unlawful campaigning. Table 5–4 shows this not to be the case. There was no category of potential union voters in which those who voted company were more likely to report unlawful campaigning than those who voted union.

PERCEPTION OF UNLAWFUL CAMPAIGNING AND UNION SENTIMENTS

While potential union voters were not influenced to vote against union representation by unlawful campaigning, they were sensitive to such tactics. The difference is most striking as to reprisals. Table 5–5 shows that 34 percent of the employees intending to vote union reported reprisals as compared to 10 percent of those who intended to

Table 5-4

Perception of Unlawful Campaigning by Potential Union Voters Who Voted Company Compared to Those Who Voted Union

Type of Potential Union Voter	Percent Reporting Reprisals	r	Percent Reporting Benefits	r	Percent Reporting Any Unlawful Campaigning	r	N
Intent undecided							
Vote company	.09		.19		.26		43
Vote union	.15		.35		.45		20
		.08		.18		.19	
Intent union							
Vote company	.22		.26		.41		88
Vote union	.36		.32		.53		397
		.12*		.05		.09	
Attitude predicted union vote							
Vote company	.17		.26		.37		92
Vote union	.39		.34		.57		351
		.18*		.07		.16*	
Card-signer							
Vote company	.15		.28		.38		138
Vote union	.36	.21*	.34	.06	.54	.15*	351

*$p \leq .01$

NOTE: Every significant difference is contrary to that assumed by the Board.

Table 5-5

Perception of Unlawful Campaigning by Potential Union Voters Compared to Potential Company Voters

Measure of Predisposition	Percent Reporting Reprisals	r	Percent Reporting Benefits	r	Percent Reporting Any Unlawful Campaigning	r	N
Intent							
Company	.10		.19		.26		410
Undecided	.11		.24		.32		63
Union	.34		.31		.51		485
		.28*		.15*		.26*	
Attitude							
Company	.11		.18		.27		561
Union	.34		.33		.53		443
		.28*		.17*		.27*	
Card-sign							
Did not sign	.12		.17		.26		568
Signed	.30		.32		.49		489
		.23*		.17*		.24*	

*$p \leq .01$

vote company ($r = .28$). Unlawful benefits were reported by 31 percent of those intending to vote union and 19 percent of those intending to vote company ($r = .15$). Employees' pre-campaign sentiments thus predict how they will perceive the employer's campaign.

The data in Table 5–6 indicate that the relationship between reporting unlawful behavior and vote is similar to the relationship between such reports and predispositions. Thirty-four percent of the union voters, but only 10 percent of the company voters, reported reprisals ($r = .25$). Unlawful benefits were reported by 32 percent of the union voters and 18 percent of the company voters ($r = .13$).

The relationship between reporting unlawful behavior and vote is not caused by union voters' generally greater awareness of the company campaign. Union voters were not generally more familiar with the company campaign than were company voters.[17]

Nor is the relationship between vote and reports of unlawful prac-

[17] See Chapter 4, p. 85.

Table 5-6

**Perception of Unlawful Campaigning by Union Voters
as Compared to Company Voters**

Vote	Percent Reporting Reprisals		Percent Reporting Benefits		Percent Reporting Any Unlawful Campaigning		N
		r		r		r	
Company	.10		.18		.25		590
Union	.34		.32		.51		477
		.25*		.13*		.23*	

*$p \leq .01$

tices affected by whether or not such practices were found. Whether they were or not, union voters reported unlawful practices significantly more often than did company voters.

Employee sentiments for or against union representation are also related to their views of why other employees voted against the union. Union voters, significantly more often (17 percent) than company voters (4 percent) attributed other employees' anti-union votes to reprisals ($r = .22$). There were no significant differences in the frequency of benefit attributions by company or union voters. Only 3 percent of the employees referred to benefits as reasons others had voted against the union.

The evidence that union voters were significantly more likely than company voters to report unlawful campaign tactics, particularly those of a threatening nature, suggests that employees may be reporting the employer's campaign tactics in terms consistent with their preconceptions of him. Those favoring union representation knew the employer was opposed to their position. Indeed, since we studied primarily elections in which the employer campaigned vigorously against union representation, they knew he was strongly opposed.[18] The data show that union voters were also aware of the employer's economic power to affect their wages, working conditions, and continued employment. Regardless of whether or not the employer threatened to use or

---

[18] During the pre-test, employees were asked whether the employer opposed unionization and if so to what extent. We dropped the question, because virtually all employees reported that the employer was strongly opposed.

used his economic power in an unlawful manner, many union voters reported that he had. Union supporters, knowing of the employer's opposition to unionization and his economic power over them, might expect him to use, or at least threaten to use, that power to punish those supporting unionization and reward those opposed.

Company supporters, whose stand on unionization is the same as the employer's, are more favorable toward him. Their attitudes should dispose them to expect the employer to act in a fair manner. They are probably as aware as the union supporters of the employer's economic power over them and his opposition to unionization, but they have less to fear from him than do union supporters. They would thus be less likely to perceive the employer's statements and actions as designed to frustrate unionization or retaliate against union supporters.

The greater tendency of company voters to report benefits than reprisals may also be due to their predisposition to view the employer's campaign in a favorable light. Reprisals are universally condemned, while company supporters may view increased benefits as based on the employer's awareness of employee needs, rather than his desire to keep the union out.[19]

The evidence that employee perceptions of the employer's campaign are influenced by their expectations is not limited to reports of unlawful campaigning. As shown in Chapter 4, union supporters, possibly anticipating the employer's hostility, were more sensitive than company supporters to employer criticisms of the union and to employer campaign themes suggesting that jobs might be lost if the union won the election. Company supporters, knowing of the union's hostility toward their choice, were more sensitive than union voters to union criticisms of the employer. Expectations thus appear to be affecting the campaign perceptions of all employees.

The relationship between expectations and perceptions of unlawful campaigning may, to some extent, account for the lack of a significant relationship between Board findings and employee perceptions of unlawful campaigning. Union supporters tend to perceive unlawful campaigning even when the Board does not find it has occurred; company supporters tend not to perceive it even when the Board finds it has occurred.[20]

---

[19] The question directed to benefits was "Did this employer give or promise benefits to employees to get them to vote against the union?" (Wave II Interview Schedule, question 19a, Appendix C.)

[20] Our explanation of the differential perception of unlawful campaigning draws heavily upon theories of cognitive consistency. These theories assume that there

DISCHARGES OF UNION SUPPORTERS

Acts of reprisal, particularly discriminatory discharges, are assumed to be among the most effective employer tactics to discourage union support. There were eight elections in which union supporters were discharged during the card-signing campaign.[21] In two elections, the discharges or layoffs were widespread. In election 8, six employees were laid off in the initial stages of the union organizing campaign and another seventy-six were laid off in the period between the union's filing of a petition for an election and the date of the election. In election 28, thirteen employees were discharged on the day the union began picketing for recognition. Unfair labor practice charges or post-election objections were filed in each of these elections. The Board's regional director issued a complaint based on the charges in three elections, indicating his view that there were reasonable grounds to believe the discharges had been motivated by the employee's union sentiments or activities. Two of the complaints were settled; one (in election 28) was dismissed by an administrative law judge after a hearing.[22] In another case, the employer admitted in the post-election interview that he had discharged employees because of their union support.

Employees in elections in which union supporters were discharged were significantly more likely than employees in other elections to report that the employer had discharged employees because of their union support ($r = .29$). They were also more likely to report that the employer had threatened or taken retaliatory action generally than were employees in other elections ($r = .16$). This difference was not associated with the amount of evidence that the discharge had been discriminatorily motivated. There were as many reports of un-

---

is a tendency to resolve cognitive inconsistencies because inconsistent information is threatening to prior attitudes and belief. Congruity theory, one of the cognitive consistency theories, assumes that a subject (employee) brings prior attitudes towards the source (employer) and the concept (union representation) to a communication situation. When the source's message about the concept is inconsistent with the subject's prior attitudes toward the source or the concept, a state of disequilibrium exists. There are a number of ways to resolve the inconsistency. Apparently union and company supporters are not changing their evaluation of the source or the concept but are distorting the meaning of the message, so as to be consistent with their prior attitudes toward the source and the concept. See R. P. ABLESON, E. ARONSON, W. J. McGUIRE, T. M. NEWCOMB, M. J. ROSENBERG, and P. H. TANNENBAUM (eds.), THEORIES OF COGNITIVE CONSISTENCY: A SOURCEBOOK (1968), particularly Tannenbaum, *The Congruity Principle*.

[21] Elections 3, 8, 11, 16, 18, 19, 28, and 32.

[22] One settlement provided for the employer to offer reinstatement and back pay to the discharged employee; the other provided for a second election.

lawful discharge in elections in which no complaint was issued as in elections in which a complaint was issued. In short, whenever an employer discharges union supporters during an organizing campaign, employees tend to view that discharge as having been motivated by the employer's anti-union sentiments.

It was primarily union supporters, not company supporters, who tended to view the discharges as having been discriminatorily motivated $(r = .35)$. The union supporters were not, however, coerced into voting against the union. There were no more card-signers who switched to vote for the company in discharge elections than in other elections. Furthermore, those card-signers who did vote company in discharge elections were no more likely to report that the discharges had been discriminatorily motivated than those card-signers who voted union.

In sum, any discharge of union supporters during the organizing campaign is likely to be viewed by other union supporters as having been discriminatorily motivated. That view does not, however, coerce them into voting against the union.[23]

DEMOGRAPHIC AND EMPLOYMENT CHARACTERISTICS AND UNLAWFUL CAMPAIGN TACTICS

The Seventh Circuit Court of Appeals has stated that young, old, unskilled, or part-time employees are more susceptible to coercion by unlawful tactics than are other employees.[24] That court has also assumed that the impact of an unlawful campaign practice can be determined in part by the size of the city in which the company is located.[25]

The data do not support these assumptions. There was no group of employees defined by a demographic or employment characteristic that was less likely to vote union in unlawful elections than clean elections. Only one demographic or employment characteristic, age, correlated significantly with the report of unlawful campaign tactics. Younger employees were significantly more likely to report unlawful

---

[23] There were no elections in which the Board found that discriminatory discharges took place. There were, however, a number of elections in which union supporters were discharged. Since Board findings of unlawful behavior are generally unrelated to employee perceptions of unlawful behavior, we believe that analysis of the relationship between discharges of union supporters, perceptions, and loss of union support is appropriate.

[24] See, e.g., NLRB v. Kostel Corp., 440 F.2d 347, 352 (1971). See also NLRB v. Copps Corp., 458 F.2d 1227 (1972).

[25] NLRB v. Kostel Corp., *supra,* note 24.

tactics than were older employees ($r = -.14$). This is not wholly due to younger employees' tendency to vote union ($r = -.11$) and union voters' tendency to report significantly more unlawful practices than company voters. Controlling for vote, the correlation between age and report of unlawful campaigning is still significant ($r = -.08$). Since, however, younger employees were significantly more likely to vote union than older employees, their greater sensitivity to unlawful campaigning did not dispose them to vote against union representation.

EMPLOYER KNOWLEDGE OF UNION SUPPORT OR ACTIVITIES

Board rules prohibiting the employer from interrogating employees about their union sympathies or activities and from keeping union activities under surveillance assume that employees will be deterred from union support or activity if they believe the employer knows or can discover their union sympathies. Board decisions prohibiting threats of selective reprisals against union supporters rest on the same assumption.

Illegal interrogation took place in sixteen elections involving over four hundred employees. Employer counsel in many of these elections reported that interrogation was widespread. Yet, only twenty-nine employees in these elections reported that interrogation had taken place. The few reports of interrogation compared to the extent of its probable occurrence suggest that employees were not generally sensitive to interrogation. It thus seems unlikely that interrogation was a substantial deterrent to union support or activity.[26]

Despite the apparent unconcern of most employees with interrogation, belief that the employer knew employees' union sentiments was widespread. Forty-three percent of the union voters thought the employer knew their position on unionization, as did 33 percent of the company voters.

Of those union voters who believed their sympathies to be known, 76 percent had told the employer themselves. They did so either directly, in conversation, or indirectly, by openly engaging in union organizing activity or by wearing union buttons or other insignia. Of those union voters who attended union meetings and believed the

---

[26] Employees were not asked directly whether they had been interrogated about their union activities or sympathies. Reports of interrogation were in response to our asking whether the employee had been spoken to by any employer representative or whether the employer knew which side the employee favored in the election.

employer knew of their union sentiments, 75 percent (117/156) had told the employer of those sentiments. This degree of voluntary reporting suggests that some employees do not fear employer knowledge of their union support and activities.

The possibility that fear of employer knowledge deterred other employees from supporting the union and attending union meetings cannot be ruled out. Of those employees who did not attend union meetings, however, only 1 percent (7/829) gave fear of employer surveillance as a reason for not attending.

The data suggest even more strongly that fear of employer knowledge does not deter employees from voting for the union. Sixty-two percent of the voters did not believe the employer knew whether or not they supported union representation. Obviously, those employees were not deterred from voting for the union by fear the employer would discover how they voted. Of the 402 employees who thought that the employer knew which side they had supported in the election, only one believed the employer knew by looking at his ballot. The risk that the employer will discover and take reprisals against union voters thus appears to be no deterrent to voting for union representation in a secret ballot election.

CONCLUSION

In every election, the employer made statements that could be interpreted as threats of reprisal or promises of benefit. Whether or not these statements were found by the Board to be unlawful, many employees, particularly union voters, perceived them as unlawful.

These findings are, to some extent, consistent with Board and court assumptions that employees will interpret ambiguous statements by an employer to contain threats and promises.[27] The data do not, however, support the Board's assumption that unlawful campaign practices affect the voting behavior of union sympathizers. The unions did not lose significantly more support in unlawful elections than in clean elections. Nor is there evidence that the perception of unlawful campaign tactics, whether or not found by the Board, is associated with switching to the company by potential union voters.[28]

---

[27] See, e.g., Singer Co., 199 NLRB 1195 (1972); NLRB v. Federbush Co., 121 F.2d 954 (2nd Cir. 1941) (L. Hand, J.).

[28] Analysis of the effect of opinion leaders on voting behavior was beyond the scope of this study. If, however, opinion leaders were influenced by unfair campaigning and, in turn, influenced others, unfair campaigning should have affected vote generally. No such effect appears in the data.

The apparent failure of unlawful campaign tactics to affect vote does not mean that some employees are not deterred from supporting union representation for fear of the employer's reaction. The data suggest, rather, that most employees susceptible to coercion have been weeded out before the pre-election campaign takes place. They know of many employers' hostility toward unions and of their employer's economic power over them. Rather than risk the exercise of that power, they decide, as soon as they learn of the union organizing campaign, to have nothing to do with the union.

Those employees who do become associated with the union are equally aware of the employer's hostility to the union and his economic power. They anticipate that he may use that power, or at least threaten to do so, and are sensitive to any intimations to that effect in the campaign. They are unaffected by what they perceive as reprisals or benefits, however, as they have discounted such responses in their initial decision to vote union. Threats or acts of reprisal are taken as confirming their need for the protection of a union; promises or grants of benefit are regarded as untrustworthy or inadequate to obviate the need for unionization.[29]

SUMMARY

Most Board decisions finding particular campaign tactics unlawful rest on the assumption that those tactics will coerce employees into voting against union representation. The data do not support this assumption. Potential union voters did not vote against union representation in significantly greater numbers in bargaining order elections than in clean elections or elections characterized by lesser unlawful campaigning. Nor did a greater proportion of employees report unlawful campaigning when the Board found it had occurred than when the Board did not find it had occurred. Employees who intended to vote union were more likely to report unlawful campaign tactics than employees who intended to vote company. Those potential union voters who switched and voted company were not, however, sig-

---

[29] In order for a persuasive communication to change behavior it most likely must first affect attitude. In congruity theory terms, attitude change occurs when the subject deals with an inconsistent message by changing his evaluation of the source, the concept, or both. In processing the message, the subject must evaluate the source's credibility and the message's consistency with prior attitudes and beliefs. Only that inconsistent information that is judged to be credible is likely to affect prior attitudes and change behavior. Of course, prior attitudes are likely to affect the judgment of credibility and consistency. See ABELSON, et al., *supra,* note 20, especially Pepitone, *The Problems of Motivation in Consistency Models.*

nificantly more likely to report unlawful campaigning than those who voted union.

Any discharge of union supporters during the organizing campaign was viewed by other union supporters as having been discriminatorily motivated. That view did not, however, result in their voting against the union.

Employees were not generally sensitive to interrogation. Of those union voters who believed the employer knew of their sympathies, a substantial majority had told the employer themselves. Hardly any employees believed that either party was able to violate the secrecy of the ballot box.

CHAPTER 6

Union Authorization Cards and Vote

At the start of an organizing drive the union typically asks employees to sign cards authorizing it to represent them in bargaining with their employer. These authorization cards are most often used to satisfy the Board's rule that a petition for a representation election must be supported by 30 percent of the employees. If, however, the Board finds the employer to have engaged in serious unfair labor practices preventing a fair election, and a majority of the employees have signed cards, the Board will order the employer to bargain with the union on the basis of its card majority.[1]

The central assumption underlying the Board's treatment of authorization cards is that card-signers want union representation, nonsigners do not or are uncertain. There has, however, been considerable controversy as to whether signing an authorization card is a reliable indicator of union sentiment.[2] Courts and commentators have charged that employees may sign and not revoke cards in the belief the cards will be used to obtain an election, in order to get the union organizer to stop bothering them, or because everyone else is signing. Under any of these circumstances, the cards might not accurately represent employee sentiments about unionization.[3]

It has also been argued that employees frequently sign cards without having heard the employer's arguments against unionization. If they do, the card, though accurately representing employee choice at the time it was signed, would be based on incomplete information. The assumption is that with full information the choice might be different. The unreliability of authorization cards is said to be demonstrated by the frequency with which unions lose elections in units in which they had a card majority.[4]

---

[1] NLRB v. Gissel Packing Co., 395 U.S. 575 (1969).

[2] NLRB v. Gissel Packing Co., *supra* at 602, n. 19.

[3] See, e.g., NLRB v. Swan Super Cleaner Inc. 384 F2d 609, 620 (6th Cir. 1967); Braune, *Obligation to Bargain on Basis of Card Majority*, 36 GA L. REV. 334 (1969); Comment, *Union Authorization Cards*, 75 YALE L.J. 805 (1966).

[4] Comment, *Union Authorization Cards*, 75 YALE L.J. 805 (1966). NLRB Chairman Frank W. McCulloch reported that of 202 elections conducted by the

The Board and the Supreme Court have accepted elections as the preferred measure of employee choice. An employer who does not engage in unlawful campaigning need not bargain with a union that possesses authorization cards signed by a majority of his employees, but may insist on an election.[5] The secrecy and formality of voting in a government-conducted election are thought to be conducive to a sober and thoughtful decision. The pre-election campaign supposedly insures that employees have an opportunity to hear the opposing arguments of employer and union. The employee may then evaluate those arguments and vote in a way that represents his informed view of the desirability of union representation.

Authorization cards, nonetheless, have been accepted as sufficiently reliable to justify a bargaining order when egregious unlawful campaigning has occurred. The Supreme Court, in *Gissel*, assumed that in most instances employees who sign cards will first have been exposed to the employers' arguments against union representation. Additionally, the Court assumed that the same group pressures alleged to detract from the reliability of cards are present in elections.[6]

CARD-SIGNING AS AN INDICATION OF EMPLOYEE CHOICE

The data demonstrate that card-signing is an accurate indicator of employee choice at the time the card is signed. Forty-six percent of the voters (489/1067) signed union authorization cards. Of those, 82 percent reported that they wanted union representation at the time they signed the card, 14 percent said they were uncertain, and 4 percent said they did not want union representation.

The data also support the assumption that employees who are asked, but do not sign cards, are generally opposed to union representation or uncertain. Thirty-eight percent (216/568) of the non-signers were asked to sign cards. Of these, 73 percent reported that they had not

---

Board's Atlanta office in 1962, the unions won 74 percent when they had 71–100 percent of the cards (57 elections), 57 percent when they had 51–70 percent of the cards (87 elections) and 19 percent when they had 30–50 percent of the cards (58 elections). McCulloch, *A Tale of Two Cities: Or Law in Action* in Proceedings, Section of Labor Relations Law, American Bar Association 14, 17 (1962). Of the thirty-one elections in our sample, the unions won 62 percent when they had 51–100 percent of the cards (13 elections) and 7 percent when they had 30–50 percent of the cards (14 elections). There were too few elections in which union had over 70 percent of the cards to warrant separate analysis. In two elections, there was no card-signing campaign: once because the election was a re-run; once because it had been postponed due to a pending unfair labor practice charge.

[5] Linden Lumber Div., Summer & Co., 190 NLRB 718 (1971); aff'd, 419 U.S. 301 (1974).

[6] 395 U.S. at 604.

signed because they did not want union representation at the time or were undecided, 9 percent cited a desire for privacy, and 18 percent gave other reasons.

Card-signing is a reasonably accurate predictor of vote ($r = .51$). Seventy-two percent (351/489) of the card-signers voted for union representation; 79 percent (448/568) of the non-signers voted against union representation. The tendency of non-signers to vote against union representation was similar whether or not they had been asked to sign.

PRESSURES WHICH MAY CONTRIBUTE TO THE CARD-SIGNING DECISION: THEIR EFFECT ON RELIABILITY

In *Gissel*, the Court indicated that whatever pressures may cause an employee to sign and not revoke an authorization card may also lead the employee to state and not vary from a voting intent. This conclusion was predicted on three assumptions: (1) elections are held most often in small units; (2) in such units the union sentiments of virtually every voter can be determined; (3) an employee whose union sentiments are known will be deterred from switching, even though his opinion as to the desirability of unionization has changed.

The Court's assumption about unit size is uncontestably accurate; almost 60 percent of the elections conducted by the Board are in units of under thirty employees, and 85 percent are in units of under one hundred.[7] If the Court's remaining assumptions are valid, the proportion of employees who believe that their sentiments regarding unionization are known to the employer or union should decrease as the size of the unit increases. The proportion of employees who vote differently from their stated intent should be greater in larger units due to the employees' belief in anonymity.

Employees in small units (under thirty employees) were more likely to perceive their sentiments as known to the employer or union than employees in medium units (thirty-one to ninety-nine employees) or large units (one hundred or more employees) ($F = 7.00$; $p \leqq .01$). Contrary to the Court's assumption, however, employees in the smaller units were not deterred from switching. While the likelihood of switch from intent to vote is generally low, it was not significantly lower in small units than in medium or large. Switching from card-sign to vote was also unrelated to the size of the unit.

In sum, the Supreme Court sought to defend the use of cards on the theory that voters in secret ballot elections are under the same pres-

---

[7] 40 NLRB ANN. REP. 246 (1975).

sures to vote in accord with their stated intent as are card-signers not to revoke their cards. These pressures were assumed to be caused by public knowledge of union sentiments in small units. The data do not indicate, however, that unit size is related to vote switch or card-sign switch. Thus, cards may be used to determine the extent of union support if a fair election cannot be held, albeit not for the reasons given by the Court.

The finding that public knowledge of union sentiments does not deter card-signers from voting against a union they subsequently do not want is also inconsistent with *Savair Mfg. Co. v. NLRB*.[8] In that case, the Supreme Court assumed that an employee who signs an authorization card solely to take advantage of an initiation fee waiver, yet does not want union representation, may subsequently vote for the union because of the commitment inherent in signing. The data indicate that employees who want union representation when they sign are not deterred from voting against the union by public knowledge of their signing. It is thus unlikely that public knowledge would deter an antiunion vote by an employee who did not want union representation at the time he signed the card.[9]

EMPLOYER KNOWLEDGE OF CARD-SIGNING

The employers also argued in *Gissel* that authorization cards should not be treated as evidence of union support, because they are frequently signed before the employer has had a chance to present his side of the unionization issue. The employers asserted that such cards do not accurately reflect employee choice, since they are based on incomplete information. The unstated assumption underlying this assertion is that many card-signers, after hearing the employer's arguments, will vote against union representation.

---

[8] 414 U.S. 270 (1973).

[9] Since the sample included no elections in which the union waived initiation fees for pre-election card-signers, only one other *Savair* assumption could be tested. The Court assumed that employees signing cards solely to take advantage of a fee waiver may mislead other employees into voting union. The Court's reasoning was that non-signers would be impressed with the union's strength as shown by a large number of card-signers. If employees are influenced to vote union by the union's show of authorization card strength, unions with a substantial proportion of cards should gain more support among non-signers, or at least lose the support of fewer signers, than unions with a lower proportion of cards. In fact, however, there was no significant relationship between the proportion of cards signed and the extent to which the union gained or lost strength between card-sign and election.

The Court responded

> Normally, however, the union will inform the employer of its organization drive early in order to subject the employer to the unfair labor practice provisions of the Act; the union must be able to show the employer's awareness of the drive in order to prove that his contemporaneous conduct constituted unfair labor practices on which a bargaining order can be based if the drive is ultimately successful.[10]

In eighteen elections we were able to determine the proportion of authorization cards signed before the employer knew about the card-signing drive. In ten of these elections, all cards were signed before the employer was aware of the card-signing drive; in four, 50–75 percent were signed before the employer found out; and in four others nearly all cards were signed after employer knowledge.

It appears, then, that in most elections the employer does not know about the card-signing drive in time to respond before a majority of the cards have been signed. It does not follow, however, that cards do not represent reasonably firm union sentiments. As noted previously, 72 percent of all card-signers voted for union representation, even though few of them had heard the employer's side of the unionization issue at the time they signed a card. Furthermore, as shown in Chapter 4, campaign familiarity was generally low. Those card-signers who did switch to the company were no more familiar with the company campaign than those who voted union.

In sum, the voting decision, made after hearing the employer's arguments, is not substantially more informed than the card-signing decision. Nor, for most employees, are the two choices different. For those few employees for whom the card-sign choice and the election choice are different, that difference is not associated with greater familiarity with the company campaign. Accordingly, the fact that most employees sign cards before having heard the employer's arguments ought not prevent the issuance of a bargaining order based on cards.

ELECTIONS AND BARGAINING ORDERS

The preference for elections rests initially on doubts as to whether an employee who signs an authorization card wants union representation at the time he signs. Those doubts are unwarranted. Regardless of what other pressures may contribute to the decision to sign a card, nearly all card-signers reported that they wanted the union at the time they signed the card.

---

[10] 395 U.S. 575, 603 (1969).

The preference for elections is also based on the view that employee choice made after hearing the arguments of both parties is more fully informed and seriously considered. This implies that an informed choice might be different. However, when voting choice is different from card-sign choice, there is no evidence that the change is due to the employees' obtaining more information. Switching to the company was not associated with familiarity with the company campaign.

Nonetheless, the employer's campaign may affect choice by activating or reinforcing positive attitudes toward working conditions or negative attitudes toward unions. The employer who addresses himself to employee dissatisfaction may persuade employees that he should be given an opportunity, free of unionization, to remedy the causes of that dissatisfaction. The mere passage of time and the imminence of an election may lead some card-signers to realize that they do not really want union representation, either because of their attitudes toward the job or unions. If an employee who has signed a union authorization card votes against union representation for any of these reasons, the election choice would represent a more considered, if not more informed, judgment than the card-sign choice.

Finally, there exists a powerful non-empirical argument supporting the preference for elections. The concept that each party should have a roughly equal opportunity to persuade the voters is fundamental to the democratic process. If the card-signing decision is treated as final, an employer may believe he has been denied a fair opportunity to be heard. The interest in encouraging peaceful acceptance of employee choice is furthered if employers are given an opportunity to campaign before employees make their final decision. The campaign may not affect that decision, but the democratic principle of equality of opportunity to persuade supports the argument that it should take place.

The arguments supporting the preference for elections do not, of themselves, undercut the issuance of bargaining orders when the Board determines that the employer's unlawful campaigning renders a fair election unlikely. Most attacks on the Board's power to issue bargaining orders are without merit. Authorization cards are a highly accurate reflection of employee choice at the time they are signed. They are also a reasonably good predictor of vote.

The most powerful argument against the issuance of bargaining orders is the lack of evidence that employer campaigning prevents a fair election. As shown in Chapter 5, potential union voters did not switch in significantly greater numbers in bargaining order elections than in those elections marked by lesser or no unlawful campaigning.

Moreover, potential union voters who did switch were no more sensitive to unlawful campaigning than those who voted union. These data suggest that if the bargaining order is to be retained as a remedy, it must be on grounds other than that certain unfair labor practices prevent a fair election from taking place.

SUMMARY

The data support the Board's assumptions about union authorization cards. Card-signing is an accurate indication of employee choice at the time the cards are signed. Card-signing is also a reasonably accurate predictor of vote. Contrary to the Supreme Court's assumption in *Gissel*, however, cards generally are signed before the employer has had a chance to present his side of the unionization issue.

CHAPTER 7

An Alternative Model of Voting Behavior: The Legal Implications

THE BOARD'S MODEL

Underlying Board regulation of union representation elections is an implicit model of the employee voter and a set of assumptions about the effect of the campaign on vote. The Board assumes that most employees know little about unions and have no firm opinions about whether or not they should vote for union representation. The pre-election campaign is assumed to provide employees with facts about union representation and the arguments for and against voting union so that they can make an informed choice. If the campaign is conducted in a calm and unemotional atmosphere, referred to by the Board as "laboratory conditions," the employee voter will listen carefully to the arguments of each party and make a reasoned decision based on these arguments.

Employee predispositions for or against unionization are assumed to be so tenuous and their voting decision so dependent on the campaign that if "laboratory conditions" are disrupted, employees may vote contrary to their own desires. The employer's threatened or actual use of his economic power is presumed to be extremely destructive to the appropriate campaign atmosphere. Because employees are economically dependent upon the employer, they are expected to interpret ambiguous statements as threats of reprisal if they vote for the union and promises of benefit if they do not. Employees, once reminded of the employer's economic power in an unlawful fashion, are expected to vote against union representation, not because of a change in sentiments, but out of fear of reprisal or to gain benefits. Employee voters also need protection from emotional appeals not based on the employer's economic power over them if they are to exercise a free and reasoned choice.

THE VALIDITY OF THE BOARD'S ASSUMPTIONS

Employees Are Unsophisticated about Unionization, So Their Sentiments Are Tenuous and Easily Changed by the Campaign

The data contradict the Board's assumption that employees are generally naive about union-management relationships and have no firm pre-campaign sentiments. Many of the employees we interviewed had personal experience with unions and union organization. Forty-three percent had been union members elsewhere; 30 percent had voted in a previous NLRB election. Even those without prior union experience tended to have firm opinions about whether or not they wanted a union. These opinions may not have been based on a full understanding of the effect of being organized. But, people typically respond affectively to situations, even ones that have only recently become salient and with which they have had little previous experience.[1]

Employees' attitudes toward working conditions and unions strongly predisposed them to vote for or against union representation. Attitudes and intent correctly predicted the votes of 81 percent of the employees. Even authorization card-signing, which took place an average of three months before the election and, for most employees, without having heard the employer's arguments against unionization, accurately predicted the votes of 72 percent of the employees.

Employees Are Attentive to the Campaign and Base Their Decisions on the Parties' Arguments

Employees are not generally attentive to the campaign. The average employee remembered fewer than 10 percent of the company campaign themes and 7 percent of the union themes. Although 71 percent of the employees recalled the union issue that it could improve wages and 64 percent that it would prevent unfairness, these were both issues that were salient to employees prior to the campaign. Even so, only 22 percent of the employees recalled union wage claims accurately.

Recall of particular employer campaign themes was also low. No issue was recalled by more than 40 percent of the employees in elections in which the issue was raised. There is no evidence that specific issues of the employer's campaign were related to vote. Initial union supporters who switched to the company were no more familiar with the company campaign than those who did not switch.

---

[1] McGuire, *The Nature of Attitudes and Attitude Change* in G. LINDZEY & E. ARONSON (eds.), HANDBOOK OF SOCIAL PSYCHOLOGY, vol. 3, 157 (2d ed. 1969).

Only the few employees who initially were company supporters but switched and voted for union representation may fit the Board stereotype of the employee who is convinced by the issues of the campaign. These employees were significantly more familiar with the union campaign than company supporters who did not switch. It is impossible to determine, however, whether their decision to vote union caused them to attend closely to the union's campaign or whether attending closely to the union's campaign convinced them to vote union.

Reprisals and Benefits Will Coerce Union Supporters into Voting against Union Representation

In every election studied, the employer referred to the harmful consequences of unionization and the advantages of remaining non-union. Regardless of whether or not these statements were found by the Board to constitute threats of reprisal or promises of benefit, many union supporters interpreted them in this fashion. The Board is correct in assuming that some employees will interpret ambiguous statements as threats or promises, but its judgment as to when they will do so is faulty.

The assumption that union supporters who perceive reprisals or benefits will vote for the company is not supported by the data. Employees who intended to vote union were more likely than those who intended to vote company to perceive unlawful campaigning by the employer, but they did not switch to the company as a result. Those union supporters who did switch reported no more unlawful campaigning than those who did not switch.

Finally, those elections in which the Board found unlawful campaigning to have taken place were not the ones in which the union's loss of support was greatest. Indeed, the unions did not lose significantly more of their initial supporters in bargaining order elections than in elections in which the Board found no unlawful campaigning.

AN ALTERNATIVE MODEL

Attitudes and the Campaign

Employees have attitudes toward working conditions and unions long before the union organizing drive makes those attitudes salient. Those employees who are dissatisfied with wages and working conditions have few alternatives. They may appeal directly to the employer to change their situation, or they may quit their jobs.

Alternatively, they may consider unionizing. Union representation would seem most appealing to dissatisfied employees who are generally favorable toward unions, believing that unions can compel the employer to improve wages and working conditions.

A union organizing campaign capitalizes on feelings of dissatisfaction by offering union representation as a means of improving the work situation. The union card-signing drive serves to stimulate favorable union attitudes and, for those employees without prior union experience, to disseminate information about the alternative that union representation provides. Some employees who are dissatisfied with working conditions and favorable toward unions become firm union supporters. Other employees, spurred by the immediacy of events and group allegiance, may sign authorization cards because their latent negative feelings about the work situation are aroused, even though they may not be wholly favorable toward unions. Still others, though not too dissatisfied with current working conditions, may be persuaded that union representation can only improve conditions.

Whether or not an employee signs an authorization card, the card-signing drive and the employer's response, if any, act to stimulate or reinforce existing attitudes toward working conditions and the desirability of union representation. These attitudes form strong and stable predispositions to vote, regardless of subsequent campaigning.[2]

Attitudes provide a convenient cognitive structure into which campaign information can be assimilated. Since beliefs are a basic component of attitudes, it would seem that attitudes could be easily altered when challenged by new information. Actually, attitudes are not very sensitive to new information. Instead, they serve a stabilizing function by providing a baseline for the assimilation of new information.[3] Because attitudes have apparent subjective validity, new information that is inconsistent with currently held attitudes is seldom given enough weight to cause much attitude change.[4]

Employees use several different techniques to deal with the cam-

---

[2] The fact that attitudes, which are based on experience, are more important to vote than the campaign is consistent with the findings of political voter studies. Key has stated: "As voters mark their ballots they may have in their minds impressions of the last TV political spectacular of the campaign, but more important they have in their minds recollections of their experiences of the past four years." V. O. KEY, THE RESPONSIBLE ELECTORATE 9 (1969).

[3] McGuire, *supra* note 1, at 158.

[4] Pepitone, *The Problem of Motivation in Consistency Models* in R. P. ABLESON, E. ARONSON, W. J. McGUIRE, T. M. NEWCOMB, M. J. ROSENBERG & P. H. TANNENBAUM (eds.), THEORIES OF COGNITIVE CONSISTENCY: A SOURCEBOOK (1968).

paign without succumbing to its persuasive impact. Predispositions for or against union representation and expectations of campaign content are a major factor in each. Although expectations refer to predictions about events, and attitudes to desires or hopes about events, they are usually highly correlated.[5] Thus, an employee who is for union representation is likely to expect the employer to be against and expect the employer to campaign accordingly.

Attention

The campaign does not influence many employees to vote contrary to their predispositions, because employees do not pay close attention to the campaign. Employees whose minds are already made up do not need to know the arguments of their own side to reinforce their decision and have little interest in the other party's campaign, which they know is designed to persuade them. They know and report those few campaign issues that are salient to their initial decision and little more.

The fact that employees do not pay close attention to the campaign does not mean that the voting decision is irrational. An employee who votes consistently with his pre-campaign attitudes is acting in a wholly rational manner. His choice, to be sure, may not be reasoned in the sense in which the Board contemplates—based on a careful weighing of the campaign arguments put forth by each party—but that does not make it any the less rational.

Selective Exposure

Company supporters, for the most part, are not influenced by the union campaign because they avoid it. Meetings are the communications medium most highly related to familiarity with issues in both company and union campaigns, but few company supporters attend union meetings. This may be due to the tendency for people to expose themselves to communications that are consistent with their existing attitudes and avoid situations in which their beliefs might be challenged.[6] Alternatively, company supporters, whose interest in the campaign is low or whose decision about unionization is firm, may find the effort to attend union meetings after working hours and away from the workplace greater than the anticipated return.[7]

---

[5] McGuire, *supra* note 1, at 152.

[6] J. T. KLAPPER, THE EFFECTS OF MASS COMMUNICATIONS 19 (1960).

[7] In evaluating the controversial literature on selective exposure, Sears and Freedman conclude that the expected utility of the information likely to be com-

Selective exposure is not characteristic of union supporters with respect to company meetings. It is unlikely that this is because they are unaware of the employer's opposition to union representation or that the meeting is designed to challenge their union sympathies. Nor is it likely that union supporters attend company meetings more frequently than company supporters attend union meetings because they are less confident in their initial opinions than company supporters.[8] Union supporters who do attend company meetings are no more likely to switch to the company than those who do not. Union supporters apparently attend company meetings because they are convenient and typically they receive paid time off work to attend. Moreover, they are rarely, if ever, told that they have the option of not attending.[9]

Perceptual Distortion

Union supporters are not influenced by the employer's campaign, because they interpret the employer's arguments as reasons why they need a union not reasons why they should vote against the union. Their expectation that the employer is anti-union and their confidence in their own beliefs prepare them to resist being persuaded by distorting the meaning of the employer's speech so that it conforms to their own opinions. The union's campaign may also help union supporters resist the employer's propaganda by warning them of the employer's likely arguments and providing them with responses to those arguments.[10]

In order for a communication to persuade, its content must be judged inconsistent with current attitudes and beliefs and the communicator must be believed reliable. Pre-warning and pre-exposure to counter arguments prepare the union supporters to find the employer's arguments consistent with their expectations (though not their own opinions) and the employer himself unreliable.[11] Union supporters expect the employer's campaign behavior to be motivated by his desire to keep the union out and interpret it as confirming their opinion that they need a union. Threats or acts of reprisal intended to coerce them into abandoning the union are viewed as evidence that they

municated compared to the effort necessary to obtain that information may account for many of the selective exposure findings. Sears & Freedman, *Selective Exposure to Information: A Critical Review,* 31 PUBLIC OPINION QUARTERLY 210 (1967).

[8] *Id.* at 209.

[9] This is another example of the utility phenomenon, only one for which the effort necessary to gain exposure to the information is minimal.

[10] McGuire, *supra* note 1, at 185, 264.

[11] Pepitone, *supra* note 4, at 323.

need a union for protection. Promises or grants of benefit are either discounted as unreliable in view of the employer's prior unresponsiveness to their grievances or as inadequate compared to the expected benefits of unionization.

The apparent failure of unlawful campaign tactics to cause union supporters to switch does not mean that fear of the employer's power does not exist. Many employees decide to have nothing to do with the union as soon as they hear about the union organizing campaign. For some, this decision may be due to fear of the employer's economic power and his ability to use it against union supporters. This fear may keep employees susceptible to coercion from ever supporting the union. This, too, would explain why loss of union support is unrelated to both Board findings and employee perceptions of reprisals and benefits. Those employees who do support the union may discount the likelihood of this behavior at the time they decide to do so.

Switching

Voting contrary to one's initial predispositions may be due to a change in attitudes. An employee may acquire new information during the campaign that requires reassessing previous attitudes. Alternatively, attitudes may change enough to cause a change in behavior without new information but simply by becoming more intense.

Those few company supporters who ultimately voted for the union may have been affected by the union's campaign. These employees attended union meetings more frequently and were more familiar with the union campaign than company supporters who did not switch. Switching to the union, then, is related to obtaining information about the union. To the extent that company supporters perceive their newly gained information about the union as valid, but inconsistent with their prior attitudes, they may be forced to reevaluate those attitudes, thus precipitating a vote switch.[12]

Switching to the company is more likely to be due to the intensification of currently held attitudes than to new information conveyed in the employer's campaign. There is no evidence that switching to the company is associated with specific issues raised by the employer, even those likely or intended to coerce union supporters to switch. Rather, the effect of the employer's campaign is to stimulate favor-

---

[12] The new information may cause company supporters to reinterpret their attitudes about union representation in their particular situation. This could occur without their opinions of unions in general changing. Consistency theory would predict, however, that general attitudes toward unions would eventually change to be consistent with voting for union representation. McGuire, *supra* note 1, at 266, 268.

able attitudes toward working conditions and unfavorable attitudes toward unions. For those employees who switched to the company, the balance of attitudes toward working conditions and unions tipped enough so that their prior intent to vote for union representation was no longer justified. Consistency theory predicts that an individual will adjust his attitudes and behavior to maintain a harmonious system of attitudes, beliefs, and actions.[13] If the employer's campaign does no more than remind employees that things are pretty good without the union, it may gain the support of some employees not wholly satisfied with working conditions, but also not wholly in favor of unions.

Summary

Employees have strong predispositions for or against union representation that are based on their attitudes toward working conditions and unions. Their ultimate votes are largely a function of these predispositions. The campaign does not cause most employees to switch, because their predispositions insulate them from influence attempts. Company supporters rarely attend union meetings, though when they do they are more likely to switch to the union than those who do not, perhaps because they are convinced by the union's campaign. Union supporters distort the employer's campaign, perceiving his attempts to influence their vote by economic power as evidence that they need a union, not as a reason to switch. There is no evidence that union supporters who do switch are coerced. Rather, their dissatisfaction with working conditions apparently lessens, indicating that a vote for the union is no longer reasonable.

RECOMMENDATIONS FOR CHANGE IN
NLRB ELECTION REGULATION

The assumptions on which the Board regulates campaigning are not supported by the data. Contrary to the Board's assumption, the campaign plays a limited role in the employees' decision to vote for or against union representation. Similarly inaccurate is the assumption that certain types of campaigning are likely to have a coercive impact. Voting behavior in elections involving campaign tactics believed to be coercive is not significantly different from voting behavior in campaigns that conform to the Board's standard of "laboratory conditions."

---

[13] McGuire, *supra* note 1, at 268.

Many of the Board's rules governing campaign tactics can be eliminated. Those campaign regulations that are preserved should not require the Board to make impact judgments. The data indicate that the Board has no basis on which to find that some campaign practices have a coercive impact on employees generally or on particular groups of employees. Nor can the Board determine the impact of particular campaign tactics in individual cases. Its efforts to do so on the basis of the intuition or experience of Board members have been wholly unsuccessful. Board members disagree with one another as to impact; the courts disagree with the Board; and the data show no relationship between Board findings and employee perceptions of coercive behavior.

The Board could hardly attempt to assess the impact of unlawful campaigning in individual cases by questioning employees as to how they voted and why. An employee's assertion that he voted against union representation because of unlawful campaign tactics would be highly suspect. Unless the Board knew that the employee planned to vote for the union before the conduct in question, it could not possibly conclude that that conduct caused him to vote contrary to his wishes. Questioning by government agents in advance of each election as to how employees planned to vote would, however, be both impractical and inconsistent with the statutory requirement of a secret ballot.

Regulation of Speech

Threats and Promises

Since union supporters are not coerced by threats of reprisal or promises of benefit into voting against union representation, neither threats nor promises should be a basis for setting aside an election or for finding an unfair labor practice. Section 8 (a) (1) of the Act, which is used to regulate speech, makes it unlawful for an employer to "interfere with, restrain or coerce" employees in the exercise of their right to select or reject union representation. Speech, whether of a threatening or promising nature, is unlikely to have that effect. Employees who want union representation vote for the union despite threats or promises designed to cause them to do otherwise.

Some might argue for continued Board regulation of threats and promises, but with more restrictive standards. Sanctions could be imposed only when threats or promises are clear, explicit, or egregious. The assumption underlying such regulation would be that clear threats and promises have a greater impact on vote than implied or ambiguous threats and promises.

The findings do not justify this assumption. The data show that union supporters perceive threats and promises even though the employer's statements are ambiguous. They are not affected by these attempts to persuade, probably because they disbelieve the promises and anticipate the threats. There is no reason to suppose that more explicit threats or promises would have an impact on union supporters. If an employee interprets a statement to contain an implied threat or promise, that employee has received the message. If that message does not change his vote when implicit, there is no reason to suppose it will when made openly.

Still other factors suggest that threats of selective reprisal against union supporters and promises of benefit to union opponents are unlikely to be more effective if made explicitly:

1. Nearly all employees believe that their vote is secret. Thus, as far as the employees are concerned, the employer is unable to administer selective reprisals or benefits based upon vote. Employees who support the union, but fear reprisals or desire benefits, might be expected to conceal their union sympathies, but not to vote against union representation.

2. The great majority of those employees who believed the employer knew of their union sympathies either told the employer or openly supported the union. This lack of secrecy indicates that these employees have determined not to let the employer's economic power affect their open union support. It would be surprising, then, if their behavior in the secrecy of the voting booth could be controlled by threats or promises.

3. Union support generally indicates a belief that a union can make employers take action favorable to employees. To the extent that employees who have such attitudes perceive the employer as threatening reprisals or promising benefits, they could be expected to count on the union's victory to protect them.

Misrepresentations

Current Board doctrine provides for setting aside any election in which the winning party makes an assertion of fact or law that is "a substantial departure from the truth . . . which . . . may reasonably be expected to have a significant impact on the election."[14] Implicit in the Board's approach is the assumption that it is capable of assessing the impact of campaign statements on vote, an assumption shown by the data to be wholly without foundation.

---

[14] Hollywood Ceramics Co., 140 NLRB 221, 224 (1962).

Board decisions setting aside elections on misrepresentation grounds are also based on the assumption that employees attend closely to the campaign and that their vote is likely to be influenced by campaign assertions. The data, however, indicate that employees are not generally attentive to the campaign. Even union claims as to wages obtained elsewhere are remembered with reasonable accuracy by fewer than 25 percent of the employees. More important, there is little evidence that the precise details of campaign propaganda play a substantial role in influencing vote. Approximately 80 percent of the sample voted as they had planned prior to the campaign. Even those who switched displayed little familiarity with the campaign of the party for which they ultimately voted. There is scant justification for the Board to scrutinize campaign propaganda more closely than do employees in order to protect employee choice.

Interrogation

Board decisions that prohibit employers from interrogating employees about their union sympathies or their reasons for wanting union representation rest on the assumption that such questioning will be taken as containing implied threats of reprisal or promises of benefit. The Board also assumes that employees are likely to inform each other about the questioning so that it will affect even those employees not immediately involved.

Although interrogation took place in over half the elections studied, it was rarely reported by employees as an employer campaign tactic. This suggests that interrogation does not have a great impact on either the employees questioned or other employees. Accordingly, it is our recommendation that questions about employees' union membership or activity or their reasons for wanting a union should not constitute an unfair labor practice or grounds for setting aside an election.

An employee who wishes his sentiments about unionization to remain secret ought not, however, be forced to disclose those sentiments. Accordingly, we recommend no change in existing law by which an employee may not be punished for his refusal to answer questions about his union sentiments.

Other Board Doctrines Resting on the Assumption of Fragility of Choice

As part of its effort to achieve "laboratory conditions," the Board has developed a variety of rules that can only be explained on the assumption that employee choice is tenuous and easily manipulated by the campaign. Employer campaigning in the locus of management authority or during home visits is deemed to be coercive without regard to content.[15] Speeches made by either side to massed assemblies of employees during the twenty-four hours preceding the election are thought to have "an unwholesome and unsettling effect."[16] Elections have been set aside because of employer speeches stressing the futility of voting for the union[17] or the inevitability of strikes.[18] Inflammatory appeals to racial prejudice have also been a basis for setting aside elections.[19] All these rules are inconsistent with the finding that employee predispositions for or against union representation are generally firm and not susceptible to campaign manipulation. Accordingly, we recommend that they no longer be enforced.

Summary

The Board should no longer set aside elections or find unfair labor practices based on written or oral campaign communications by employers or unions. Speech in union representation elections should be as free of governmental restraint as speech in political elections. The government has no role in determining what is "good" and "bad" campaign propaganda in political elections. The parties in such elections are allowed to use whatever campaign appeals they wish, short of malicious defamation.[20] Each side is also free to point out the weaknesses in the other's arguments. The voters, not the government, then decide which assertions are valid and relevant, which invalid or irrelevant. The data do not suggest that the employee voter is less capable of performing that function than the political voter. Both the employee voter and the political voter appear less interested in the campaign than traditional theory would have it, but that, if anything, suggests less need for government regulation of speech, not more.[21]

---

[15] Peoria Plastics Co., 117 NLRB 545 (1957); General Shoe Corp., 77 NLRB 124 (1948).

[16] Peerless Plywood Co., 107 NLRB 427, 429 (1953).

[17] Dal-Tex Optical Co., 137 NLRB 1782 (1962).

[18] Unitec Industries, 180 NLRB 51 (1969).

[19] Sewell Mfg. Co., 138 NLRB 66 (1962).

[20] The Supreme Court has held that a person who knowingly defames another in the course of a political election campaign is liable for damages ((N.Y. Times v. Sullivan, 376 U.S. 254 (1964)); the same is true in a union representation election (Linn v. Plant Guards, 383 U.S. 53 (1966)).

[21] A more modest reform is also possible. The Board might decline to entertain objections based on speech in those cases in which the margin of victory is greater than 20 percent of the electorate. The data indicate that no matter what type of speech employees are exposed to, the votes of approximately 80 percent are pre-

Regulation of Conduct

Grants of Benefit

It is unlawful for an employer to grant benefits to employees during the pre-election campaign for the purpose of discouraging them from voting for union representation.[22] Such grants, though commonplace in the elections studied, had no demonstrable effect on vote. Employees who reported promises and grants of benefit were actually more likely to vote for union representation than were other employees. The data also do not support the Supreme Court's theory that employees will infer a threat of reprisals from a grant of benefits. A grant of benefits, then, ought not be grounds on which to set aside an election. For the same reason, a grant of benefits should not be held to violate Section 8 (a)(1) of the Act, which prohibits only that conduct that serves to interfere with, restrain, or coerce employees in the exercise of their free choice.

Acts of Reprisal

Discharges or layoffs of union supporters during the card-signing campaign took place in eight elections. In one election, charges were filed alleging that eighty-two employees had been laid off because of their union activities. In another election, similar allegations were made as to the discharge of fourteen employees. While the discharges in only one election were found to have been based on union sentiments, hence unlawful, union supporters tended to perceive all such discharges as having been based on union sentiments. Nonetheless, there was no evidence that such perceptions led to a loss of union support. Card-signers did not vote against the union in significantly greater numbers in discharge elections than in other elections. Em-

---

dictable on the basis of pre-campaign attitudes. Indeed, the data suggest that the actual number of employees influenced by the campaign is far less. Since no more than 20 percent, and probably far fewer, are subject to campaign influence, the Board would be on exceedingly safe ground if it were to refuse to entertain objections based on speech unless the margin of victory was less than 20 percent. By this rather simple change in its practice, the Board could eliminate a portion of its caseload of objections with little risk that employee rights of free choice were being injured.

One cannot be certain whether this more modest reform would have any meaningful impact. Data are not available as to the proportion of Board elections in which the margin of victory is greater than 20 percent. When the margin is greater than 20 percent, the loser may tend not to file objections, believing that after a loss of such magnitude, it would be unlikely to win a rerun election. Yet it is only in this situation that the more modest reform would preclude the filing of objections.

[22] NLRB v. Exchange Parts Co., 375 U.S. 405 (1964).

ployees who reported that the employer discriminatorily discharged union supporters were even more likely to have voted for the union than those who did not report such action.

Since union supporters tend to view discharges during the organizational campaign as motivated by an intent to discriminate against them, regardless of whether or not the Board finds such a motive, the remedy, other than that provided the individual, ought not turn on the employer's motive. If employees are not coerced into voting against the union by discharges they view as unlawful, no reason exists to set aside the election because the Board finds the discharge to be unlawful. The same reasoning necessarily applies to less drastic types of employer conduct.

We recommend no change in existing law with regard to the rights of the employee who is discharged or against whom other action is taken. Those rights will continue to rest on the employer's motive. If the employer is not motivated by anti-union sentiments, there is no reason, as far as the policies of the Act are concerned, to limit his freedom to discipline. If he is improperly motivated, the employee is entitled to an appropriate remedy. An employee discriminatorily discharged, for example, is entitled to reinstatement with back pay. An employee discriminatorily deprived of benefits given to others should receive those benefits.[23]

Appearance of Fairness in the Election Process

Some Board rules are aimed primarily at preserving the appearance of fairness in Board elections rather than employee free choice, while others appear designed to serve both of these goals. The Board's rule prohibiting its agents from fraternizing with representatives of the parties is one designed primarily to preserve the appearance of fairness, as is the rule against Board agents leaving a ballot box unattended.[24] Falling into the group of rules designed to preserve both the appearance of fairness and employee free choice is that prohibiting the alteration of official Board documents to suggest that the

---

[23] Threats of reprisal and promises of benefit will continue to be used as evidence of the employer's motive. This is not inconsistent with our recommendation that threats and promises should be free of regulation. That recommendation is not based on the view that these tactics serve a desirable function in the campaign, but that they do not affect vote generally and the Board is incapable of determining if they do affect vote in particular cases.

[24] See Athbro Precision Engineering Corp., 166 NLRB 966 (1967); Austill Waxed Paper Co., 169 NLRB 1109 (1968).

Board endorses one party rather than the other. Also in this category is the Board's rule forbidding electioneering near the polls.[25]

To the extent the foregoing rules rest on the assumption that employee free choice is fragile, they are as unsupported by the data as other Board rules resting on the same assumption, hence ought not provide a basis for setting aside the results of an election in which employees have expressed their choice. To the extent these rules rest on the Board's desire to preserve the appearance of fairness in its processes, they may be justifiable, but there would appear a more satisfactory remedy for their violation than setting aside the results of an election that the Board does not even contend was influenced by the conduct involved.[26] The Board can enforce rules relating to the conduct of its own agents by appropriate internal disciplinary procedures. Rules regulating the conduct of the parties, such as those prohibiting the alteration of Board documents or tampering with a Board ballot box, can be enforced by the passage of laws specifically prohibiting such conduct.

Bargaining Orders and Other Remedies

The Preference for Elections

Union authorization cards are a highly accurate reflection of union sentiments when signed and a reasonably good predictor of vote. Nonetheless, the Board's preference for elections is justified. The election choice differs from the card-sign choice for approximately 25 percent of the employees and may well represent a more considered, if not more informed, judgment. The value that each party should have a roughly equal opportunity to present its case to the voters also supports the preference for elections. The Board should continue to permit an employer who does not engage in unlawful campaigning to insist on an election, even if the union possesses authorization cards signed by a majority of his employees.[27]

The Bargaining Order as a Remedy for Unlawful Campaigning

The theory underlying the bargaining order as a remedy for unlawful campaigning is that the impact of some employer campaign tactics is so great that a fair election cannot be held. Accordingly, the union

---

[25] See Allied Electric Products, Inc., 109 NLRB 1270 (1954); Rebmar, Inc., 173 NLRB 1434 (1968); Milchem Inc., 170 NLRB 362 (1970).

[26] See, e.g., Athbro Precision Engineering Corp., *supra* note 24.

[27] Linden Lumber Div., Summer & Co., 190 NLRB 718 (1971), aff'd, 419 U.S. 301 (1974).

is awarded bargaining rights without an election or, in some cases, after an election in which it has been defeated.

The data provide no evidence that unlawful campaigning regarded by the Board as sufficiently serious to warrant a bargaining order affects vote. Potential union voters did not vote against union representation significantly more often in bargaining order elections than in clean elections or those characterized by lesser unlawful campaigning. Reports of unlawful campaigning were not significantly more frequent in bargaining order elections than others. Elimination of the bargaining order as a remedy for unlawful campaigning should thus be considered.

The principle that the expressed will of the voters should be ignored and the fruits of victory awarded to the losing party is, as far as we know, unique to Board-conducted union representation elections.[28] Other systems of election regulation provide for voiding the results of one election and holding another if the winner has engaged in misconduct, but none reverses the election outcome on the basis of assumptions as to the likely impact of the winner's conduct, which is the practical effect of a bargaining order.[29]

It may be thought advisable to retain the bargaining order, while using it sparingly, in order to deter those employers who might, absent the risk of such an order, engage in wholesale violations of the Act. Some commentators argue that if a bargaining order is occasionally imposed against the will of a majority of employees, the harm done to those employees is minimal compared to the general deterrent value of bargaining orders. The union's bargaining authority can be challenged by holding another election a year later. The union thus should be motivated to negotiate a contract that will satisfy a majority of the employees. If it fails to do so, the employees may vote it out.[30]

If the bargaining order is to be retained as a remedy on the

---

[28] Some state labor boards, modeled after the federal Board, have also adopted the bargaining order. See WERC v. City of Evansville, 89 LRRM 2989 (Wisc. Sup. Ct. 1975); MERC v. Mugerian, 88 LRRM 3513 (Mich. Ct. App. 1975).

[29] Election results are sometimes reversed and a new winner installed when it is determined that but for illegally counted or rejected votes, the supposed loser would have won. See *Developments in the Law: Voting*, 88 Harv. L. Rev. 1111, 1317 (1975). However, where legal voters have been subject to improper influence, the courts have been unwilling to install a new winner. *Id.* at 1321–1322.

[30] See Lesnick, *Establishing Bargaining Rights Without an Election*, 65 Mich. L. Rev. 857, 862 (1967); Bok, *The Regulation of Campaign Tactics in Representation Elections Under the National Labor Relations Act*, 78 Harv. L. Rev. 38, 135 (1964).

grounds of its deterrent value, the Board should not be required, as it presently is, to find that the employer has engaged in campaign practices that make a fair election unlikely or impossible. The data indicate that the Board is incapable of making such judgments. Hence, the bargaining order, if it is to be retained, should be triggered automatically by those practices it is intended to deter. For example, if the bargaining order is intended to deter discriminatory discharges, any such discharge should result in the issuance of a bargaining order, assuming the union involved has a card majority. Additionally, the union might be required to win a specified proportion of the vote, say 25 percent, on the theory that a union with less support could not engage in meaningful bargaining.[31] The crucial point is that bargaining orders, if used, should be based upon predetermined criteria, not upon case-by-case judgments concerning impact.

Because a bargaining order is likely to involve the sacrifice of majority choice, the Board should consider other remedies that might serve to deter undesirable campaign practices. Focussing again on the discriminatory discharge, one alternative would be to impose on the employer the burden of proving the absence of a discriminatory motive for any discharge during the organizational campaign.[32] The employer might be discouraged by this burden from exercising his power to discharge, but he would retain the power to do so if, for example, a union supporter engaged in an outright refusal to work. Furthermore, the duration of the limitation would be brief. It would begin with the initiation of the card-signing drive and end with the election, normally a period of approximately ninety days.[33] The Board could be required to institute immediate injunctive proceedings to obtain reinstatement of any employee discharged during this period, with the burden of proof on the employer in these proceedings as well. The election could be delayed, at the union's option, until fifteen to thirty days after the court had ruled on the Board's request for reinstatement. Finally, in the event an employer was found to have discharged an employee because of his union sentiments or activity,

---

[31] The 25 percent would have to include discriminatorily discharged employees to prevent the employer from avoiding the bargaining order by discharging all union supporters.

[32] Present law places on the Board's General Counsel the burden of proving the employer's discriminatory motive by a preponderance of the evidence. See Stratford Lithographics, 168 NLRB 469 (1967).

[33] One might require the union, as a condition to obtaining this protection, to notify the Board or the employer of the date it will begin its card-signing drive and limit it to thirty days of card-signing prior to filing a petition for an election.

he might be required to pay that employee three times his lost earnings, in addition to offering reinstatement.[34]

Other remedies could undoubtedly be devised to deal with those few employers who flagrantly and persistently violate the commands of the Act.[35] Such an employer might, for example, be declared ineligible for government contracts. The point is that if one wishes to deter violations of the Act, there are remedies that may do so without the risk of impinging on majority choice or requiring impact judgments that the Board is institutionally incapable of making.

Equal Opportunities for Organizational Communication

In *NLRB* v. *United Steelworkers of America (Nutone, Inc.)*,[36] the Supreme Court held that an employer did not necessarily violate the Act by campaigning against the union on working time or premises while preventing similar campaigning on behalf of the union. The Court stated, however, that if the combined effect of the employer's campaigning and his refusal to allow similar union campaigning was to create an imbalance in opportunities for organizational communication, the Board could find the employer's conduct unlawful. The data show that such an imbalance normally exists. The employer who uses working time or premises to campaign against the union and denies those facilities to the union effectively communicates with a substantially greater proportion of the employees than does the union.

The employer's advantage is primarily due to the powerful correlation between campaign familiarity and attendance at meetings. Employees who attended meetings conducted by either party were significantly more familiar with that party's campaign than employees who did not attend meetings. The employer tends to be far more successful in attracting employees to meetings on working time and premises than does the union in attracting them to meetings outside working hours and away from company premises. Eighty-three percent of the sample attended company meetings, while only 36 percent attended union meetings. Furthermore, those employees who attended union meetings tended to be union supporters. The company, then, has a great advantage in communicating with the undecided and those not

---

[34] Treble or punitive damage remedies are common for violation of federal statutes. See e.g., 15 U.S.C. Sec. 7 (anti-trust violations), 35 U. S. C. Sec. 284 (1970) (patent violations), 17 U.S.C. Sec. 1 (1970) (copyright violations), 42 U.S.C. Sec. 3612 (1970) (civil rights violations). The use of such a remedy under the NLRA would require amendment of the Act.

[35] See, e.g., J. P. Stevens & Co. v. NLRB, 406 F.2d 1017 (4th Cir. 1968).

[36] 357 U.S. 357 (1958).

already committed to it. This advantage is particularly important since attendance at union meetings is significantly related to switching to the union. If the union could communicate with more of those not already committed to it, it might do significantly better in the election.

In order for each party to have an equal opportunity to present its views, an employer who holds campaign meetings on working time and premises should be required to allow the union (or unions) to hold such meetings on working time and premises. A similar requirement should be imposed on an employer who permits supervisors to campaign against the union on company premises, whether in individual or small group meetings with employees. Campaign familiarity is also significantly related to personal contacts. If employers could campaign individually or in small groups on company premises, without the necessity of offering the union an opportunity to campaign under similar circumstances, they would be tempted to switch to such campaigning. In view of the employer's ability to contact all employees on company premises, if the union were restricted to off-premises contacts, it would be at the same disadvantage as under existing law. Accordingly, if supervisors are allowed to engage in individual campaigning on company premises, union organizers must also be allowed to do so.

This recommendation does not rest solely on the evidence that campaign familiarity is related to switching to the union. It is fundamental to the democratic process that each party should have a roughly equal opportunity to communicate with the electorate, regardless of the effectiveness of that communication. This principle supports the employers' preference for determining employee choice by secret ballot election rather than authorization cards; it also supports the union's request for an opportunity to respond, on company time and premises, to employer campaigning on company time and premises.

An opportunity for unions to respond on company premises to antiunion campaigning on those premises is particularly important if the Board, as we recommend, is to cease regulating speech. Campaign regulation in political elections is based on the assumption that each party will be able to point out to the voters those aspects of the other party's campaign it believes to be untruthful or unfair. Unions will have that ability only if they have the opportunity to campaign on equal terms with the employer on company premises.

Neither Section 8(c) of the Act nor the First Amendment to the Constitution would be violated by requiring an employer who campaigns on company time or premises to allow the union similar campaign opportunities. The First Amendment and Section 8(c) protect the employer's freedom to express his opinions regarding unionization. They do not, however, permit him to use his ownership of working premises to deny the union the same right, when utilization of those premises is critical to the union's ability to communicate. The Supreme Court's decision in *Nutone*, sustaining the Board's power to permit union campaigning on company premises when necessary to prevent an imbalance in opportunities for organizational communication, makes this point clear.[37] So, too, the Court has indicated in other circumstances that a property owner who uses his property for the communication of ideas may be required to allow others to do the same.[38]

Enforcement of these equal access requirements presents practical problems, but they are not insuperable. The union should be free, if it wishes, to pay employees for the time spent attending a union meeting on company premises during working hours. Overhead costs incurred during the period of the union speech should be borne by the employer. Overhead costs are unlikely to be great in comparison to wage costs, and agreement on the amount of these costs, if the union were required to pay, is unlikely. Such a requirement might thus lead to petty and harassing litigation.

If supervisors engage in individual solicitation, union organizers should be allowed access to employees in non-working areas from the date of the first supervisory solicitation to the election. If, for example, supervisory solicitation begins two weeks prior to the election, the union should have two weeks for purposes of solicitation. Allowing the union only an equal number of hours in which to solicit would require it to keep track of the amount of time spent in supervisory solicitation, an impossible task. If there are no non-work areas on the premises, the union must be allowed access to employees wherever they spend their non-work time. Other enforcement problems can be dealt with in a manner that comports with the basic principle that an employer who uses company premises for anti-union campaigning must allow the union equal opportunities for organizational communication.

A violation of the equal opportunity requirement should constitute both grounds on which to set aside an election and an unfair labor practice. Enforcement should be through injunctive relief pursuant to Section 10(j) of the Act. There will be no necessity for Board findings as to impact, so difficult issues of fact or law are unlikely. Prompt injunctive relief would minimize any delay in holding the elec-

---

[37] Compare the concurring and dissenting opinion of Chief Justice Warren, 357 U.S. at 365.

[38] Red Lion Broadcasting Co. v. F.C.C., 395 U.S. 367 (1969).

tion while the union takes advantage of its opportunities for communication.[39]

Summary and Conclusion

We recommend that the Board cease regulating speech and, for election purposes, nearly all conduct. Employees harmed by discriminatory grants of benefit or acts of reprisal should continue to receive the individual remedies provided by existing law. Such conduct should not, however, provide a basis for setting aside the results of an election. The only basis on which objections to the election should be entertained and second elections held should be for conduct that interferes with union access to employees. An employer who campaigns on company premises should be required to allow union campaigning on company premises. Bargaining orders, if retained, should be triggered automatically by the conduct they are intended to deter.

There are, to be sure, arguments against substantial deregulation of the campaign. There may be some cases in which the speech and conduct we propose to leave unregulated will frighten some employees into voting against union representation who would not be frightened by presently lawful campaigning. These coerced votes, on occasion, may provide the margin by which a union loses an election it would otherwise have won. We do not believe that this risk justifies maintaining the existing system of Board regulation.

There are not likely to be many cases in which the number of votes affected by employer campaigning will be sufficient to deprive the union of a victory it would have gained under existing law. The data show clearly that union supporters perceive both reprisals and benefits whether the employer campaigns lawfully or unlawfully. They do not, however, vote against the union as a result of those perceptions. Some employers might, absent Board regulation, be more explicit in their threats and promises, but there is no reason to suppose that more explicit threats or promises will have a greater impact than those currently used. The failure of threats and promises to affect vote does not appear due to the union supporters' failure to perceive them, but to their ability to absorb those threats and promises into their cognitive

---

[39] The Board's requirement that the employer supply the union with a list of employee names and addresses (Excelsior Underwear, Inc. 156 NLRB 1236 (1966)) is supported by considerations similar to those justifying an equal access requirement. It is also like the equal access requirement in that its enforcement does not require the Board to make findings on a case-by-case basis as to the effect of the employer's conduct on free choice. Accordingly, we recommend retention of the *Excelsior* rule.

systems without changing their behavior. That ability should not be affected if the employer's threats and promises become more explicit.

Moreover, the absence of direct legal restraints on threats and promises is not likely to result in substantial changes in current modes of campaigning. Nearly all employer counsel whom we interviewed stated that they would not recommend using explicit threats of reprisal even if they were legal. Some believed such campaigning could backfire by persuading employees that they need a union for protection. Others stated that the potential gains of explicit threats of reprisal were outweighed by the impediment they might present to establishing a satisfactory bargaining relationship with the union if it should win the election.[40] Those few lawyers who stated that, absent legal restraint, they would recommend explicit threats of reprisal were the same ones who said they currently used such tactics if they thought the risk of a union victory was sufficiently great.

The possibility of an increase in explicit promises and grants of benefit following deregulation seems greater. Some employer counsel stated that they would advise promising benefits if the employer were willing to grant those benefits. We do not regard this as a cause for concern. While the Board characterizes a grant or promise of benefits by an employer as a form of "pressure and compulsion,"[41] we reject this characterization. An employee is free to choose union representation despite promises or grants of benefit by the employer. He may not lawfully be penalized for doing so. If, under these circumstances, an employee wishes to rely on the employer's promises or grants of benefit as a reason for rejecting union representation, his decision would appear wholly free. A contrary conclusion could rest only on an assumption that promises or grants of benefit will be understood by employees to contain an implied threat of reprisal (the "fist inside the velvet glove" theory) or that employees are incapable of maintaining a previously formulated intention to vote union, however strongly held, in the face of a grant or promise of benefits designed to persuade them to vote company. Neither of these assumptions is supported by the data.

Continued regulation of discriminatory acts of reprisal and grants of benefit provides another deterrent to substantial changes in current modes of campaigning. Threats or promises would continue to be used as evidence of improper motive in the event that an employer's conduct was challenged as discriminatory. Unless the employer intends

---

[40] Admittedly, these statements can be dismissed as self-serving. They should, however, be evaluated in light of the fact that most employer counsel were quite candid in their interviews with us.

[41] Hudson Hosiery, 72 NLRB 1434, 1436 (1947).

to act in an exemplary fashion throughout the campaign, the possibility that explicit threats or promises might be used as evidence of discrimination might discourage him from using them, particularly if the remedy for discriminatory conduct were stringent.

Still another weakness in the current system of regulation is its failure to provide adequate sanctions against those few employers who engage in such flagrant violations of the Act as the mass discharge of suspected union supporters. To be sure, the results of this study do not indicate that discriminatory discharges cause union supporters to abandon the union. It may well be, however, that such conduct, if engaged in at the very outset of the union organizing campaign, or in prior campaigns, will discourage many employees from openly supporting unionization or even giving it serious consideration. It is with such conduct that the Board should be concerned, not with employer speech. Indeed, a central weakness of the existing regulatory scheme is that it provides employees with unnecessary protection against speech, while failing to provide sufficient protection against retaliatory behavior.

Prompt and effective remedies for any retaliatory actions engaged in by an employer may serve ultimately to establish a climate in which fear of reprisal is less of a factor in some employees' initial response to a union organizing drive. The Board does not now provide such remedies. The changes we propose, while depriving the Board of the power to regulate speech, to set aside elections, and to issue bargaining orders based on impact determinations, would in no way lessen the Board's power to provide prompt and effective relief. To the contrary, the additional remedies we propose—injunctive relief to obtain reinstatement of discharged employees, treble damages for lost earnings and loss of government contracts—should strengthen the Board's power to protect the organizational rights of those employees who have been denied their rights under the current regulatory system.

Any argument in favor of continued Board regulation of electioneering must take into account the costs of such regulation. Regulation of election campaigns has contributed substantially to the Board's increasing caseload. In fiscal 1975, objections were filed in 2,230 of 8,916 elections.[42] While 206 of these objections were withdrawn and only 220 of the remaining 1,024 objections were sustained,[43] each objection that is not withdrawn requires an administrative investigation that may be followed, if the objection has prima facie merit, by a trial-type

---

[42] 40 NLRB ANN. REP. 227, 228 (1975).
[43] *Id.* at 229.

hearing before an administrative law judge, an appeal to the Board, and a further appeal to the courts.

Commentators have suggested that the Board's caseload has lowered the quality of its decisions and impaired its ability to enforce the act.[44] The parties pay the costs of campaign regulation through the financial burden of litigating election challenges and the delay resulting from such challenges. Both are substantial. If the union wins the election, the employer's duty to bargain is, as a practical matter, suspended while he pursues his objections through the Board and the courts, a process that can consume as much as two years.[45]

The problems associated with Board regulation of the campaign cannot be solved merely by directing the Board to exercise restraint in deciding which speech or conduct warrants setting aside an election. The data provide no evidence that particular types of speech or conduct have a generally coercive impact, and the Board possesses no tools for making impact judgments on a case-by-case basis, however stringent the standards it applies. Any regulatory system that operates on the assumption that the Board is capable of making impact judgments is inviting a continuation of the existing system under which such judgments are either a product of untested behavioral assumptions or rationalizations for decisions reached on other grounds. We intend no attack on the competence or good faith of Board members, past or present. They have been given an impossible task and, as might be expected, have adapted themselves to the system. We recommend a system that will, at very least, relieve Board members of a task beyond the institutional competence of the Board.

If these recommendations are followed, the Board's regulatory task

[44] "As delays have diminished the effectiveness of the Board's decrees, the temptation to ignore the law has increased, thus threatening to provoke further violations which will add still more to the workload of the Board. There are other, less tangible ways by which a heavy workload may affect the quality of the law. Complaints may be dismissed too readily by the regional director; investigations may be handicapped through lack of time and money; opinions may be written too hastily; records reviewed too briefly." Bok, *supra* note 30, at 60–66. See also R. WILLIAMS, P. JANUS & K. HUHN, NLRB REGULATION OF ELECTION CONDUCT 438 (1974); Samoff, *NLRB Elections: Uncertainty and Certainty,* 117 U. PA. L. REV. 228, 238–239 (1968). One commentator who supports Board regulation of election campaigns conceded that such regulation consumes "untold time and energy." Pollitt, *NLRB Re-Run Elections: A Study,* 41 N.C.L. REV. 209, 222 (1963).

[45] Sections 10(e) and (j) of the NLRA vest the Board with the power to petition for a temporary injunction requiring the employer to bargain pending judicial review, but in 1971–75, the most recent five-year period for which statistics are available, only three such petitions were filed and one granted. Letter to Stephen B. Goldberg from John C. Truesdale, Executive Secretary, NLRB, April 14, 1976.

will be lessened, yet more effective. The Board will no longer be required to rely on untested assumptions about the impact of speech or conduct. Speech will be wholly free, as in any political election. Discriminatory acts of reprisal and grants of benefit will be redressed without regard to their presumed effect. Bargaining orders, if retained, will be automatic. Unions will be assured of equal access to employees and will be able to respond in their own fashion to employer campaigning.

The majority of the changes we recommend do not require legislative action. The Board has broad discretion to determine which speech or conduct warrants setting aside an election, finding a violation of Section 8(a)(1), or issuing a bargaining order. For the Board to limit the grounds on which it will take those actions is within that discretion.

Appendix A

DEMOGRAPHIC AND JOB EXPERIENCE CHARACTERISTICS OF THE SAMPLE

Age

No Answer	24 Years or Less	25–34 Years	35–44 Years	45–54 Years	55–64 Years	Over 64	Total
2	305	272	257	236	147	20	1239
.2%	24.6%	22.0%	20.7%	19.0%	11.9%	1.6%	

Sex

No Answer	Male	Female	Total
3	738	498	1239
.2%	59.6%	40.2%	

Race

No Answer	White	Minority (Black and Spanish-speaking)	Total
64	1027	148	1239
5.2%	82.9%	11.9%	

Education Level

No Answer	1–4 Years	5–8 Years	Some High School	High School Grad.	Some College	College Grad.	Total
5	23	234	355	456	151	15	1239
.4%	1.8%	18.9%	28.6%	36.8%	12.2%	1.2%	

Political Preference

No Answer	Democratic	Republican	Other	Independent	None	Total
30	546	246	8	290	119	1239
2.4%	44.1%	19.9%	6%	23.4%	9.6%	

Marital Status

Not Married	Married	Total
338	901	1239
27.3%	72.7%	

Tenure

Less than 1 Year	Less than 3 Years	Less than 10 Years	10 or More Years	Total
343	244	412	240	1239
27.7%	19.7%	33.2%	19.4%	

Hours (per week)

No Answer	Less than 25 Hours	25–34 Hours	35–44 Hours	More than 44 Hours	Total
3	30	55	695	456	1239
.2%	2.4%	4.4%	56.1%	36.8%	

Wage Rate (per hour)

No Answer	Under $2	$2.00–2.25	$2.26–2.50	$2.51–2.75	$2.76–3.00
35	145	65	77	142	131
2.8%	11.7%	5.2%	6.2%	11.5%	10.6%

$3.01–3.25	$3.26–3.50	$3.51–3.75	$3.76–4.00	$4.01–4.25
117	150	102	67	44
9.4%	12.1%	8.2%	5.4%	3.6%

$4.26–4.50	$4.51–4.75	$4.76–5.00	Over $5	Total
59	35	19	51	1239
4.8%	2.8%	1.5%	4.1%	

Previous Union Member

Not Previously *Employed*	*No*	*Yes*	*Total*
233	474	532	1239
18.8%	38.2%	42.9%	

Spouse, Father, or Mother Previous Union Member

No	*Yes*	*Total*
309	930	1239
24.9%	75.1%	

Voted in Previous NLRB Election

No	*Voted against* *Union*	*Do Not Recall*	*Voted for* *Union*	*Total*
862	173	30	174	1239
70%	14.0%	2.4%	14.0%	

Appendix B
EMPLOYEE INTERVIEW SCHEDULE

UNIVERSITY OF ILLINOIS SURVEY RESEARCH LABORATORY

Sample No.   Study of NLRB Elections

Wave I

1. How long have you been employed by this Company?
   - Under 1 year...................................1
   - At least 1 year but less than 3 years................2
   - At least 3 years but less than 10 years..............3
   - 10 years or longer..............................4

2. On the average, over the last month or two, how many hours per week did you work? This includes overtime.
   - Under 25.......................................1
   - 25–34...2
   - 35–44...3
   - Over 44.......................................4

3. If for some reason you were to decide to quit your job with this Company, do you think it would be easy or difficult for you to find as good a job elsewhere?
   - Easy..3
   - Difficult.......................................1
   - (Don't know, uncertain, neither easy nor difficult).....2

4a. Have you ever been employed by another Company?
   - Yes...3
   - No (Skip to Q.5)...............................1

b. Have you ever been a Union member while employed by another Company?
   - Yes...3
   - No (Skip to Q.5)...............................1

c. For how many years were you a Union member?
   - Under 1 year...................................1
   - At least 1 year but less than 3 years................2
   - At least 3 years but less than 10 years..............3
   - 10 years or longer..............................4

169

5. I would now like to read to you a number of statements made by workers in other plants with regard to unions. We would like to know whether, in general, you agree or disagree with each of these statements.

	Agree	Disagree	(Don't know, uncertain)
a. Unions are becoming too strong. Do you agree or disagree? 1		3	2
b. Unions make sure that employees are treated fairly by supervisors. Do you agree or disagree? 3		1	2
c. Unions help working men and women to get better wages and hours. Do you agree or disagree? 3		1	2
d. Unions interfere with good relations between companies and workers. Do you agree or disagree? 1		3	2
e. Union dues are too high. Do you agree or disagree? 1		3	2
f. When a strike is called, it is generally for a good reason. Do you agree or disagree? 3		1	2
g. Unions are a major cause of high prices. Do you agree or disagree? 1		3	2

6. Taking everything into consideration, would you describe your overall attitude toward unions as favorable or not favorable?
Favorable 3
Not favorable 1
(Uncertain, don't know) 2

7. Now I would like to ask you a few questions about your job.

a. Are you satisfied or not satisfied with your wages?
Satisfied 3
Not satisfied 1
(Uncertain, don't know) 2

b. Do the supervisors in this Company play favorites or do they treat all employees alike?
Play favorites 1
Treat alike 3
(Uncertain, don't know) 2

c. Are you satisfied or not satisfied with the type of work you are doing?
Satisfied 3

Not satisfied 1
(Uncertain, don't know) 2

d. Do your supervisors show appreciation when you do a good job or do they just take it for granted?
Show appreciation 3
Take it for granted 1
(Uncertain, don't know) 2

e. Are you satisfied or not satisfied with your fringe benefits, such as pensions, vacations, holiday pay, insurance, and sick leave?
Satisfied 3
Not satisfied 1
(Uncertain, don't know) 2

f. Do you think there is a good chance or not much chance for you to get a promotion in this Company?
Good chance 3
Not much chance 1
(Uncertain, don't know) 2

g. Are you satisfied or not satisfied with job security at this Company? (If R asks: "Job security" = "risk of losing job or being laid off.")
Satisfied 3
Not satisfied 1
(Uncertain, don't know) 2

8. Taking everything into consideration, would you say you were satisfied or not satisfied with this Company as a place to work?
Satisfied 3
Not satisfied 1
(Uncertain, don't know) 2

9. On the whole, would you describe the people you work with as friendly or not friendly?
Friendly 3
Not friendly 1
(Uncertain, don't know) 2

10. How much have you talked to people at work about the Union or the election—very much, some, or not at all?
Very much 3
Some 2
Not at all 1

11. Has the Union been able to get good people at this Company to support it? (If R asks: "Good people" = "people you respect.")
Yes 3
No 1
(Don't know, uncertain, some good people) 2

12. How many, if any, of the people you know at work do you think will vote for the Union—most, some, or none of them?

    Most 3
    Some 2
    None 1
    (Don't know, uncertain) 8

14a. Not too long ago, the Union was asking people to sign Union cards. Did you sign one of those cards? (If R asks: "Union cards" = "Union authorization cards.")

    Yes 3
    No (Skip to Q. 14e) 1
    (Don't remember—Skip to Q. 15a) 8
    (Refused to answer—Ask b and c, then skip to Q. 15a) .9

   b. If you can remember, was it an employee of this Company or someone else who asked you to sign the card?

    Employee 1
    Someone else 2
    (Both) 3
    (Nobody asked, I asked for card, I volunteered
      to sign) 4
    (Don't know, uncertain, can't remember) 8

   c. What was said to you when you were asked to sign the card? (If R responds "Nothing," ask "Had anything been said to you previously about why people should sign cards?")

   _____

   d. At the time you signed the card, did you, or did you not, want the Union to get in at the Company?

    Did want Union in 3
    Did not want Union in 1
    (Uncertain, don't know) 2

                   (SKIP TO Q.15a)

   e. Were you asked to sign a card?

    Yes 3
    No, don't remember (Skip to Q.15a) 1

   f. If you can remember, why didn't you sign the card?

   _____

15a. Would you say that the Union has acted fairly or not fairly in its efforts to organize the employees of this Company?

    Fairly (Skip to Q.16a) 3
    Not fairly 1
    (Uncertain, don't know—Skip to Q.16a) 2

   b. In what way do you think the Union has acted unfairly?

   _____

16a. Have you taken part in any way in the election campaign by trying to get people to vote for or against the Union?
(If R asks: "Taken part" = "done anything.")
Yes...3
No (Skip to Q.17a)................................1

b. Which way have you tried to persuade people to vote—for the Union or against the Union?
For the Union....................................3
Against the Union...............................1

17a. Have you ever voted in an NLRB election before this one, that is, an election to decide if there should be a union where you work?
Yes...3
No (Skip to Q.18)................................1
(Don't know, don't remember—Skip to Q.18)........2

b. Was it while working for this Company, another Company, or both?
This Company....................................1
Another Company...............................3
Both..2

c. Did you vote for or against the Union then?
For the Union....................................3
Against the Union...............................1
(Sometimes for, sometimes against) 2
(Don't remember)................................8
(Refused to answer)..............................9

18. Do you think it would be a <u>good</u> thing if the Union were voted in, a <u>bad</u> thing, or do you think it would make <u>no real difference?</u>
Good...3
Bad...1
No real difference (don't know)....................2

19a. If the election were held tomorrow, would you vote <u>for</u> or <u>against</u> the Union?
For the Union (Skip to Q.20)......................3
Against the Union (Skip to Q.20)..................1
(Wouldn't or couldn't vote—Ask 19c)...............7
(Refused to answer—Skip to Q.20)................9
(Don't know—Ask 19b)...........................2

b. Well, even though you don't know for sure how you would vote, which way are you leaning now—toward voting <u>for</u> or <u>against</u> the Union?
For the Union....................................3
Against the Union...............................1
(Don't know, uncertain)..........................2
(Refused to answer)..............................9

(SKIP TO Q.20)

c. Well, even though you don't think you will (could) vote, which way would you vote if you did (could)—<u>for</u> or <u>against</u> the Union?

```
For the Union.......................................3
Against the Union...................................1
(Don't know, uncertain)............................2
(Refused to answer)................................9
```

20. This final group of questions doesn't relate directly to the Union or the election, but gives us information we need to compare your answers with the answers of people like yourself who work for other companies.

    (IF TELEPHONE INTERVIEW, ASK FOLLOWING)
    First of all, what was your age as of your last birthday?
    (Read categories)

    (IF PERSONAL INTERVIEW, ASK FOLLOWING)
    First of all, we need to know your age. Would you look at this and tell me what the letter is next to your age. (Show R Q.20)

```
    A.  24 years or under.............................1
    B.  25-34 years..................................2
    C.  35-44 years..................................3
    D.  45-54 years..................................4
    E.  55-64 years..................................5
    F.  65 years or over.............................6
```

21. Are you presently married?

```
    Yes.............................................3
    No.............................................1
```

22. Including yourself, how many people are you supporting? (Circle one.)

```
    1          2          3          4          5 or more
```

23. (IF TELEPHONE INTERVIEW, ASK)
    What was the last year of school you completed? (Read categories)

    (IF PERSONAL INTERVIEW, ASK)
    Would you look at this and tell me what the letter is next to the last year of school you completed? (Show R Q.23)

```
    A.  1-4 years grade school.......................1
    B.  5-8 years grade school.......................2
    C.  Some high school.............................3
    D.  High school graduate.........................4
    E.  Some college................................5
    F.  College degree..............................6
```

24a. Which of the following is the best description of the city or town you lived in most of the time before you were 18?
    (Show R Q.24a and read categories)

```
    A large metropolitan city—100,000 or more.... ......1
    Suburb of a large city.............................2
    A medium sized city—50,000-99,999.................3
```

A small city—10,000–49,999. .4
A small city or town, but not on a farm,
 of less than 10,000. 5
On a farm. 6

b. What state (or country) was that in?

_____

25. Which one of the political parties do you generally support?
Democratic. 1
Republican. 2
Independent; support man, not party. 3
Other. 4
None. 5

26. What is your religious preference?
Catholic. 1
Protestant. 2
Jewish. 3
Moslem. 4
Other. 5
None. 6

27. Have any of the following members of your family ever been Union members?

		Yes	No	(Don't remember)	Never married
a.	Spouse? (Circle one).	3	1	2	8
b.	Father? (Circle one).	3	1	2	—
c.	Mother? (Circle one).	3	1	2	—

(INTERVIEWER: THE FOLLOWING THREE QUESTIONS FOR TELEPHONE INTERVIEWS ONLY. IF PERSONAL INTERVIEW, SKIP TO QUESTION 28a.)

28. On an hourly basis do you earn more than $3.50 or less than $3.50?
(If more, ask and circle number when R answers "No") (If less, ask and circle number when R answers "No")
(If exactly $3.50, circle 07)

More than $3.75. 08	Less than $3.25. 07
More than $4.00. 09	Less than $3.00. 06
More than $4.25. 10	Less than $2.75. 05
More than $4.50. 11	Less than $2.50. 04
More than $4.75. 12	Less than $2.25. 03
More than $5.00 {No. . . .13 {Yes. . . .14	Less than $2.00 {No. . . . . .02 {Yes. 01

29. After taxes and other deductions is your usual weekly take home pay more than $100 or less than $100? (If exactly $100, circle 04)

(If more, ask and circle   (If less, ask and circle
number when R answers   number when R answers
"No")   "No")
More than $125........05   Less than $75...........04
More than $150........06   Less than $50...........03
More than $175........07   Less than $25 {No.......02
More than $200 {No.....08   {Yes.......01
                {Yes....09

30. Of what race or ethnic group do you consider yourself a member—
    white, black, or other? (Record answer at Question 32.)

    (INTERVIEWER: THE FOLLOWING TWO QUESTIONS FOR
    PERSONAL INTERVIEWS ONLY.)

28a. What is the letter next to the amount you earn per hour? (Show R
     Q.28a)
     A. Under $2.00..................................01
     B. $2.00–$2.25.................................02
     C. $2.26–$2.50.................................03
     D. $2.51–$2.75.................................04
     E. $2.76–$3.00.................................05
     F. $3.01–$3.25.................................06
     G. $3.26–$3.50.................................07
     H. $3.51–$3.75.................................08
     I. $3.76–$4.00.................................09
     J. $4.01–$4.25.................................10
     K. $4.26–$4.50.................................11
     L. $4.51–$4.75.................................12
     M. $4.76–$5.00.................................13
     N. Over $5.00..................................14

29a. What is the letter next to your usual weekly take home pay, after
     taxes and other deductions? (Show R Q.29a)
     A. Under $25...................................01
     B. $25–$50....................................02
     C. $51–$75....................................03
     D. $76–$100...................................04
     E. $101–$125..................................05
     F. $126–$150..................................06
     G. $151–$175..................................07
     H. $176–$200..................................08
     I. Over $200..................................09

Thank you very much for your cooperation. We would like to talk
to you by telephone once again right after the election on

_____   _____
        (Day)   (Date)
Will you probably be home that evening so that I or one of our
staff members could call you?

If telephone:
Best day and time (approximate) to call:_____
Any day and time not to call:_____
Telephone number (Be <u>certain</u> to get if we have no phone number.
If R has no phone, see if he can be reached at another phone).

Additional information that might be helpful to second wave
telephone interviewer:_____
If personal:
Day and time of appointment:_____
Telephone number (in case interviewer delayed, etc.):_____
Additional information that might be helpful to second wave
interviewer (e.g., description of R's home and/or directions if
difficult to locate):_____
If no second interview arranged:
Why was R unwilling:_____
Is there any reason not to send an interviewer to try again after
the election?_____

(INTERVIEWER: IF R HAS REFUSED TO ANSWER THE
QUESTION AS TO HIS VOTE INTENT (Q.19), TRY IN A
VERY LOW-KEY MANNER TO GET AN ANSWER NOW. IF
YOU GET VOTE INTENT INFORMATION HERE, CIRCLE
APPROPRIATE ANSWER CATEGORY IN Q.19.)

INTERVIEWER QUESTIONS
(Complete immediately after leaving respondent)

31. What was the respondent's sex?
Male..1
Female..2

32. What was the respondent's race?
White...1
Black...2
Other...3

INTERVIEWER: GO OVER THE ENTIRE INTERVIEW SCHED-
ULE NOW AND MAKE CERTAIN THAT ALL QUESTIONS HAVE
BEEN ASKED AND AN ANSWER CATEGORY CIRCLED. IF ANY
QUESTIONS NOT ANSWERED, PLEASE RETURN AND GET AN-
SWERS (UNLESS, OF COURSE, R HAS REFUSED TO ANSWER
A PARTICULAR QUESTION, IN WHICH CASE THE "REFUSED
TO ANSWER" CATEGORY SHOULD BE CIRCLED OR YOU
SHOULD WRITE "REFUSED TO ANSWER"). ALSO MAKE CER-
TAIN THAT YOUR HANDWRITING IS LEGIBLE AND THAT
WHAT YOU HAVE WRITTEN MAKES SENSE ON ALL OPEN-
ENDED QUESTIONS.

Appendix C

EMPLOYEE INTERVIEW SCHEDULE

UNIVERSITY OF ILLINOIS SURVEY RESEARCH LABORATORY

Study of NLRB Elections

Wave II

INTERVIEWER: WHENEVER R REFERS TO THE POSSIBILITY OF HARM COMING ABOUT IF THE UNION SHOULD WIN, OR BECAUSE THE UNION WON, YOU MUST PROBE: "IF YOU CAN TELL ME, WHY DO YOU THINK THE (HARM MENTIONED) WILL/WOULD COME ABOUT IF THE UNION WON/BECAUSE THE UNION WON."

I would like to begin by asking you some questions about the election campaign. First, I will ask you a few questions about what the Company said and did, then a few questions about what the Union said and did. That way we can get a pretty good idea of what happened.

1a. First, did you, at any time before the election get any letters or other written material from the Company discussing the Union or the election?

Yes..3
No, don't know (Skip to Q.2a).....................1

b. What did they say?_____(☐ R read)

2a. Did any foremen, supervisors, or persons at higher management levels speak to you by yourself about the Union or the election?

Yes..3
No, don't know (Skip to Q.3a).....................1

b. What did he (they) say?_____

3a. Did any foremen, supervisors, or persons at higher management levels speak to you together with other employees about the Union or the election? This could have been either at a meeting or at an informal discussion.

Yes..3
No, don't know (Skip to Q.4).....................1

179

b. How many such meetings or informal discussions have you been present at? (Circle one.)

        1   2   3   4   5 or more

c. What was said by the person from the Company at that meeting or discussion (those meetings or discussions)?

_____

4. (SKIP TO Q.5a IF R HAS NOT BEEN SPOKEN TO BY COM-PANY, I.E., BOTH Q.2a AND Q.3a ANSWERED "NO")
I have one question about where this meeting (these meetings) were held. Did anyone from the Company ever speak to you by yourself or to you and other employees in the office of any foreman, supervisor, or person at a higher management level?

           Yes..3
           No...1

5a. Did the Company express its views about the Union or the election in any other way? This could have been either on posters, bulletin boards, buttons, leaflets, or in some other way.

           Yes..3
           No, don't know (Skip to Q.7a).......................1

b. In what ways?

_____

c. What did they say?

_____(☐ R read)

(NO Q. 6)

7a. Now let's turn to the Union campaign. Did you get or see any letters or other written material from the Union?

           Yes..3
           No (Skip to Q.8a)................................1

b. What did they say?_____(☐ R read)

8a. Have you been to any Union meetings?
           Yes (Skip to 8c)................................3
           No...1

b. Any particular reason why not?_____
(SKIP TO Q.9a)

c. Can you tell me what was said there?_____

9a. Apart from any Union meetings, has anyone talked to you, either in person or on the telephone, about why you should join or vote for the Union?
           Yes..3
           No (Skip to Q.10a)................................1

b. Approximately how many times have you been talked to about this? (Circle one)

Once..1
Twice...2
Three times.....................................3
Four times......................................4
More than four times............................5
(Don't remember)................................8

c. Was the person (any of the people) who talked to you an employee of this Company or was he someone who works for the Union as an organizer?

Employee..1
Organizer.......................................2
(Both)..3
(Don't know)....................................8

d. What did he (they) say to you about why you should join or vote for the Union?

_____

10a. Did the Union compare wages at this plant with what it has been able to get for employees at unionized plants?

Yes...3
No, don't know (Skip to Q.11a)..................1

b. To the extent that you can remember, what did the Union say it got for employees in such plants? (INTERVIEWER: GET FIGURES IN DOLLARS AND CENTS IF R CAN PROVIDE THEM.)
_____(☐ R read)

11a. Do you think the Union acted fairly or not fairly in its efforts to persuade people to vote for the Union? (If R asks: I know we asked you this question at the last interview, but a lot has happened since then and we'd like to know what you think now.)

Fairly (Skip to Q.12a)..........................3
Not fairly......................................1
(Don't know—Skip to Q.12a).....................2

b. In what way do you think the Union acted unfairly?

_____

12a. (INTERVIEWER: SKIP TO Q.12b IF ELECTION RESULTS NOT AVAILABLE.)

The Union appears to have (won/lost) the election. Do you think this represents a good or a bad decision on the part of the employees?

Good..3
Bad...1
(Don't know, uncertain)........................2
(Refused).......................................9

(SKIP TO Q.13)

b. We don't know yet if the Union won or lost the election. Do you think it would be a good thing or a bad thing if the Union won?
Good 3
Bad 1
(Don't know, uncertain) 2
(Refused) 9

13. How about you? Did you vote <u>for</u> or <u>against</u> the Union?
For the Union 3
Against the Union 1
(Didn't vote—Skip to Q.16) 6
(Refused—Skip to Q.15) 9

14. Why did you vote (for/against) the Union?

---

15. How long before the election did you definitely make up your mind which way to vote—during the week before the election, more than one week before the election, or as soon as you heard the Union was trying to get in? (<u>INTERVIEWER</u>: REPEAT QUESTION IF NECESSARY.)
During week before election 1
More than one week before election 2
Soon as heard Union trying to get in 3
(Don't know, don't remember) 8

16. Let me ask you one question about those employees who voted against the Union. Why do you think they voted against the Union?

17a. Do you think that either the Company or the Union knows which side you were in favor of in the election?
Yes 1
No (Skip to Q.18a) 3
(Don't know—Skip to Q.18a) 2

b. Who do you think knows which side you were in favor of—the Company, the Union, or both the Company and the Union?
The Company 1
The Union 3
Both 2
(Don't know—Skip to Q.18a) 8

c. How do you think the (Company/Union) knows this?

18a. Sometimes an employer, during the course of a campaign, will either take harmful action against Union supporters or will threaten harmful action against them. Did this employer take or threaten harmful action against union supporters? (If R asks: "Harmful action" = "Bad things.")
Yes 3
No, don't know (Skip to Q.19a) 1

b. What did the Company do?

_____

c. Do you think that what the Company did was effective in getting people to vote against the Union?

Yes..3

No...1

(Don't know)..................................2

19a. How about benefits? Sometimes an employer will give employees new benefits or promise them new benefits so they will vote against the Union. Did this employer give or promise benefits to employees to get them to vote against the Union? (If R asks: "Benefits" = "good things.")

Yes..3

No, don't know (Skip to Q.20).....................1

b. What did the Company do?

_____

c. Do you think that what the Company did was effective in getting people to vote against the Union?

Yes..3

No...1

(Don't know)..................................2

20. The last time you were interviewed, we asked you whether you agreed or disagreed with a number of statements made by workers in other plants with regard to unions. I'd like to ask you just a few of them again.

a. Unions help the working man to get better wages and hours. Do you agree or disagree?

Agree...3

Disagree...1

(Don't know, uncertain)..........................2

b. Unions interfere with good relations between companies and workers. Agree or disagree?

Agree...1

Disagree...3

(Don't know, uncertain)..........................2

c. Unions make sure that employees are treated fairly by supervisors. Agree or disagree?

Agree...3

Disagree...1

(Don't know, uncertain)..........................2

21. In general, would you describe your overall attitude toward unions as favorable or not favorable?

Favorable..3

Not favorable....................................1

(Uncertain, don't know)..........................2

22. Now let me finish up by repeating a few questions about your job.

   a. Do the supervisors in this Company play favorites or do they treat all workers alike?
      Play favorites....................................1
      Treat alike.......................................3
      (Uncertain, don't know)...........................2

   b. Are you satisfied or not satisfied with your wages?
      Satisfied...3
      Not satisfied.....................................1
      (Uncertain, don't know)...........................2

   c. Are you satisfied or not satisfied with your fringe benefits, such as pensions, vacations, holiday pay, insurance, and sick leave?
      Satisfied...3
      Not satisfied.....................................1
      (Uncertain, don't know)...........................2

23. Taking everything into consideration, would you say you were satisfied or not satisfied with your job?
      Satisfied...3
      Not satisfied.....................................1
      (Uncertain, don't know)...........................2

INTERVIEWER:

A. IF R HAS ANSWERED QUESTION AS TO HOW HE VOTED (Q.13), ASK Q.24.

B. IF R HAS REFUSED TO TELL HOW HE VOTED, ASK AGAIN NOW.
   (1) IF R STILL WILL NOT ANSWER, END INTERVIEW.
   (2) IF R NOW GIVES VOTE INFORMATION, CIRCLE APPROPRIATE ANSWER CATEGORY IN Q.13 AND ASK Q.24.

24. INTERVIEWER: CHECK VOTE INTENT FROM WAVE I, QUESTION 19a, b, or c AND ACTUAL VOTE FROM WAVE II, QUESTION 13. IF R VOTED THE SAME WAY AS HE INTENDED, END INTERVIEW. IF R SWITCHED, ASK:
   I notice that you voted for/against the Union, while you told us earlier that you planned to vote for/against the Union. What happened to make you change your mind?

That's all the questions I have. Thank you for your cooperation, and once again let me assure you that all this will be treated confidentially.

INTERVIEWER: PLEASE GO BACK OVER THE INTERVIEW SCHEDULE NOW AND MAKE CERTAIN THAT ALL QUESTIONS HAVE BEEN ANSWERED AND THE ANSWER INDICATED ON THE INTERVIEW SCHEDULE. IF ANY QUESTION HAS NOT BEEN ANSWERED, CALL BACK AND GET AN ANSWER (UN-

LESS, OF COURSE, THE RESPONDENT REFUSED TO ANSWER, IN WHICH CASE THE "REFUSED TO ANSWER" CATEGORY SHOULD BE CIRCLED OR YOU SHOULD WRITE "REFUSED TO ANSWER"). ALSO MAKE CERTAIN THAT YOUR HAND-WRITING IS LEGIBLE AND THAT WHAT YOU HAVE WRITTEN MAKES SENSE ON ALL OPEN-ENDED QUESTIONS.

Appendix D

100 Series—Harmful Economic Consequences of Unionization

110 Series—Benefits

*110 = *Loss of benefits (retaliation):* Benefits (any type) will/may be cut/taken away *in retaliation* for union victory.

111 = *Loss of benefits (other); economic/non-economic harm:* Benefits (any type) will/may be cut/taken away for reasons other than retaliation/reasons unknown. Benefits have been cut elsewhere after union victory. All benefits up for discussion may go down as well as up. Unionization will/might lead to economic/non-economic harm for reasons other than retaliation/reasons unknown.

130 Series—Plant Closing/Moving

*130 = *Plant closing/moving (retaliation):* Will/may take place in retaliation for union victory.

131 = *Plant closing/moving (other):* Will/may take place for other reasons. Has taken place elsewhere after union victory.

150 Series—Discharges/Layoffs

*150 = *Discharges/layoffs (retaliation):* Employer will/may discharge/ lay off employees in retaliation for union victory/support.

151 = *Discharges/layoffs (other):* Employer will/may discharge/lay off employees for other reasons. Have taken place at other plants after union victory.

200 Series—Strikes (Negative aspects; for positive or neutral aspects, see 960 series)

210 Series—Likely/Possible/Certain

210 = *Strike likely/certain:* If union wins, there will/may be strike.

213 = *Elsewhere:* This union has been involved in strikes elsewhere.

214 = *Strike already called:* Union strike at this plant/store shows union irresponsible; ignores orderly processes of law.

---

* = Unlawful campaign tactic

220 Series—Loss of Jobs/Benefits

220 = *Loss of jobs (general):* Strike will/may lead to loss of jobs for any reasons other than discharge of strikers.

*221 = *Loss of jobs (discharge):* Employer will/may fire strikers.

230 Series—Other Economic Consequences of Strikes

230 = *Unemployment compensation:* Strikers will be ineligible.

231 = *Employment elsewhere:* Other companies will not hire strikers.

232 = *Loss of wages/benefits:* Strikers will lose wages/job benefits; have no income during strike. Perhaps lose more than gain by strike.

234 = *Strike benefits:* Union strike benefits insubstantial.

250 Series—Impact on Employer

250 = *Little or none:* Little or none; employer can hire other people to do work of strikers.

251 = *Substantial:* Strike will hurt employer and thus hurt employees.

252 = *Never yield:* Employer will never yield to strike.

260 Series—Other

261 = *Union not hurt:* Union does not lose/is not harmed by strike; employer/employees lose by strike, not win.

262 = *Picket duty:* Strikers may/must walk picket lines.

269 = *Other:* Other statements about strikes or their effects.

300 Series—Unionization Unnecessary, Futile or Harmful (Non-economic Harm)

300 Series—Wages/Working Conditions Good; Don't Need Union

300 = *Wages good:* Wages are now good; are equal to/better than those under union contracts elsewhere; will stay good without union.

301 = *Hours/days/work schedule good:* Hours/days/work schedule are now good, etc. (same as 300).

302 = *Pensions/profit-sharing:* Are now good, etc. (same as 300).

303 = *Holidays/Vacations:* Holidays/vacations are now good, etc. (same as 300).

304 = *Sick leave/insurance:* Sick leave/insurance are now good, etc. (same as 300).

306 = *Misc. specific working conditions/fringe benefits good:* Misc. specific working conditions/fringe benefits (e.g., funeral leave, jury duty pay, etc.) now good, etc. (same as 300).

308 = *Wages/working conditions good (particular employees):* Wages/working conditions now good for particular employees; they don't need union.

---

* = Unlawful campaign tactic

309 = *Wages/working conditions (general) good:* Wages/working conditions generally good; are equal to/better than those under union contract elsewhere; will stay good without union. [Emphasis on 310/360 when overlap with 309.]

310–320 Series—Wages/Working Conditions Improvement Unrelated to Unionization

310 = *Improvements not dependent on unionization:* Union cannot guarantee jobs/improvements; cannot keep promises that it can. Only employer can bring about improvements by getting/keeping customers. Will try to do that. Employer will pay what is right/feasible; cannot be compelled to pay more; under no obligation to agree.

313 = *Company in bad financial condition:* Company in bad financial condition; cannot afford union.

*315 = *Wages/working conditions will improve:* Employer admitted past mistakes. Will/said he will improve/try to improve wages/working conditions.

316 = *Recent improvements:* Recent improvement in wages/working conditions indicate improvements can be made without unionization.

330 Series—Bargaining

*330 = *No bargaining:* Employer will not bargain with/deal with/ sign contract/permit/accept union.

331 = *No bargaining pending judicial review:* Employer will contest union victory before labor board/courts; no bargaining until complete which may take years.

334 = *Bargain in good faith:* Employer will bargain in good faith.

340 Series—Employer/Employee Relationship

*340 = *Loss of individual treatment (retaliation):* Employer will/may stop giving special consideration for individual problems/ treat all alike/operate strictly by rules/follow strict senority system in *retaliation* for union victory.

341 = *Loss of individual treatment (other)/interference with relationships between and among employers and employees:* Union victory will lead to loss of individual treatment (as in 340)for reasons *other* than retaliation. Will/may harm employer/ employee, employee/employee relationships. Employees can represent selves; don't need union. Union is outsider; will/ may interfere with efficient operation of business.

*343 = *Loss of individual freedom of discussion:* Unionization will/ may lead to loss of individual employee freedom to deal/ confer/discuss directly with employer as to wages/hours/ working conditions.

---

* = Unlawful campaign tactic

344 = *Advancement on merit:* Promotions now made without regard to race, sex, religion, etc.

345 = *Job classification:* Union will insist on job classification. Prevent employer from working employees out of classification as alternative to short work week/layoffs.

346 = *Shop committee:* Problems can be resolved through shop committee; don't need union.

360 Series—Fair/Good/Equal Treatment

360 = *Fair treatment/concern:* Employer has treated employees fairly/well/equally. Cares about employees' well-being. Loyalty/fairness to employer should lead to vote against union.

361 = *Fair/good/equal treatment (named/specified individual):* Named/specified individual has treated employee(s) fairly/well/equally; is liked by employee(s).

370 Series—Other

371 = *Phase II:* Union cannot increase wages more than would increase without union; Phase II prevents. Employer willing to/has raise(d) to 5.5 level without union.

372 = *More/harder work:* Union will cause employees to work more/harder/faster, etc.

373 = *Legal effect of union victory on wage increase:* If union wins, legally impossible for employer to grant wage increase employees have right to expect.

374 = *Increase in minimum wage:* Congress is increasing minimum wage; no need for union.

375 = *Word as good as contract:* Employer's word is just as good as any union contract.

376 = *Phase IV increases:* Phase IV regulations permit price/income increases.

400 Series—Criticisms of Union Movement/Organizers/Supporters Campaign

410 Series—Dues/Initiation Fees/Assessments/Fines

410 = *Financial costs of unionization outweigh gains/costs too high:* Union dues/initiation fees/assessments greater than value of union representation; financial gains of unionization will be offset by cost of dues, etc.; dues, etc., too high. All employees may/will be forced to join union/pay union dues/initiation fees/assessments.

412 = *Fines:* Union can/may/will fine employees who fail to perform union duties (e.g., strike, picket, attend meetings.)

419 = *Other:* Other criticisms relating to dues amount/initiation fees/assessments/fines.

420 Series—Lack of Concern for Employees

420 = *Lack of concern for employees:* Unions are not concerned with welfare of employees; union only interested in getting money through dues (see also 410); does not help employees when need help.

421 = *Using employees as stepping-stones:* Union not concerned with this unit; wants victory to impress employees elsewhere.

422 = *Arbitrary/unresponsive grievance processing:* Union will/may be arbitrary/unresponsive in pressing grievances/making other decisions.

423 = *Lack of local control:* Union would be controlled by people from other cities/states/bargaining units.

424 = *Discharges:* Union can/has/will cause employees to be discharged.

430 Series—Organizers, Supporters, Officials

430 = *Radical, communistic/un-American:* Union has too many radicals/communists; too radical/communist/un-American in goals.

431 = *Blacks:* Too many Blacks in union; union supports goals of Blacks.

432 = *Crooks:* Too many crooks in union.

433 = *Supporters undesirable:* Union organizers/supporters/officials are generally undesirable persons; good workers don't need unions; unions only protect bad/lazy workers.

434 = *High salaries:* Union officials receive high/exorbitant salaries/expenses.

435 = *Top seniority/special privileges:* If union wins, union officers/stewards will have top seniority/special privileges.

439 = *Other:* Other criticisms of organizers/supporters/officials.

440 Series—Campaign

440 = *Campaign lies:* Union lied to employees/tried to deceive employees; made promises it couldn't keep. (Refers only to specific lies, not to general statements that union cannot keep promises. For latter, see 310.)

442 = *Campaign too strong:* Union campaign was too strong/hard; too much pressure; too many contacts.

443 = *Campaign too weak:* Union did not campaign hard enough.

444 = *Campaign too selective:* Union played favorites in campaigning; did not talk to people it assumed were firmly for/against union.

445 = *Talking down to employees:* Union talked down to employees/treated employees as unintelligent; employees too smart to fall for union propaganda.

446 = *Use of obscene/vulgar language:* Union organizers/supporters used obscene/vulgar language.

449 = *Campaign otherwise unseemly/unfair/improper:* (In respects not treated above).

450 Series—Union Strength/Demands

450 = *Union too weak:* This union too weak to help employees.

451 = *Union(s) too strong:* Union(s) too strong/powerful; may once have served useful purpose. If union wins, it may get too strong/powerful.

452 = *Demands too great:* Union demands on employer are/may be too great/unrealistic.

453 = *Union did not obtain improvements elsewhere:* This union did not obtain improvements elsewhere.

454 = *Union financially weak:* Union financially weak; too weak to afford expense of arbitration/other expenses.

455 = *Few employers organized:* Unionization of no value if only few shops organized; must have many/all.

460 Series—Other

460 = *Violence:* Unions use violence as a tactic.

461 = *Inflation:* Unions contribute to inflation/rising prices: are harmful to economy.

462 = *Tried to prevent some employees from voting:* Union tried to prevent some employees from voting; challenged eligibility of some employees.

463 = *Union internal labor problems:* Union has own internal labor problems; laid off own employees; struck by own employees.

464 = *Union unfair labor practices/other unlawful conduct:* Union has committed unfair labor practices/other unlawful conduct. (References to violence to be coded 460.)

465 = *Obligations of union membership:* Union members must attend meetings/serve on union committees.

466 = *Union constitution/by-laws:* Discussed/described union constitution/by-laws/history/organization.

467 = *No compassion:* This/other union has no compassion for people in trouble.

469 = *Other:* Other criticisms of union (use only if cannot use 419, 439, or 449; use those if criticism in area covered by those).

500 Series—Other Statements/Reasons Why Employees Should Not/Will Not/Did Not Vote for Union; Other Statements as to Harmful Consequences of Unionization

510 Series—Company Characteristics/Actions/Wishes

510 = *Company too small:* Unions unnecessary in small companies.

511 = *New company/management/operating methods:* New company taking over/has recently taken over; changes in management/ operations; wait and see what it does. New company/changes in management/operations will/may provide increased benefits without need for union.

512 = *Company wishes:* Company does not want union. (Use this category only if no other responses to Q. 1–5.)

513 = *Company campaign:* Company campaign has convinced employee(s) union not desirable (*Note:* Use only if reference to campaign. See also 512).

514 = *Bad company experience elsewhere:* Company had bad experience with union at other plant/store/etc.

515 = *Nonprofit/public service employer:* Employer is nonprofit/ public service in character. Unionization will/may lead to higher prices, with consequent impairment of ability to serve public. (Compare 111 in which emphasis on economic harm to employer/employees.)

516 = *Company will fight:* Company will fight union in all possible ways/as hard as legally can.

519 = *Others:* Other company characteristics/actions/wishes leading to vote against union.

520 Series—Union Characteristics/Actions/Wishes

520 = *Union may not/will not win:* Union may not/will not win election.

521 = *Union difficult to get out:* If employees choose union and later become dissatisfied with union, it will be difficult to get rid of union; easy to get in, hard to get out.

522 = *Respondent's prior unfavorable experience with unions:* Past experience of employee has shown unions undesirable. (See also 540.)

525 = *Union inappropriate:* This union inappropriate for this unit.

529 = *Other:* Other union characteristics/actions/wishes leading to vote against union.

530 Series—Employee Characteristics/Actions/Wishes

530 = *Short time (junior):* Employees who have been with company for short time against union; union (seniority system) will hurt them.

531 = *Black:* Blacks against union; union will not help blacks.

532 = *White:* Whites against union; union will not help whites.

533 = *Other racial/ethnic group:* Group against union, union will not help group.

534 = *Old:* Old people against union; union will not help old.

535 = *Young:* Young people against union; union will not help young.

536 = *Female:* Females against union; union will not help females.

537 = *Male:* Males against union; union will not help males.

538 = *Part-time:* Part-timers against union; union will not help part-timers.

539 = *Long-time (senior):* Employees who have been with company for many years (senior in terms of service) against union; union will not help long-time employees.

540 Series—Advice/Experience Other Employee/Friend/Relation

540 = *Union experience other employee/friend/relation:* Other employee/friend/relative had prior unfavorable experience with union (any union).

541 = *Advice of other employee:* Other employee advised vote against union. (*Note:* Should always be followed by another code for reason why advised vote against union.)

542 = *Advice of friend:* Friend (non-employee) advised vote against union. (*Note:* Same as 541.)

543 = *Advice of relative:* Relative (non-employee) advised vote against union. (*Note:* Same as 541.)

544 = *Advice of friend in management:* Friend in management (foreman/supervisor/boss) advised vote against union. (*Note:* Same as 541.)

545 = *Rejected elsewhere:* This union rejected by employees at other plants.

546 = *Rejected here:* This/other union(s) previously rejected by employees at this plant.

548 = *Can get union in year:* Wait and see; can always get union in a year.

549 = *Advice of other/unspecified person:* Individual whose status not clear/not specified above advised vote against union. (*Note:* Same as 541.)

550 Series—Other

550 = *Other:* Other statements/reasons why employees should not/will not/did not vote for union; other statements as to harmful consequences of unionization (*Note:* Use only if cannot use 519, 529, or 549).

551 = *Don't like unions/afraid of change:* I/some people don't like unions; don't/didn't know what union will be like; don't/didn't want to take chance.

553 = *Not primary wage earner:* Against union because doesn't really need money; husband/wife employed elsewhere.

600 Series—Other Employer Statements/Questions/About Union/Election

610 Series—Interrogation   (Limited to Oral Interrogation)

*610 = *Interrogation (grievances/union supporters/respondent's views):* Employer asked what were employee complaints/demands/ grievances; why employees wanted union; which employees wanted union; whether respondent wanted union; what respondent thought of union.

*613 = *Opinion survey:* Employer had outside individual/organization conduct survey of employee opinions of wages/hours/ working conditions.

619 = *Interrogation (other):* Employer interrogation not covered by above.

620 Series—Election

620 = *Election process/date:* Employer described election process; announced election date/time.

621 = *Secret ballot:* Ballot will be secret.

622 = *Vote:* Employees should be certain to vote (includes statements designed to turn out vote).

624 = *NLRB election open to all:* You do not have to be a union member or sign a union card to vote in the NLRB election.

625 = *Names and addresses:* We are required by law to furnish the NLRB with your names and addresses.

626 = *Cannot answer questions orally:* Because of NLRB regulations, employer can only answer questions in writing.

629 = *Other:* Other statements as to election process.

630 Series—NLRB Voting Study

630 = *Encouraged cooperation:* Praised study; encouraged employees to cooperate with study.

631 = *Neutral on cooperation:* Advised employees of freedom to cooperate or not as they wished.

632 = *Discouraged cooperation:* Attacked study; discouraged employees from cooperating with study.

633 = *Criticized union cooperation:* Criticized union for cooperating with study.

639 = *Other:* Other statements as to study.

640 Series—Facts

640 = *Get facts before deciding/decide for selves/employer will accept decision:* Employees should get facts from both sides before deciding how to vote; should decide for selves how to vote; should become familiar with campaign issues. Employer willing to provide facts; discuss/answer questions. Employer will accept/abide by employee decision as to organization.

642 = *Offered to debate union:* Employer offered to debate union.

* = Unlawful campaign tactic

643 = *Right to own opinion:* Each person entitled to own opinion about union; employees should not get angry at those with views other than theirs.

650–670 Series—Other

650 = *Effect of pending election on promises/grant of benefits:* Employer barred by pending election from promising to improve/improving wages/hours/working conditions.

651 = *No retaliation:* If union loses, company will not retaliate against union supporters.

652 = *No campaign:* Company has not campaigned against union representation.

654 = *Union good points:* Employer discussed/recognized good points of union/unionization.

655 = *Card signing and vote:* Employees who signed union authorization card are under no obligation to vote for union.

656 = *No retaliation (if union wins):* If union wins, company will not retaliate by moving plant/closing plant or in any other way.

657 = *Card signing and union representation:* Union can use cards to get in without election.

658 = *No advantages for union voters:* Those who vote for the union will get no special advantages if the union wins the election.

659 = *Other:* Other employer statements/questions about union/election. (*Note:* Use only if cannot use 619, 629, or 639.)

*660 = *Suggested forming committee:* Suggested forming employee committee to discuss problems with employer.

661 = *Free to engage in union activity:* Employees are free to engage in union activity on own time; to wear union buttons.

663 = *Free to refrain from union activity:* Employees are free to refrain from engaging in union activity.

664 = *Layoffs/discharges, etc. economically motivated:* Layoffs/discharges/other economic action based on economic considerations, not retaliation for union activities (or bribe to keep union out).

665 = *NLRB sustained employer contentions:* NLRB has sustained employer position (includes all types of favorable decisions by regional director, trial examiner, NLRB).

666 = *Don't sign cards:* Employees who do not want union should refuse to sign cards.

667 = *Suggestion box:* Employer asked employees to submit questions/suggestions in written (anonymous) form.

668 = *Will put statements in writing:* Anything we say, we will put in writing.

669 = *Go to union meeting:* Employees should go to union meeting, ask questions.

---

* = Unlawful campaign tactic

670 = *Decision important:* Your decision is very important. Will significantly affect your future, that of employer/other employees/family/etc.

671 = *History/organization of company:* Discussed history/organization of company.

700 Series—Employer Actions Intended to/Likely to Discourage/Prevent Employees from Supporting/Voting for Union

(*Note:* Employer *motive* of discouraging/preventing union support and *effect* of discouraging/preventing union activity/support are interchangeable in all categories in which reference is made to motive of discouraging/preventing union support.)

710 Series—Discharges/Layoffs

*710 = *Discharges/layoffs/refusals to hire:* Discharged/laid off/refused to hire employees because of union activity/support.

711 = *Discharges/layoffs/refusals to hire (motive/effect uncertain):* Discharged/laid off/refused to hire employees for reasons/with effect uncertain/unspecified.

720 Series—Deprivation of Benefits (Economic Matters)

*720 = *Deprivation of benefits (general):* Deprived employees of benefits generally because of union activity/support.

*721 = *Deprivation of benefits (particular employees):* Deprived particular employees of benefits to discourage union activity/support.

722 = *Deprivation of benefits (motive/effect uncertain):* Deprived some/all employees of benefits for reasons/with effect uncertain/unspecified.

730 Series—Grant of Benefits (Economic Matters)

*730 = *Grant of benefits (general):* Granted benefits to employees generally to discourage union activity/support.

*731 = *Grant of benefits (particular employees):* Granted benefits to particular employees to discourage union activity/support.

732 = *Grant of benefits (motive/effect uncertain):* Granted benefits to some/all employees for reasons/with effect uncertain/unspecified.

*733 = *Formation/domination of employer committee:* Employer formed/dominated employee representation committee.

*734 = *Grant of benefits (elsewhere):* Granted benefits to employees at other non-union stores to discourage unionization at this store.

740 Series—Good Treatment of Employees (Non-economic Matters, e.g., Attitude)

*740 = *Good treatment (general):* Treating employees well generally to discourage union activity/support/vote.

---

* = Unlawful campaign tactic

*741 = *Good treatment (particular employees)*: Treating particular employees well to discourage union activity/support.

742 = *Good treatment (motive/effect uncertain)*: Treating some/all employees well for reasons/with effect uncertain/unspecified.

750 Series—Harsh Treatment of Employees (Non-economic Matters)

*750 = *Harsh treatment (general)*: Treating employees generally harshly to discourage union activity/support/vote.

*751 = *Harsh treatment (particular employees)*: Treating particular employees harshly to discourage union activity/support.

752 = *Harsh treatment (motive/effect uncertain)*: Treating some/all employees harshly for reasons/with effect uncertain/unspecified.

760 Series—Union Discussion/Solicitation (Including Authorization Cards)

760 = *No solicitation (working time)*: Employer prohibited union discussion/solicitation on working time.

*761 = *No solicitation (non-working time)*: Employer prohibited union discussion/solicitation at all times on company premises.

762 = *No solicitation (unclear)*: Scope of no solicitation rule as to time unclear/unspecified.

*763 = *No solicitation (limited to union)*: Employer prohibited *only* union discussion/solicitation; other types allowed. (*Note:* Use only if respondent explicitly states that other forms of solicitation/discussion allowed to continue.)

770 Series—Distribution of Union Literature

770 = *No distribution (working areas)*: Employee prohibited distribution of union literature in working areas of plant/stores.

*771 = *No distribution (non-working areas)*: Employer prohibited distribution of union literature in non-working areas of plant/store.

772 = *No distribution (area unclear)*: Scope of no distribution rule as to areas of plant/store unspecified/unclear.

773 = *No distribution (working time)*: Employer prohibited distribution of union literature during working time.

*774 = *No distribution (non-working time)*: Employer prohibited distribution of union literature at all times on company premises.

775 = *No distribution (time unclear)*: Scope of no distribution rule as to time unclear.

*776 = *No distribution (limited to union)*: Employer prohibited *only* distribution of union literature; other types allowed. (*Note:*

---

* = Unlawful campaign tactic

Use only if respondent explicitly states that other types of distribution allowed to continue.)

777 = *No distribution (access road):* Employer prohibited distribution of literature on access road leading to plant.

780–790 Series—Other

*780 = *Strict enforcement of rules:* Tightened up on rules; enforced rules more strictly to discourage union activity/support/vote.

781 = *Older employee/foremen pressure:* Had older employees/foremen put pressure on employees.

*782 = *Surveillance:* Tried to find out which employees supported union/what employees were saying about union; watched suspected union supporters.

783 = *Juggling/trying to alter voter eligibility/voting unit:* Employer promoting/transferring employees to affect eligibility to vote; seeking to get particular employees into/out of unit.

784 = *Turned out vote:* Actions designed to encourage employees to vote in election.

785 = *Union dues:* Actions designed to demonstrate amount of union dues (e.g., two paychecks).

786 = *Hired new/temporary employees:* Hired new/temporary employees to show that employees could be replaced easily if struck.

*787 = *Employee pressure:* Allowed/encouraged anti-union employees to coerce/harass/intimidate pro-union employees.

788 = *Party/dinner:* Had party/dinner for employees.

789 = *Guarantee sheet:* Handed out sheet for union representative to sign to guarantee promises.

*798 = *Other:* Other actions intended to/likely to discourage/prevent union activity/support/vote.

799 = *Other (motive/effect uncertain):* Other actions for reasons/with effect uncertain/unspecified.

800 Series—Statements/Reasons as to Why Employees Should/Will/Might/Did Support/Vote for Union; Statements as to Favorable Consequences of Unionization

810–820 Series—Wages/Hours/Working Conditions

810 = *Wages:* Wages unsatisfactory (includes too slow/infrequent raises/promotions); union will improve.

811 = *Hours/days/work schedule:* Hours/days/work schedule unsatisfactory; union will improve.

812 = *Pensions:* Pensions unsatisfactory; union will improve.

813 = *Holidays/vacations:* Holidays/vacations unsatisfactory; union will improve.

---

* = Unlawful campaign tactic

814 = *Sick leave:* Sick leave/insurance unsatisfactory; union will improve.

816 = *Safety:* Safety conditions unsatisfactory; union will improve.

817 = *Cleanliness:* Cleanliness unsatisfactory; union will improve.

818 = *Production:* Production requirements unsatisfactory (includes employees must work too fast, produce/lift/carry too much).

819 = *Job classification:* Jobs presently unclassified; job functions undefined. Union will require classification/definition; protect employee from being required to work outside classification/do work not within job definition.

820 = *Fair treatment (including grievance procedure/seniority system/job security):* Company has treated employees unfairly, without consideration; played favorites. Union will insure fairness/consideration in treatment of employees; prevent favoritism/arbitrary action/unjustified disciplinary action; protect employees from employers; set up grievance procedure/seniority system/job security.

821 = *Efficiency/equipment:* Company presently disorganized/inefficient; uses poor equipment; union will improve organization/efficiency; require company to provide better equipment.

822 = *Pay periods:* Employees paid too infrequently/at inconvenient time; union will improve.

823 = *Premium pay:* Premium rate for over-time/holidays not paid/unsatisfactory; union will improve.

824 = *Sex discrimination:* Employer paying women less than men for same work; union will improve.

825 = *Guaranteed jobs/no discharges:* Union will prevent employer from firing employees.

826 = *Other (specific):* Other (specific) working conditions unsatisfactory; union will improve.

829 = *Other (general):* Other (general) working conditions unsatisfactory; union will improve.

830 Series—Union Strength

830 = *Union strength:* Strength of union will balance employer strength; union will provide employees with voice in determining wages/working conditions.

831 = *Company fears union strength:* Fact that company fighting union so hard, granting/promising benefits means company fears union can really accomplish something for employees.

832 = *Appropriate union:* This is appropriate union for employees in this industry/company.

833 = *Cannot lose with union:* If union wins election, employees cannot lose/only gain.

834 = *Union better because outsider:* Union, as outsider, not obligated to company; is in better position to bargain.

840 Series—Employee Characteristics

840 = *Blacks:* Blacks for union; union will help blacks.

841 = *Whites:* Whites for union; union will help whites.

842 = *Other racial/ethnic group:* Group for union; union will help group.

843 = *Old/senior:* Old/senior people for union; union will help old/senior employees.

844 = *Young:* Young people for union; union will help young.

845 = *Female:* Females for union; union will help females.

846 = *Males:* Males for union; union will help males.

847 = *Part-timers:* Part-timers for union; union will help part-timers.

848 = *Full-timers:* Full-timers for union; union will help full-timers.

849 = *Other:* Other group for union; union will help group.

850 Series—Advice/Experience Other Employee/Friend/Relation

850 = *Union experience other employee/friend/relation:* Other employee/friend/relation had prior favorable experience with union (any union).

851 = *Advice of other employee:* Other employee advised vote for union. (*Note:* Should always be followed by another code for reason why advised vote for union.)

852 = *Advice of friend:* Friend (non-employee) advised vote for union. (*Note:* Same as 851.)

853 = *Advice of relative:* Relative (non-employee) advised vote for union. (*Note:* Same as 851.)

854 = *Advice of other/unspecified person:* Individual whose status not clear/not specified above advised vote for union. (*Note:* Same as 851.)

855 = *Advice/opinion religious groups/leaders/other respected persons:* Religious groups/leaders/other respected persons support unionization.

856 = *Unionized employees elsewhere support union:* Letter from unionized employees elsewhere supporting union.

860 Series—Characteristics of Union

860 = *Employees choose union leaders:* Employees will choose union leaders/officers/stewards/negotiating committee.

861 = *Participation in union decisions:* Union bargains for what employees want; is democratic institution; is not "outsider," but creation of employees. Contract will be submitted to employees for vote.

862 = *Technical assistance:* Union will provide technical assistance in grievance handling, negotiations, etc.

863 = *Financial records:* Union financial records open to inspection by members/public officials/public.

864 = *Appeals:* Members can appeal local decisions to Public Review Board.

865 = *Scholarships:* Union provides scholarships for members/ children of members.

866 = *Not communist:* Union is not communist affiliated/dominated.

867 = *History/organization/growth of union:* Union described history/organization/growth of union.

868 = *Unionization and professionalism:* Union not inconsistent with professionalism.

869 = *Other:* Other statements about employee rights within union/ about union as responsible/respectable organization.

870–890 Series—Other

870 = *Company can afford better wages/working conditions:* Company making profit/can afford better wages/working conditions; union will force it to provide better wages/working conditions.

871 = *Experience with unions:* Employee's prior favorable experience with unions. (See also 850.)

872 = *Recent harmful change:* Company has recently taken action to make wages/hours/working conditions unsatisfactory/less satisfactory; union will correct/improve.

873 = *No promises:* Union made no promises; will bargain for what it can get.

874 = *Prevent retaliation:* If union loses, employer will/may punish union supporters; union victory will protect employees from retaliation.

875 = *Union will/may win; everyone/majority for union:* Employees should/will/did vote for union because it will/may win; because everyone/majority for union.

876 = *Union gains elsewhere:* Union has obtained good wages/good working conditions elsewhere.

877 = *Employer promises/good treatment will not/may not continue without union/contract:* Company promises/good treatment began when union came on scene/started organizing; no guarantee/certainty without union/union contract that employer will keep promises/continue good treatment; only union/union contract provides guarantee of wages/hours/ fringes/working conditions.

878 = *Phase II:* Union can obtain wage increases during Phase II greater than could be obtained without union.

879 = *Union demands reasonable:* Union demands reasonable/will take account of company's financial situation; union not

going to force company to lay off/close. Union will not change good features of company.

880 = *Employer moving/sold/may be sold; job retention:* Employer moving location/sold/may be sold; union will protect/retain employee jobs.

881 = *Union not run business:* Union does not run/want to run company's business.

882 = *Racism:* Company officials/supporters discriminate on race grounds; speak disparagingly of non-white employees.

883 = *Social justice:* Union has fought for social justice.

884 = *Employer joins organizations, so can employees:* Employer is member of employer organizations; ought not oppose employees joining union.

870–890 Series—Other

885 = *Employer contract/salaries:* Employer officers have contract/ good salaries; so should union officers/members.

886 = *Employer unconcern:* Employer not really concerned with welfare of employees.

887 = *Employer behind times:* Employer is twenty years behind times.

888 = *Vote for union:* Employees should vote for union. (Use this category *only* if no other responses to Q. 7–9.)

889 = *Other:* Other statements/reasons as to why employees should/ will/might/did support/vote for union; statements as to favorable consequences of unionization.

890 = *NLRB sustained union contentions:* NLRB has sustained union position (includes all types of favorable decisions by regional director, trial examiner, NLRB).

891 = *Union representative honest:* Union representative is honest.

892 = *Other plants/shops will follow:* If this shop goes union, others will follow.

900 Series—Other Union Statements/Questions About Employer/ Employees/Election

910 Series—Interrogation

910 = *Interrogation (employee grievances):* Union asked what were employee complaints/grievances about job/employer; asked what employees wanted in contract.

911 = *Interrogation (other):* Union asked, e.g., if any questions about union/election; whether respondent/others wanted/ supported/planned to vote for union.

920 Series—Election Process/Rules; Labor Law

920 = *Election process/date:* Union described election process; announced election date/time.

921 = *Secret ballot:* Ballot will be secret.

922 = *Vote:* Employees should be certain to vote.

923 = *Legal right to unionize/bargain:* Employees have legal right to engage in union activity; employer cannot punish/ threaten to punish for union activity. Employer has legal duty to bargain with employee representatives.

925 = *Confidentiality of authorization cards:* Cards are confidential/ secret; employer does not know identity of card-signers.

926 = *Right to solicit, distribute union literature:* Employees have legal right to solicit for union; distribute union literature on own time on company property.

927 = *Open books:* Law requires employer to open books to union if pleads inability to meet union financial demands.

928 = *Unlawful to interrogate:* Employer cannot lawfully question employees as to union attitude/card-signing.

929 = *Other:* Other statements as to election process/rules/law.

930 Series—NLRB Voting Study

930 = *Encouraged cooperation:* Praised study; encouraged employees to cooperate with study.

931 = *Neutral on cooperation:* Advised employees of freedom to cooperate or not as they wished.

932 = *Discouraged cooperation:* Attacked study; discouraged employees from cooperating with study.

933 = *Criticized employer cooperation:* Criticized employer for co-operating with study.

934 = *Independent:* Voting study independent of company and union.

935 = *Described:* Described voting study; told employees about study.

939 = *Other:* Other statements as to study.

940 Series—Facts

940 = *Get facts before deciding/decide for selves:* Employees should get facts from both sides before deciding how to vote; should decide for selves how to vote.

941 = *Union willing to provide facts:* Union willing to provide facts/ discuss/answer questions.

942 = *Union guarantee:* Union guarantee, signed and notarized, as to dues and strikes.

950 Series—Company Campaign

950 = *Campaign lies:* Employer lied to employees/tried to deceive employees.

951 = *Campaign too strong:* Employer campaign was too strong/ hard; too much pressure; too many contacts.

952 = *Campaign too weak:* Employer did not campaign hard enough.

953 = *Campaign too selective:* Employer played favorites in campaigning; did not talk to people it assumed were firmly for/against employer.

954 = *Talking down to employees:* Employer talked down to employees/treated employees as unintelligent.

955 = *Don't be frightened:* Employer will seek to persuade/frighten employees into voting against union/to divide and conquer; employees should stand together, not be frightened, misled, disturbed.

956 = *Used obscene/vulgar language:* Company officials/supporters used vulgar/obscene language.

957 = *Violated NLRA elsewhere:* Company violated NLRA elsewhere.

958 = *Violated NLRA:* This employer violated NLRA in effort to keep union out.

959 = *Campaign otherwise unseemly/unfair/improper:* (In respects not treated above.)

960 Series—Strikes

960 = *No strike without vote:* No strike is/will be called unless employees vote to go on strike; employees decide whether there will be strike.

961 = *No strike without reason:* Strikes are not called without reason/unnecessarily; only if employer conduct makes necessary.

962 = *Strike benefits:* Employees will strike/receive strike benefits from union.

963 = *Gains of strike outweigh costs:* Gains of strike outweigh costs/disadvantages.

964 = *Secondary picketing/boycott:* Secondary activity can be used in support of strike.

965 = *International approval necessary:* International must approve local strike to get strike sanction.

969 = *Other:* Remarks about strike not covered above (favorable or non-critical).

970 Series—Dues and Initiation Fees

970 = *Reasonable:* Dues/initiation fees are reasonable/not too high in view of benefits.

971 = *Initiation fee waiver:* Initiation fees will not be required of employees presently employed.

972 = *Fines/assessments:* Union does not fine/assess members or does so only under limited circumstances.

973 = *No dues until contract:* No dues obligation until contract signed/ratified.

974 = *Payment necessary to participate in contract negotiations:* Only employees who pay dues/initiation fee will be allowed to participate in contract negotiations.

975 = *Employees will set own dues:* Employees in this local will set their own dues.

979 = *Other:* Remarks about dues/initiation fees not covered above (favorable or not critical).

980 Series—Other

980 = *Union meeting:* Announced/invited employees to union meeting.

981 = *Union easy to get out:* Employees can easily get rid of union if dissatisfied; can vote union out in NLRB/decertification election.

982 = *Personal criticism of employer:* Criticism of employer unrelated both to arbitrary/unfair treatment of employees covered in 820 series and unsatisfactory wages/hours/working conditions covered in 810 series.

983 = *Debate/speech on company premises:* Union offered to debate employer; requested opportunity to reply to company speech on company premises; employer declined above offer/request.

984 = *Employer stalling:* Employer trying to stall election to discourage organization.

985 = *Sign authorization card/participate in union activity:* Employees should sign authorization cards/encourage others to sign/participate in union activity.

986 = *Refusal to bargain:* Employer refused to bargain with union.

987 = *Authorization cards/election:* Authorization cards will be/have been used to get NLRB election.

988 = *Authorization cards/bargaining/representation:* Cards will/may be used to get bargaining rights; signing a card means you want to be represented, not merely for election.

989 = *Other:* Other union statements/questions not covered by 919, 929, 939, 959, or 979.

990 = *Employer notified of union members/supporters/card-signers:* Union notified employer of identities of union members/supporters/card-signers.

991 = *Non-signers can vote union:* Employees who have not signed authorization cards can vote for union.

992 = *Baby book:* Union distributed book of baby photos, ridiculing employer opposition to unionization.

993 = *Union withdrawal:* Discussed possibility of union withdrawal.

000 Series—Miscellaneous

000 Series—Answers Lacking in Substance

000 = Not applicable (the respondent was not supposed to be asked the question).

001 = *Denied vote switch:* Respondent denied having switched vote from Wave I to Wave II.

003 = Respondent indicates disbelief in all campaign propaganda.

006 = Respondent refused to answer.

007 = No second mention (only legal in columns assigned for second mentions).

008 = Don't know.

009 = Not ascertainable. (Coder cannot code because, e.g., respondent misunderstood question; answer does not make sense; question should have been asked but was not.)

010 Series—Respondent Criticism of Employer Campaign (to Be Used Only for Respondent's Personal Criticisms; for Respondent's Report of Union Criticisms, Use 950 Series)

010 = *Campaign lies:* Employer lied to employees/tried to deceive employees. (Use whenever respondent indicates disbelief in employer statement.)

011 = *Campaign too strong:* Employer campaign was too strong/ hard; too much pressure; too many contacts.

012 = *Campaign too weak:* Employer did not campaign hard enough.

013 = *Campaign too selective:* Employer played favorites in campaigning; did not talk to people it assumed were firmly for/ against employer.

014 = *Talking down to employees:* Employer talked down to employees/treated employees as unintelligent.

015 = *Used obscene/vulgar language:* Company officials/supporters used vulgar/obscene language.

019 = *Campaign otherwise unseemly/unfair/improper:* (In respects not treated above).

020 Series—Respondent Criticism of Union Campaign (to Be Used Only for Respondent's Personal Criticisms; for Respondent's Report of Employer Criticisms, Use 440 Series)

020 = *Campaign lies:* Union lied to employees/tried to deceive employees. (Use whenever respondent indicates disbelief in union statement.)

021 = *Campaign promises:* Union made promises it couldn't keep.

022 = *Campaign too strong:* Union campaign was too strong/hard; too much pressure; too many contacts.

023 = *Campaign too weak:* Union did not campaign hard enough.

024 = *Campaign too selective:* Union played favorites in campaigning; did not talk to people it assumed were firmly for/ against union.

025 = *Talking down to employees/acted childish:* Union talked down to employees/acted childish/treated employees as unintelligent; employees too smart to fall for union propaganda.

026 = *Use of obscene/vulgar language:* Union organizers/supporters used obscene/vulgar language.

027 = *Conducted union business on company time/interfered with work:* Union/employees conducted union business on company time; passed out union cards on company time; interfered with work.

028 = *Racism:* Union organizers/supporters made racist statements.

029 = *Campaign otherwise unseemly/unfair/improper:* (In respects not treated above).

030 = *Personal attacks on management:* Union organizers/supporters engaged in personal attacks on management personnel.

031 = *Campaigning within twenty-four hours:* Union campaigned within twenty-four hours of election; company cannot.

Appendix E

TYPICAL CAMPAIGN PROFILE

Employer Campaign

111 —— It is our sincere belief that this union would be contrary to the best interests of our employees as well as to the best interests of the company. Under the law, all present benefits are a subject for bargaining. A union can, and may, trade away present benefits for other things, for things the union wants, such as a union shop.

130 —— If union wins, company might move plant.

131 —— The loss of business flowing from a strike could force the com-

151 —— pany to move or close. Other plants have closed as a result of union demands and strikes. Also, unionization could lead to layoffs.

210 —— With a union, there is always the possibility of a strike.

220 —— A company can permanently replace employees who strike.

232 —— You will lose more wages in a strike than can be made up in a long time.

251 —— A strike can badly hurt the company.

261 —— A strike does not hurt the union organizer.

269 —— A strike could cost this community dearly through lost buying power. Would also cause ill will and bad feeling in plant.

300 —— Our wages are competitive with those in other plants.

303 —— We have a good vacation and holiday program.

304 —— We have provided hospitalization, accident, and life insurance.

306 —— Employees have only been terminated for good cause.

309 —— Working conditions and benefits are competitive with other shops.

310 —— Union cannot guarantee improvements or security. We are not required to agree to any union demands, but retain the power to say "no." Our policy is to pay good wages based upon sound business judgment, and no union can force us to do more than that. Union claims that it will improve conditions are nonsense. We will improve working conditions when we can.

334 —— We will bargain in good faith.

341 —— My door has been open and will remain open to each one of you. The union is a stranger. You have been capable of thinking and speaking for yourselves in the past, and you can continue to do so in the future.

360 —— We have treated employees fairly. We have given you benefits, because we were concerned with your personal security. We are really interested in your welfare.

371 —— In the past two years, your wage increases have been the maximum permitted under federal law. $3.50 exemption did not take effect until April 30, 1973.

375 —— Our word is just as good as any union contract.

410 —— The union will want dues and initiation fees.

412 —— The union has the power to fine employees who do not carry out its wishes.

420 —— The union is only interested in you because it wants money.

434 —— Union bosses are getting rich.

440 —— Union lied by saying you have to pay union dues to be eligible to vote.

620 —— Election date and details.

621 —— Election will be by secret ballot.

622 —— Be sure to vote.

624 —— You do not have to be a union member or sign a union card to vote in the NLRB election.

625 —— We furnished the NLRB with your names and addresses. We are required by law to do this.

626 —— Because of NLRB regulations, I cannot answer any questions orally, but only in writing.

629 —— Under the law, unions can't bargain for supervision or try to force a company to deal with a supervisor any particular way.

640 —— You are the one who must decide how to vote. Ask yourself where your best interests lie.

650 —— Once the union files its petition, an employer cannot grant wage increases without the threat of violating a law.

651- —— The company will guarantee you no one will discriminate against
656　　 you whether you are for or against the union. We will not move out of this community—union or no union.

655 —— You can vote against the union even if you have signed a union authorization card.

663 —— If the union calls upon you at home, you may refuse to talk to them if you wish. It is unlawful for anyone to threaten, coerce, or attempt to force you to join a union.

785 —— Gave out two paychecks, one in the amount of union dues.

Union Campaign

810 —— Wages are low; union will improve.

811 —— Overtime is excessive; union can provide some relief.

812 —— There is a good union pension plan.

814 —— Union will improve sick and accident insurance plan.

816 —— Plant has unsafe conditions; union will improve.

817 —— Plant is unclean; union will improve.

820 —— Foremen do not treat people with respect; union will improve; will file grievances if necessary.

829 —— Working conditions are poor; union will improve.

830 —— Organizing a union is a team effort. We must work together.

833 —— You have everything to gain and nothing to lose by joining the union.

860 —— Employees will elect by secret ballot a committee from both plants to represent you in negotiations with the company.

861 —— Employees will vote on their own contract. You make your own decision. You vote on everything that goes into the contract.

862 —— Union will provide assistance in negotiations.

875 —— Vast majority of employees have joined union.

876 —— Union has gained substantial benefits at other plants.

884 —— Employer joins organizations, but does not want employees to do so.

920 —— Announced filing of petition, hearing, post-election procedures.

923 —— Employees have right to join union without employer interference. Company cannot take away any benefits because employees join the union. Foreman will lose job if he repeats threat to move plant.

926 —— Company cannot bar employees/union representatives from soliciting employee membership during nonworking hours.

928 —— Employer may not ask employees about confidential union matters, meetings, union sentiments.

950 —— Employer is lying to employees.

955 —— Employer will try to confuse employees, try to make them forget low wages and bad working conditions.

960 —— No strike without vote of employees.

961 —— Strikes are rarely called by union; only if necessary.

962 —— Union provides $35 a week in strike benefits after a two-week waiting period.

965 —— International must approve local strike to get strike sanctioned.

970 —— Dues/initiation fees are reasonable. Employee must pay only $5 prior to negotiation of union contract.

972 —— No fines or assessments by this union.

973 —— No dues until contract is ratified by employees.

974 —— Only employees who pay $5 will be allowed to participate in contract negotiations.

975 —— Employees will set their own dues.

980 —— Announced meeting.

985 —— Get other employees to sign union authorization cards.

986 —— Company refused to recognize union.

Appendix F

VOTE CATEGORIES BY ELECTION

Election Number	Company Voters	Union Voters	Card-signers Voting Company	Card-signers Voting Union	Non-signers Voting Company	Non-signers Voting Union	Intent Union, Vote Company	Intent Company, Vote Union	Intent Uncertain, Vote Company	Intent Uncertain, Vote Union	Predict Union Vote Company	Predict Company, Vote Union
1	44	53	12	46	32	7	4	2	3	0	4	12
2	9	7	5	7	4	0	2	1	0	0	2	1
3	10	21	1	19	9	2	2	0	0	0	3	3
4	33	17	5	14	28	3	4	0	2	0	2	1
5	17	7	5	5	12	2	3	2	2	1	1	2
6	30	15	18	14	12	1	8	1	2	1	7	4
8	30	12	5	9	25	2	4	1	1	2	5	2
9	13	18	1	8	12	10	2	2	1	1	2	4
10	51	38	6	22	45	15	4	5	3	2	3	13
11	0	15	0	15	0	0	0	0	0	0	0	0
12	9	0	4	0	5	0	1	0	1	0	2	0
13	1	2	0	1	1	1	0	0	0	0	0	0
14	3	1	1	1	2	0	1	1	0	0	0	1
15	8	0	5	0	3	0	3	0	0	0	4	0
16	12	6	1	5	11	1	0	0	2	0	1	1
18	10	8	1	2	9	6	1	0	2	0	1	0
19	3	9	0	8	3	1	1	0	1	0	1	1
20	1	25	1	17	0	8	0	0	0	0	0	6
21	4	13	0	10	4	3	0	0	1	1	0	3
22	13	10	2	10	11	0	0	0	0	1	0	3
23	6	5	1	2	5	3	1	0	3	3	3	3
24	59	23	3	10	56	13	3	2	5	2	7	9
25	14	7	1	5	13	2	5	0	2	0	2	1
26	34	26	6	15	28	10	2	1	2	1	3	4
27	65	32	23	29	41	2	10	2	1	0	11	3
28	11	6	3	5	8	1	3	1	0	0	0	0
29	28	3	10	2	16	0	5	0	4	1	7	1
30	13	60	2	42	11	18	7	3	0	2	7	14
31	20	7	4	6	15	1	6	1	1	0	6	1
32	16	5	4	4	12	1	3	0	1	0	3	1
33	23	26	8	18	15	7	3	2	3	2	5	6
Totals	590	477	138	351	448	120	88	27	43	20	92	100

Index

Access to company premises. *See also* Campaign methods; Imbalance in opportunities for organizational communications
Board rules, 19–20
implications of data for, 96
recommendations for change in, 156–159
Ambiguous statements
Board and court assumptions, 9–11, 24
inconsistency of, 21
employee interpretation, 128, 141
Attitudes. *See also* Predispositions
and the campaign, 141–143, 146
changes in, 71–72, 145–146
effect of persuasive communications on, 29–32
errors in prediction, 61–64. *See also* Switchers and undecided voters
in general, 28, 53
and intent, 64–66
toward unions
data, 58–59, 60–64, 66–69, 70, 71–72, 85–87
measurement, 57–59
toward working conditions
data, 54–57, 60–64, 66–69, 70, 71–72, 85–87
measurement, 54–56
Authorization cards. *See also* Bargaining orders
Board and court assumptions, 20–21, 25–26, 131–132

data
effect of signing on vote, 133–134
employer knowledge of signing, 134–135
signing as indication of employee choice, 132–133
function, 1, 131
measurement of signing, 40–43

Bargaining orders. *See also* Authorization cards; Remedial orders
Board rules, 3
recommendations for change, 153–155
compared to elections as indicator of employee choice
Board and court preference, 132
data
elections in which issued, 112–113
employee reports of unlawful campaigning, 117–118
voting behavior, 113–116
Behavioral assumptions
about authorization card signing. *See* Authorization cards
about campaigning on company premises. *See* Access to company
consistency, lack of, 21–23
employees
attention to the campaign, 8, 140, 143

215